Library of Congress Cataloguing-in-Publication Data

Raeder, Linda C.
   The Rise and Fall of Freedom / Linda C. Raeder.
   Includes bibliographical references.
   ISBN 13-978-1545197103

Typeface: Garamond Pro

FREEDOM AND AMERICAN SOCIETY

Volume III

The Rise and Fall of Freedom

Linda C. Raeder

⚜

Sanctuary Cove Publishing
Palm Beach and Richmond

FREEDOM AND AMERICAN SOCIETY

Volume III

The Rise and Fall of Freedom

In loving memory of my father,
Howard M. Maxwell

CONTENTS

ACKNOWLEDGEMENTS

I am indebted above all to the many students at Palm Beach Atlantic University who participated in my courses in political philosophy over the past sixteen years. This work would not appear in its present form without the knowledge and understanding I have gained through my experience teaching undergraduates at PBA, and especially those enrolled in my Freedom and American Society and Roots of American Order courses. I would like to thank all those students who shared their perspectives and insights over the years and provided indispensable feedback to the ideas presented in this work.

I am further indebted to the PBA administration, particularly President Bill Fleming and Dr. Ken Mahanes, both of whom have provided unwavering support and encouragement for my scholarship and teaching. My colleagues in the Politics Department, Dr. Francisco Plaza and Dr. James Todd, have also earned my deepest gratitude, not only for their graciousness and collegiality, but also for the penetrating insight and maturity of vision that mark their scholarship and teaching. I am especially thankful for their willingness to read and comment on sections of the manuscript over the course of its development.

Thank you as well to my mother, Evelyn Pokorny Maxwell, for her steadfast love, support, and strength, and my dear animal companions, Max, Sophie, Callie, and the Muscovies, who make day-to-day existence a continual joy.

THE RISE AND FALL OF FREEDOM

The present book is the third of three volumes that comprise a comprehensive study of Freedom and American Society. Volume I, *Freedom and Political Order* explores the meaning of freedom in traditional American society and its relation law and rights. Volume II, *Freedom and Economic Order*, explores the economic dimension of freedom as historically conceived and practiced within American society. It examines the two major modern economic paradigms, capitalism and socialism, from both utilitarian and moral perspectives, especially their relation to individual freedom.

ELEVEN

LIMITED GOVERNMENT AND THE WEST

Stand fast, therefore, in the liberty wherewith Christ hath made us free, and be not entangled again with the yoke of bondage.   —Galatians V.

. . . Political as well as spiritual liberty is the gift of God through Christ.
                                                            —Thomas Paine

The great political contest of the modern world has been the contest between liberal democracy and totalitarianism, that is, between limited and unlimited government. Although characteristically conducted in the language of economics, the modern conflict involves far more than the competing claims of capitalism and socialism. Such rival economic claims are merely one particular expression of a more comprehensive conflict, famously characterized by Thomas Sowell as a "conflict of visions."[1] Modern Western society is riven by fundamentally opposing views of the nature of human existence, views arising, in the main, from opposing and irreconcilable religious or metaphysical views. On the one side, we find champions of traditional Western values and Western civilization more generally, including its specifically American expression—limited, constitutional government, the rule of law, capitalism, peace, liberty and justice for all. Such values, as previously observed, are intimately related to a particular moral and religious ethos, the Judeo-Christian or biblical worldview (*Weltanshauung*) that decisively informed the development of Western civilization. The

---

[1] Thomas Sowell, *A Conflict of Visions: Ideological Origins of Political Struggles* (New York: William Morrow & Co., 1987).

complex of assumptions, beliefs, and values that constitute the biblical worldview has been challenged in modernity by the emergence of an alternative vision of existence profoundly in conflict with that of its rival. The central assumption of the competing worldview, variously referred to as naturalistic, "secular," post-theological, post-Christian, or postmodern, is precisely its rejection of theological presuppositions, particularly those inherent to Christianity. The widespread embrace of a post-theological worldview in the West has entailed profound political and social consequences, including and especially the rise of the modern ideological movements. Communism, socialism, fascism, and their variants cannot be comprehended apart from the antitheistic impulses and convictions that inspired and impelled their advocates. Economic, political, and historical considerations undoubtedly played a role in shaping the history of the modern era, but, in the end, the modern conflict, as Sowell observed, is a conflict of visions—a conflict of religious or metaphysical visions.

We have discussed the moral and economic dimensions of the ideological or collectivist movements in previous chapters. Our present concern is the significance of the modern "abolition of God" with respect to American political and social order, in particular, the preservation of individual freedom.[2] The exploration of that significance must begin with an examination of the traditional worldview inherited by Americans of the founding period, especially its characteristic moral and political values and the role of religion in their formation. The antitheistic worldview that informed the modern ideological movements and continues to inform various political aspirations in contemporary Western society will be explored in the following chapter.

The "West"

American society did not fall from a cloud in the eighteenth century. It is rather the fruit of several thousand years of cultural development, an offshoot of a unique civilization that definitively shaped its characteristic

---

[2] The phrase is attributed to Fabian economist G.D.H. Cole. In recounting the goals he shared with fellow Fabians, he is said have proclaimed, "Why, I forgot to include the abolition of God!" Rose L. Martin, *Fabian Freeway* (Ludwig von Mises Institute, 2013, Kindle edition); Margaret Cole, *The Story of Fabian Socialism*, 1st ed (Stanford: Stanford University Press, 1961).

assumptions, beliefs, and values. The American experience can only be understood in light of the civilization that provided its foundational worldview, namely, Western civilization.

Western civilization ultimately derives its name from the actions of the third-century Roman emperor Diocletian (245-311 A.D.) During his reign, the emperor divided the Roman Empire into several distinct administrative sections. Eventually these coalesced into two chief divisions—the Western Empire centered in Rome (whose capital was Ravenna) and the Eastern Empire centered in Constantinople (formerly Byzantium, later Istanbul). "Western civilization" refers to the unique culture that developed in the western territory of the Roman Empire after its fall to the so-called barbarian or Germanic tribes (conventionally dated 476 A.D.) Over the course of centuries, this territory would develop into the nation-states comprised by contemporary Western Europe—Italy, France, Germany, England, and so on. Western civilization, then, is the conventional term for the distinctively European civilization that developed in the western regions of the former Roman Empire, including offshoots such as the United States, Canada, and Australia. Historians usually divide its chronological development into three or four main categories: the Ancient and Classical world (further subdivided into the ancient Near East, Egypt, Greece, and Rome), roughly 3000 B.C. to 476 A.D; the so-called Dark Ages, roughly the fifth to ninth centuries A.D.; the Middle Ages (subdivided into Early, High, and Late Middle Ages), roughly the tenth to sixteenth centuries; and Modernity (subdivided into Early Modern, Modern, and Postmodern), roughly the seventeen or eighteenth century to the present. Such dates and categorizations should not of course be regarded as definitive and objective demarcations but rather approximations, varying from scholar to scholar and intending merely to assist the organization of thought.

In the aftermath of the fall of Rome in the West (476 A.D.), victorious barbarian tribes succeeded in establishing various small kingdoms throughout the territory.[3] The Franks would settle in Gaul (modern

---

[3] The term "barbarian" stems from the Greeks, who used it to refer to all those persons who did not speak Greek. In the Roman context, barbarian means ignorant and uncivilized. The barbarian or Germanic tribes (Vandals, Goths, Franks, Lombards, and so on) were not necessarily violent hordes aimed exclusively on destruction but rather ignorant and unlettered people without

France), the Angles in territory eventually known as "England," the Lombards in northern Italy (Lombardy), and so on. The several tribes represented diverse ancestral and linguistic groups lacking overarching cultural unity. Their members generally spoke different languages, practiced different customs, and governed themselves by different forms of political organization. A second formative influence on the culture of the era was the remnant of Greco-Roman civilization carried by the indigenous Roman populace, all of whom did not immediately disappear with the fall of Roman administration in the western half of the Empire. The third and final important cultural influence of the period was the Christian Church. Centuries of sporadic persecution were eventually supplanted by significant social success: in 380 A.D. Christianity became the official state religion of the Roman Empire. By the fifth century, the period that witnessed the "fall of Rome," the Christian religion was well established and led by a highly educated group of church leaders, many of whom had received the classical training of the Roman elite. Over time, the blending of these three chief elements—tribal cultures, remnants of Greco-Roman culture, and Christianity—would form a distinctive culture that eventually became known as Western civilization or "the West."

The formation of a distinct civilizational entity known as Western civilization entailed a lengthy process that unfolded over many centuries. It was probably not until the tenth or eleventh century that inhabitants of the Western territories began consistently to regard themselves as members of a comprehensive and unique community. By the so-called Middle Ages, however, such was undoubtedly the case. Historians have explored the interesting question of how an initially hodgepodge collection of barbarian tribal customs and Greco-Roman traditions merged over time to form a universal cultural identity. Such a result is all the more remarkable in that such a common identity was shared by peoples who continued to speak diverse languages (French, German, English, and so on), embrace diverse local laws and customs, and govern their several communities by distinct forms of political organization. The answer to the question is provided by the third element that shaped the formation of Western civilization, that is, Christianity. Christianity

---

written language or law, utterly incapable of carrying on the sophisticated administrative machinery of Roman government.

would indeed prove the decisive influence on the development of a distinct Western culture and civilization, a fact pointedly indicated by the traditional term for that civilization, namely, Christendom. Members both within and without its sphere (such as inhabitants of Islamic civilization) well understood that the defining characteristic of "Western" civilization—that which makes it what it is and distinguishes it from other civilizations—was the more or less universal embrace of the Christian faith within its domain. Western civilization is synonymous with Christian civilization, a fact universally acknowledged throughout most of its history. To paraphrase historian Christopher Dawson, 'we do not know what sort of civilization would have emerged in the West after the fall of Rome in the absence of Christianity. What we do know, however, is that the particular civilization that did emerge was one shaped by the general commitment to Christianity'.[4]

The complex story of how Christianity ultimately and definitively shaped the entity that came to be known as Western civilization is of course beyond the scope of the present work. Our interest is confined to those developments that led to the emergence of characteristically Western political values and institutions, especially the value of individual freedom. One will search in vain beyond the orbit of Western culture for a social and political order self-consciously committed to the institutional protection of individual freedom. Freedom is a characteristically Western value.[5] Our inquiry into the source of Western political values and institutions is thus also and simultaneously an inquiry into the source of the valorization of individual freedom.

First and foremost among the developments that led to the emergence of distinctively Western values is the gradual assimilation of the biblical worldview by the vast bulk of the populace. We leave aside such intractable questions as the sincerity, depth, or intensity of religious

---

[4] Christopher Dawson, *Medieval Essays: a Study of Christian Culture* (Garden City, NY: Image Books, 1954); *Religion and the Rise of Western Culture* (New York: Image Books, 1991); *The Formation of Christendom*. 1st. ed (Sheed and Ward, 1967); *The Making of Europe* (Washington, D.C.: The Catholic University of America Press, 2002).

[5] This is not to say of course that individual freedom has not been valued by particular persons across culture and time but simply that such valorization did not achieve social and institutional significance beyond the orbit of Western culture.

belief and confine ourselves to the fact that members of what came to be called Western civilization overwhelmingly regarded themselves as Christian.

The importance of such a development is best perceived in light of the nature and meaning of "culture" in general. The word culture derives from the Latin word "cult" (*cultus*), the original meaning of which is "religious association." Religion, as we shall employ the term, is broadly conceived to include any body of thought that claims to provide *ultimate* understanding of human existence. On such a definition, atheism, for instance, is a religion, professing as it does ultimate knowledge of the nature of existence, in its case, that there is no god. Every human society, past and present, is informed by a worldview dependent upon core religious convictions so conceived. The worldview held by any individual or prevailing in any society may be implicit or tacit, involving assumptions regarding the nature of existence that have never been articulated or raised to consciousness. It may also be explicit, in which case beliefs about the nature of ultimate reality have been consciously articulated. Implicitly or explicitly, however, every human being carries an overarching worldview so conceived, one that necessarily informs his particular beliefs, values, and actions. The values and beliefs informed by the individual's worldview, moreover, include not only expressly religious or metaphysical beliefs but also beliefs seemingly unrelated to religion *per se*, for instance, regarding government, economics, law, and other mundane affairs. A particular culture, then, represents a particular complex of widely shared beliefs and values informed by a common worldview. We again recall Plato's observation: society is man writ large. The character of any society, its particular culture, manifests the assumptions, beliefs, and values—the worldview—held by its individual members, and every worldview necessarily involves religious belief broadly conceived. Every historical culture is thus ultimately a product of the religious worldview—beliefs regarding the ultimate nature and meaning of human existence—held by its members. At the root of every culture is the "cult."

It is thus not surprising or remarkable that a widespread embrace of the Judeo-Christian or biblical worldview, such as ultimately occurred in the western territories of the former Roman Empire, would produce a unique civilization known as Christendom. It should be noted in this context that acknowledgement of the determinative role of biblical religion in the formation of Western civilization is not an argument for or against the truth of biblical religion. It is simply acknowledgement of the objective fact that Christianity in the West historically achieved a measure of social success sufficient to form a distinct and overarching culture. The more or less universal embrace of the biblical worldview in the western territories meant that Judeo-Christian beliefs would inevitably shape not only the values of its inhabitants but also their institutional manifestations, moral, legal, political, economic, and religious. As we shall see, moreover, the widespread embrace of Christianity, while necessary for the development of a distinctly Christian civilization, would not in-itself prove sufficient for that development. Other cultures informed by the biblical worldview would not rise to the civilizational achievement of Christianity in the West.

The great political contest of the modern world, as previously remarked, has pitted Western liberal society, the so-called "Free World," against one form or other of totalitarian rule, famously symbolized by Winston Churchill as the "Iron Curtain."[6] The freedom quest of Western man that ultimately bore fruit in the emergence of liberal society is not a mere accident of history. It is rather an outgrowth of particular presuppositions intrinsic to Western culture, presuppositions informed by the religious vision at the core of that culture, namely, biblical religion. Individual freedom is a cultural value more or less specific to Western civilization precisely because freedom is a value more or less specific to the Judeo-Christian tradition. The free society did not emerge in Islam or ancient Egypt or China precisely because the religious presuppositions of such cultures were not conducive to such a development. The gradual emergence of institutions of freedom in the West was impelled by certain assumptions and values exclusive to the biblical worldview within a historical context shaped, as we shall see, by certain crucial if fortuitous circumstances.

American society, the very paradigm of the free society, is of course an offshoot of Western or Judeo-Christian civilization. Its characteristic

---

[6] Winston Churchill's celebrated speech at Westminster College in 1946. The term "Bamboo Curtain" later came to be applied to the communist regime in China.

institutions of freedom embody the moral and religious heritage uniquely associated with that civilization, a fact widely recognized throughout the course of American history. The intimate relation between liberal society and biblical religion is evidenced not only by the historical record but also the ideological critique of that society advanced by thinkers such as Marx. The assault on Western liberal economic and political order is closely and invariably wedded to a critique of the Western religious heritage. Indeed, the explicit attack on Christianity that emerges in the eighteenth century and rises to militant fervor in the nineteenth can scarcely be comprehended apart from its relation to the simultaneous attack on Western liberal society. The carriers of the ideological movements clearly understood the intrinsic relation between the free society and biblical religion: the dependence of the former on the latter meant that they must fall in tandem or not at all. Marx's self-proclaimed animus toward transcendent divinity—"I hate all the gods"—and Fabian socialist G. D. H. Cole's forthright demand for "the abolition of God" are inseparable from their political and economic goals. The enemies of Western liberal society clearly perceived that free institutions are rooted in Judeo-Christian soil and their destruction requires destruction at the root—the religious worldview that generated and sustains them. For this reason, the rejection of freedom at the heart of the modern totalitarian impulse is inextricably linked to its simultaneous rejection of the Judeo-Christian heritage. Such is the reason, moreover, why the general hostility toward Western civilization characteristic of the modern and contemporary Left is inseparable from its hostility toward biblical religion, particularly Christianity, the formative religion of that civilization.

Such hostility should be of concern to any individual, irrespective of personal religious belief, who cherishes traditional institutions of freedom. Whatever one's personal opinion regarding the validity of biblical religion, the fact remains that Western civilization and the free society are manifestations of Judeo-Christian presuppositions, beliefs, and values. Not only are traditional American institutions largely incomprehensible in their absence but, moreover, the continuing existence and vitality of free institutions may depend upon the preservation of such traditional religious values and beliefs in one form or another.[7]

Christianity East and West

The historical correlation of free institutions and biblical religion in Western civilization is well established. The reasons for such correlation, however, are not well understood and far from self-evident. Why did institutions of freedom emerge in the West, in Christendom, and only in the West? The question may be approached on two fronts: first, why did the Judeo-Christian worldview engender the specific demand for freedom; and, second, how was that demand historically realized in the actual development of free institutions? It should again be emphasized that exploration of such questions is not an exercise in Christian apologetics, which is beyond the range of the author's competence. It is rather an attempt to explicate the existential and historical relation between biblical presuppositions and the rise of the free society. The hope is that a better understanding of such a relation may shed light on both historical and contemporary social and political developments, including the conditions requisite to the preservation of free government.

The first issue that must be addressed is the peculiar fact that Christianity is only historically correlated with free institutions in *Western* civilization. Christianity was of course embraced and practiced in both sections of the Roman Empire, East and West, ultimately developing into two distinct faith traditions—Greek Orthodoxy in the

---

[7] "We are a religious people whose institutions presuppose a Supreme Being. . . When the state encourages religious instruction or cooperates with religious authorities by adjusting the schedule of public events to sectarian needs, it follows the best of our traditions. For it then respects the religious nature of our people and accommodates the public service to their spiritual needs. To hold that it may not would be to find in the Constitution a requirement that the government show a callous indifference to religious groups. That would be preferring those who believe in no religion over those who do believe ... We find no Constitutional requirement which makes it necessary for government to be hostile to religion to and to throw its weight against efforts to widen the effective scope of religious influence." *Zorach vs. Clauson*, United States Supreme Court (1952).

East, headed by the Patriarch of Constantinople, and Latin Christianity in the West, headed by the Pope in Rome. The two traditions are distinguished by different languages, customs, doctrine, and leadership. They are further distinguished by the failure of the Eastern Empire and its descendants, the Byzantine and Ottoman Empires, to experience the development of free institutions, as occurred in the Western territories. The reason for such failure must be attributed to the vastly different historical circumstances encountered by Christianity in East and West, circumstances that largely account for the exclusive rise of freedom in the West.

Throughout the final centuries of imperial Rome, political power was increasingly concentrated in the Eastern portion of the Empire. In the West, by contrast, Roman power eventually weakened to the point of extinction, its rule supplanted by that of the various Germanic kingdoms. The continuing strength of Roman authority in the East enabled the Eastern Empire to endure for centuries after the decline of the Western Empire. The relative strength of Roman authority in East and West would have decisive impact on the ability of Christianity to influence cultural developments in the two regions. In the Eastern Empire, Greek Orthodoxy would develop under the influence of a still-powerful Roman administration that carried forward the traditional pagan practice of political control of religion. Moreover, the conversion of Emperor Constantine in 320 A.D. had led to the establishment of Christianity as the official religion of the Roman Empire in 380 A.D; Christianity was legally wedded to the state. Both traditional Roman practice and official religious establishment meant that Christianity came under control of Roman political authority.

The result in the Eastern Empire was the emergence of a particular form of church-state relations generally referred to as *Caesaropapism*. At the risk of oversimplification, such a relation involves the establishment of religious policy by the government (Caesar), its direct transmission to Church leaders (Papacy), and indirect transmission to the body of the faithful. Christianity in the East remained, to some degree, an arm of imperial Rome. For that reason, Orthodox Christianity failed to achieve the degree of political independence needed to stand as an *autonomous* spiritual authority capable of exerting effective countervailing power against the Roman state. The failure to achieve such autonomy— independence from political control—meant that Eastern Christianity would ultimately fail to achieve the degree of political and cultural influence achieved by Latin Christianity in the West. Only the Western Church would ultimately attain the spiritual autonomy and authority necessary to shape not only the political order of society but, indeed, the formation of civilization as a whole.

The success of Western Christianity in this regard is largely due to the unique historical circumstances encountered by the Latin Church, circumstances radically different than those encountered by the Orthodox Church. Most important, Roman imperial power had been shattered in the West and supplanted by barbarian rule. Latin Christianity did not have to contend with Roman power but rather the breakdown of Roman institutions and rise of the tribal kingdoms. Such circumstances of course posed various difficulties for the Latin Church, but such did not generally include interference with either its internal administration or Christian belief and practice. The Germanic rulers, unlike the Roman, did not generally intervene in matters of religion. By the fifth century, moreover, Latin Christianity was firmly committed to a novel and distinctive view of the proper relation between political and religious authority. Christ's celebrated dictum— *Render unto Caesar the things that are Caesar's, and unto God the things that are God's* (Matthew 22: 21)—came to be interpreted by the early Church as marking a dramatic departure from previous pagan practice. Pre-Christian societies of the ancient world were characterized precisely by the *union* of political and religious authority in one person or institution. The Egyptian Pharaoh was himself regarded as a god or son of a god; the Greek polis was more or less equivalent to a church (*ecclesia*); the Roman Emperor also held the title of *Pontifex Maximus*, High Priest of the Roman religion. Pagan society was marked by a characteristic and universal belief that political rulers were simultaneously responsible for both religious and "secular" affairs (a distinction itself alien to the pre-Christian world), a responsibility that continued to be assumed and exercised, as said, by Roman authority in the East.

The novel and even revolutionary Christian emphasis on the distinction between God and Caesar turned the tables, so to speak, on the pagan concept.[8] Christianity not only insisted on a conceptual

---

[8] Certain scholars regard the Old Testament distinction between king and prophet as similarly distinguishing between "God" and "Caesar." While true,

distinction between religious and political authority and denied the religious authority of secular rulers but further claimed the superiority of religious to political authority. Western church leaders, in contrast to pagan practice, would vigorously assert the right of religious leaders to counsel or chastise political authority.[9] Indeed they came to regard the union of religious and political authority as a characteristically pagan institution and their division an essential element of Christian faith. The principled distinction between God and Caesar was central to Christianity in both its forms, Latin and Greek, but only Latin Christianity would prove capable of effectively implementing and ultimately institutionalizing a division of religious and political authority ("Church and State"). In so doing, as we shall see, it would open the door to the free society.

The distinction between God and Caesar may seem unremarkable to members of contemporary Western society. Such is only the case, however, because Western consciousness has been shaped by millennia of experience informed by such a Christian distinction. Although the differentiation of "Church" and "State" is largely taken for granted in modern society, various scholars have highlighted the unparalleled significance of such a conception, indeed regarding it as perhaps the single most important contribution of Christianity to the development of liberal society.[10] We shall explore such significance at length in a following section. The main point at present is that unique historical circumstances in the West—the breakdown of centralized Roman political power—permitted the Western Church, unlike its Eastern counterpart, ultimately and over the course of centuries, to achieve independence from political control. Freedom from political control would in turn permit Latin Christianity to achieve a degree of spiritual and social autonomy and authority sufficient to form the basis of a new civilization. Historical conditions encountered by the Eastern Church

---

such a distinction did not have determinative social import in pre-Christian society, although it did gain the Jews exemption from certain Roman laws governing religious practice.

[9] Allen Brent, *A Political History of Early Christianity* (New York: t & t Clark International, 2009), pp. 286-291. Hereinafter cited as *Political History*.

[10] M. Stanton Evans, *The Theme is Freedom: Religion, Politics, and the American Tradition* (Washington, DC: Regnery Press, 1994), 145. Hereinafter cited as *Theme is Freedom*.

did not permit such developments. For this reason, the correlation between Christianity and free institutions is confined to Western civilization, as is the quest for individual freedom more generally. Christianity, as said, would prove a necessary but not sufficient condition for the rise of free government.

Greece and Rome

The question at issue is why institutions of freedom arose within Western civilization, within Christendom, and only within that civilization. Scholars generally agree that certain building blocks of the free society first emerged in the pre-Christian world, particularly classical Greece and Rome, whose achievements are conventionally regarded as foundational to Western civilization. Classical culture would provide Western civilization with certain core values that characterize it to the present day, including, for instance, the great Western ideals of the Good, the True, and the Beautiful. The Greek valorization of human reason and rationality, of theoretical and philosophical contemplation (*theoria*), would become a further distinguishing characteristic of the Western mind.[11] The Greek passion for theorizing involved both natural and moral philosophy, the attempt to discover and systematically articulate the principles that govern existence in the realms of both nature (physical science) and ethics (moral science). We have seen that Plato is celebrated as the founder of political philosophy, the first thinker systematically to explore the moral rules that ought to govern human relations in society. His student Aristotle was among the first to study the institutional structure of political relations, a field of inquiry still practiced in the West under the academic banner of "political science."

Greece is further celebrated as the "birthplace of democracy." For the first time in history citizens were able to participate in the determination of both the laws by which they were governed and the rulers who governed them. The Greeks also emphasized the centrality of justice and first identified the attribute of *isonomia*, which, as we have seen, remains a leading element of the Western ideal of justice to the present day.[12]

---

[11] *Theoria* (θεωρία) is the Greek counterpart of the Latin contemplation, "looking at," "gazing at," "being aware of."

[12] Consider the valorization of justice in the Old Testament.

Plato, and especially his teacher Socrates, is widely acclaimed for his defense of deontological morality, the view, as we recall, that certain actions are right- and wrong-in-themselves and thus to be done or avoided for-their-own-sake, because they accord or fail to accord with the nature of being. Classical Greek culture transmitted to Rome its tradition of *paideia*, the liberal culture of the mind that would long embody the highest intellectual and educational aspirations of Western civilization. For these and other reasons, Western civilization is profoundly indebted to the remarkable achievements of the Greek mind, achievements absorbed by the Romans and transmitted to the West by remnants of Greco-Roman culture that endured beyond the political collapse of Roman authority.

Classical Greece, however, for all its significant achievements, cannot be credited with the discovery of the value upon which our discussion is focused, namely, individual freedom as historically conceived within the Anglo-American tradition. The Greeks did speak of liberty but, as we have seen, generally employed the term in a sense distinct from that of Locke and his American counterparts. To mark such a distinction, contemporary scholars, following the nineteenth-century thinker Benjamin Constant, conventionally distinguish between "ancient" and "modern" liberty.[13] We have discussed modern liberty at great length— the negative liberty valorized by the Old Whigs, voluntary action achieved by the absence of coercion and regarded by the Americans as a natural, unalienable, and individual right. Ancient liberty, liberty as conceived by the classical Greeks, generally involves, by contrast, the ability to live under rules or laws determined not by foreigners or autocratic domestic rulers but rather citizens of the polis. Ancient liberty, as we recall, involved two distinct aspects. First, it meant freedom from subjection to foreign rule, in more contemporary language, self-determination, self-government, or home rule. Athens was free provided its citizens were not subjected to laws imposed by non-Athenians, such as Spartans. The second meaning of ancient liberty is more or less equivalent to democracy—the ability of citizens to determine, through voting, the laws and political rulers by which they are governed, as well

---

[13] Benjamin Constant, "The Liberty of Ancients Compared with that of Moderns." Speech delivered to his fellow citizens in 1816. *Constant, Political Writings*, ed Biancamaria Fontana (Cambridge: Cambridge University Press, 1988).

as opportunity to themselves hold political office. An Athenian citizen was free in this sense if he himself could vote for the laws under which he lived and was himself eligible to serve in office.

As previously discussed, the conception of freedom as either home rule or democracy is different in kind from the type of freedom proclaimed by the Declaration of Independence. The Americans, however, did not reject the ancient conception of liberty *in toto*. They rather understood liberty to include both the negative individual liberty proclaimed by Locke and the corporate liberty of political self-determination legitimately exercised by the several states. The so-called dual sovereignty established by the U.S. Constitution reserves all non-enumerated powers of the federal government "to the States respectively, or to the people."

The corporate liberty held by the sovereign states involves their right to self-government, self-determination, or home rule. The people of the several states are corporately free (like the people of Athens) so long as they live under laws made by their representatives and not imposed from without (by foreign nations, the federal government, or other state governments). The Americans, however, did reject in part the second ancient meaning of freedom, that is, democracy. The political order of the United States, as we have seen, is not a pure democracy of the Greek type but rather a liberal or constitutional democracy. Modern liberal democracy presupposes a distinction between freedom and democracy, a distinction never clearly articulated by the ancient Greeks. Voluntary action was undoubtedly valued in the polis, at least to some extent, but freedom in this sense was not a self-conscious value explicitly protected by ancient constitutions. Athens, in particular, did seem to enjoy a measure of modern freedom, if the "Funeral Oration" of Pericles is an accurate representation of life in that city.[14] Nevertheless Athens, like other Greek poleis, fell far short of the standard of freedom championed by the moderns; indeed, measured by the modern standard, the Greek people were often radically unfree. Their activities were subjected to majority rule, for example, in instances that would be regarded as unacceptable and even oppressive on the modern view of freedom.[15]

---

[14] "The Funeral Oration of Pericles," in Thucydides, *On Law, Power, and Justice* (Indianapolis: Hackett Publishing Company, Inc.., 1993), 39-46.
[15] Fustel De Coulanges, *The Ancient City: A Classic Study of the Religious and Civil Institutions in Ancient Greece and Rome* (New York: Doubleday and Company, Inc., 1956), 218-23.

Moreover, the ancients never developed a concept of subjective or natural rights held by the individual against government, one of the crucial elements of modern Anglo-American freedom. Nor did they valorize economic freedom or comprehend the spontaneous ordering principles of the market process; such economic freedom as did occur was incidental rather than principled. Finally, it should not be forgotten that the institution of slavery was universal throughout the ancient world. It is estimated that even at the height of classical Greek democracy only about thirty percent of the Athenian populace held the status of citizen and thus eligibility to vote. Another thirty percent were *metics* (resident aliens without voting rights), and the remainder were slaves without protection of law.

Classical Roman civilization advanced beyond Greece in certain political respects and especially development of law. Indeed, Western civilization is indebted to Rome for one of its leading and most enduring political ideals, one of the core principles of the free society, namely, the ideal of the rule of law. The Roman genius for governing has often been remarked, and one of its most impressive manifestations is the development of the philosophy and practice of law. Roman jurisprudence is profoundly indebted to the philosophy of Stoicism, which dominated the thinking of Roman elites for six hundred years (300 B.C.-300 A.D.) and achieved its most celebrated expression in the writings of the Roman statesman Cicero (106 B.C.-43 B.C.). The advance of Roman legal thought and practice was further facilitated by the emergence of a specialized class of professional jurists (*prudentes, jurisprudentes*), a conception of legal science, and other forms of juridical practice such as the office of the praetor. Roman legal thought reached its height during the so-called classical period of Roman law, the first several centuries A.D. Such is the period of renowned Roman jurists such as Gaius (130-180 A.D.), Ulpian (c. 170-223A.D.), and others whose commentaries and treatises assisted in the principled and systematic development of law.

Roman jurists identified three types of law that long remained seminal categories in Western thought—civil law, natural law, and the law of nations (*jus civile, jus naturale,* and *jus gentium*)—and also developed a conception of rights protected by law. Roman law embodied subjective rights to liberty and property (*iura*), but these differed significantly from the natural and unalienable rights of the American tradition. For one thing, Roman rights were established by human law (and not the Creator) and, moreover, conceived as privilege, that is, a right, advantage, or immunity granted to a particular person or group of people (from *privilegium*, a law for one person). Accordingly they were far from the universal possession of every Roman citizen, let alone every human being, as the American Founders believed.[16] Individual citizens held a variety of rights depending on the particular "status" they were assigned by Roman law. Such legal status comprised a variety of classes, including, for instance, Roman citizen (in contrast to a foreigner), free person (in contrast to a slave), head of the family (in contrast to a lower member), and so on, each of which was defined by the particular individual rights enjoyed by its members. Slavery was widespread in the Roman Empire. It is estimated that between twenty to forty percent of the populace were legal slaves; their treatment varied from extreme brutality to provision of relative comfort. Certain institutions of Republican Rome would serve as models for later statesman, including and especially the American Founders. The U.S. Senate and Capitol, for instance, testify to the influence of Republican Rome on the American political imagination. Indeed, American leaders of the revolutionary period often identified with various Roman figures who struggled to save their own Republic from tyranny and dictatorship. The authors of *The Federalist Papers,* John Jay, Alexander Hamilton, and James Madison, signed their articles with Roman pseudonyms such as Cato and Brutus.

Western civilization is further indebted to Rome for its role in the transmission of Greek culture, including its emphasis on higher learning, to those who followed. The Romans developed the concept of the "humanities" (*humanitas*) and the "liberal arts"—studies reserved for free men, denied to slaves, and which remained the core of higher education in the West for most of its history. The Romans also transmitted Greek Stoicism, which, as mentioned, dominated philosophical thought for almost six hundred years. The Romans, moreover, not only transmitted Stoic philosophy but developed it in directions that would profoundly influence later Western moral thought. Roman

---

[16] Privilege: from Latin *privilegium* "law applying to one person," later "privilege," from *privus* "individual" (private) + *lex* (gen. legis) "law."

+3kkstoicism moved beyond the parochialism of Greek culture and advanced the ideal of the universal brotherhood of man governed by universal law, the "Law of Nature." The formulation of the natural law provided by Cicero would remain for centuries yet another concept central to Western moral and political thought—the concept of the natural or higher law previously encountered in our discussion of Locke and the American Founders. As Cicero writes in *De Res Publica*:

> True law is right reason in agreement with Nature. . . . [I]t is of universal application, unchanging and everlasting. . . . And there will not be different laws at Rome and at Athens, or different laws now and in the future, but one eternal and unchangeable law will be valid for all nations and for all times, and there will be one master and one rule, that is, God, over us all, for He is the author of this law, its promulgator, and its enforcing judge.[17]

The idea of the law of Nature, foundational to the Lockean and American social contract, has a distinguished and ancient pedigree. Roman Stoicism made other significant and enduring contributions to the development of the Western tradition beyond those mentioned, including the influence of late Stoicism on the development of early Christian ethics. Indeed, despite his rejection and even persecution of Christianity, the musings of the last great Stoic emperor, Marcus Aurelius, are difficult to distinguish from those of a devout Christian.[18]

We thus conclude a cursory and radically incomplete survey of the contributions of classical Greece and Rome to the development of what would become known as Western civilization. The Western debt to classical civilization is incalculable for reasons discussed, and many others. The central values informing the traditional American conception of freedom, however—the inherent worth of the individual person, divinely endowed with unalienable and natural rights, and the corollary importance of limits on governmental power—are not among them. Such conceptions are not of Greek or Roman inspiration. To

---

[17] Cicero, *The Republic and The Laws*, trans., Niall Rudd (New York: Oxford University Press, 1998), 68-69. Hereinafter cited as *Republic*.
[18] Marcus Aurelius, *Mediations* (Mineoloa, NY: Dover Publications, 1997).

discover their source and explain their development, we must look not to Greece or Rome but rather to their Western successor, to Christendom.

The Concept of Limited Government

Modern freedom, as we have seen, is crucially bound to the corollary institution of constitutional or limited government. Government, on the traditional American view, is the communal agent of coercive force, the designated executor of the right of self-defense inherently possessed by every individual. It is a trustee charged with specific duties and functions, above all, the security of the individual's natural and unalienable rights. Its power is limited both explicitly by the higher law of the Constitution and implicitly by the purpose for which it was established. In the American political tradition, freedom and limited government are inseparable, two sides of the same coin, a relationship so deeply rooted in American consciousness that it may seem self-evident.

The seemingly self-evident association between freedom and limited government, however, may blind us to an important question. Traditional American political thought and practice led the American people to take more or less for granted not only freedom but also the general notion of *limited government*, to simply assume its meaningfulness and validity. A study of human history, however, reveals the error of such an assumption. The abstract concept of limited government, like the institutional achievement of freedom more generally, would be alien to the overwhelming majority of peoples, cultures, and societies that have existed over the course of history. The concept, like the quest for freedom, is unique to Western civilization and societies within its cultural orbit. Indeed despite their many profound achievements, even pre-Christian Western cultures, classical Greece and Rome, failed to develop the general concept of limited government. One searches their literature in vain for a conception of *a priori* or principled limits to the legitimate range of political power. Plato's *Republic* is an all-embracing political community ordered by "philosopher-kings"—persons of superior virtue and knowledge who must not be bound in advance by limits on their authority.[19] For Aristotle, the *polis* was the "perfect community"—fulfillment of human association and precondition of intellectual and ethical excellence. Cicero too defined the state in normative terms; a "republic," he said, is an "assemblage [of men] associated by a common acknowledgement of right and by a community of interests."[20] Moreover, Cicero, like the majority of his peers, could conceive no higher moral obligation than "duty to the state," to Rome, embodying as it did the highest values of the community. To the classical mind, human flourishing was inextricably entwined with the flourishing of the overarching political association, the polis or the state; personal and political fulfillments were symbiotic and inseparable.[21] It did not occur to inhabitants of the ancient world to demand principled limits on political power.

The classical evaluation of the political community would undergo radical transformation upon the rise of Christianity in the West. Pre-Christian societies, as briefly discussed, were uniformly characterized by the union of religious and political authority in the same governing institution. Such a union meant, among other things, that a person's devotion to polis, state, or emperor was at the same time a kind of religious devotion. Rome is a case in point. Unitary allegiance—simultaneous allegiance to Roman government and its civic religion—was expected and even required of Roman citizens. Such posed no inherent difficulty for classical Romans because the union of political and religious authority eliminated the necessity to choose between loyalty to the state and loyalty to one's religion. The Romans, moreover, were generally tolerant of the various religious cults that existed throughout the Empire. So long as a citizen observed the legal duties required by the Roman civic religion, he was otherwise free to participate in such cults. Judaism was the principal exception to this rule; Roman law granted the Jews specific religious privileges denied to others, for instance, exemption from emperor worship and military service.

---

[19] Plato does make some concession to the ideal of the rule of law in a later work, *The Statesman*.

[20] Cicero, *Republic*, 19.

[21] Certain sections of the present chapter restate material originally published in Linda C. Raeder, "Augustine and the Case for Limited Government," *Humanitas* 16:2 (2003) and reprinted with permission of the National Humanities Institute.

The rise and expansion of Christianity in the Roman world brought matters of political and religious allegiance to greater significance. Perhaps most important, it introduced a profound dualism or tension to the minds of gentile converts to Christianity. Henceforth such converts would have to maneuver a novel and dual allegiance—to Caesar and to God, to this world and the world-to-come—a tension probably heightened for many Jewish converts as well. Conversion to Christianity did not of course instantly transport new believers to heaven. Christians, like other citizens and subjects, remained embedded within Roman society for the course of their natural lives and were expected to obey its laws, including those relating to Roman civic religion, such as public participation in the Cult of the Emperor (Jews excepted). The Christian conscience, however, could no longer regard such mundane laws and duties as absolutely obligatory, as could non-Christian Roman citizens and subjects. The Christian revelation relativized such worldly values, which paled in significance in light of the revelation of man's ultimate destiny beyond this world. Such a "re-evaluation of values." as Nietzsche would put it, held true not only for particular legal obligations but also various general ideals characteristic of contemporary Rome, such as valorization of power and glory. Indeed the relativization of worldly values would extend even beyond the realm of prevailing Roman values and virtues to include the overarching concept of the "political." The very idea of worldly or political rule would undergo dramatic re-evaluation under the Christian dispensation: in light of the unlimited value of eternal salvation promised by Christ, the value of temporal politics or government could only appear "limited."

Augustine and Limited Government

Christianity would not only challenge the normative politics of classical thought, and especially its conception of the state (polis) as the highest achievement of social existence, but led to a general and radical devaluation of the role of politics and government in human existence. The most influential early Christian thinker explicitly to reject the classical conception of the state was Augustine of Hippo (354-430 A.D.). Although Augustine, the Christian theologian and statesman, never produced a formal treatise on political philosophy, certain conceptions developed in his voluminous writings would decisively inform the Christian worldview that shapes Western social and political experience to the present day. More particularly and most important with respect to the present discussion, Augustine has been characterized by certain scholars as the "intellectual father of the concept of the limited state."[22] Both Augustine's political thought and ontology (study of the nature of being) embody a vision that intrinsically limits the authority and competence of secular government and, further, regards politics or government as inappropriate means of effecting either individual or social improvement.[23] He offers a realistic interpretation of the political realm that provides an important counterweight to political idealism or romanticism in all its varied forms, classical and modern. Augustine exerted incalculable influence on the development of Western political thought, shaping the development of Christian views on the nature and purpose of government for a thousand years and beyond. Indeed, his thought is of special relevance to the American experience: the purposes of the Founders, as we have seen, can only be understood in light of the Augustinian presuppositions that informed them. An exploration of the contribution of Christianity to the rise of limited government in the West has no better starting point than Augustine of Hippo.

Augustine's challenge to the classical conception of the state as the embodiment of the highest values of the community and ultimate object of human allegiance stemmed of course from his Christian convictions. Such classical ideals failed to impress the mystical Christian sage because he held a higher allegiance—to his God—alongside which the human state and its strictly secular concerns paled in significance (became "limited"). Moreover, his moral lucidity and realism permitted clear recognition of the nature or essence of political authority, namely, coerciveness. Augustine regarded the coercive rule exercised by secular government as a necessary aspect of human existence but certainly not

---

[22] Gerhart Niemeyer, cited in Graham Walker, *Moral Foundations of Constitutional Thought: Current Problems, Augustinian Prospects* (Princeton: Princeton University Press, 1990), 167. Hereinafter cited as *Moral Foundations*.
[23] The philosophical study of the nature of being, existence or reality in general, as well as the basic categories of being and their relations. Traditionally categorized as a part of the branch of philosophy known as metaphysics, ontology, traditionally categorized as a part of the branch of philosophy known as metaphysics, deals with questions concerning what entities exist or can be said to exist.

worthy of reverence, let alone worship. His conception of political rule is perhaps best revealed by the anecdote he himself recounts to his readers: "When [Alexander the Great] asked [a captured pirate] what he meant by infesting the sea, he boldly replied: 'What you mean by warring on the whole world. I do my fighting on a ship, and they call me a pirate; you do yours on a large ship, and they call you Commander'."[24] Augustine's clear-eyed moral realism deflated the grandiose political expectations of the classical world and, as said, remains an indispensable counterweight to political romanticism in its myriad forms. Government, for Augustine, is not the embodiment of all value or the source of all goodness and flourishing but rather the institutional embodiment of coercion. We have of course encountered such a conception in previous discussions. The Americans of the eighteenth century did not invent their conception of government from whole cloth but developed an ancient political tradition saturated with Augustinian insights.

Augustine, then, like his American descendants, held a sober and realistic conception of government and law. On his view, the coercive authority embodied in government is indispensable to the well-being, not to say preservation, of members of society. Nevertheless, government, the organized agent of coercive force, is neither a noble phenomenon nor an appropriate object of devotion. Political rule, on the contrary and quite literally, is a necessary evil; its existence is not a cause for celebration but rather a necessary consequence of mankind's fallen state. God, Augustine tells us, "did not intend that his rational creature, who was made in his image, should have dominion over anything but the irrational creature—not man over man, but man over the beasts."[25] According to Augustine, sin and sin alone brought the need for political coercion into human existence. Government and human law, he believed, exist as punishment and corrective for sin, a punishment which mankind, through the actions of Adam and Eve, brought upon itself. Political man is fallen man. Such a fact, however, does not lead Augustine to condemn secular government as such. Political coercion is indispensable to social order precisely because human beings are prone to depravity and sin. Government and law exist

---

[24] St. Augustine, *The City of God*, IV: 4, 88-89.
[25] Augustine, *City of God*, XIX: 15, 461.

to intimidate, restrain, and punish those who would do evil in order that the good may live in some semblance of peace and order. Government is the hangman or executioner that serves an essentially negative function—to restrain and punish the wicked. Political rule is indispensable but neither glorious nor enviable.

The Two Cities

Augustine's devaluation of the political realm is thus inseparable from his Christian worldview, which also informs his conception of human society more generally. Although Augustine himself did not intend such a result, his celebrated account of the "Two Cities" would provide the Christian West with one of its leading political symbols, serving to represent the principled Christian distinction between God and Caesar, religion and government, Church and State. The metaphor of the Two Cities would profoundly impress Christian consciousness; indeed the distinction it implies would become a distinguishing characteristic of the Western mind.

Augustine's metaphor refers to his belief that the human race is permanently divided into two mutually exclusive classes which, though related, remain separated by an unbridgeable gulf. These two groups of human beings constitute two "cities"—the City of God and the City of Man (Earth)—the citizenry of which are determined by the quality of their inhabitants' respective love.[26] The *civitas dei* consists of all persons who orient their love (*caritas*) and reason toward the Highest Good—communion with God.[27] The *civitas terrena,* on the other hand, is peopled by the "castoffs" of the heavenly city—those persons whose love (*cupiditas*) is exclusively oriented either toward themselves or the

---

[26] Ibid. George Sabine points out the very ancient lineage of the concept of "two cities." Augustine, he tells us, provided a "restatement, from the Christian point of view, of the ancient idea that man is a citizen of two cities, the city of his birth and the City of God" (George H. Sabine, *A History of Political Theory,* 3rd ed. (New York: Holt, Rinehart and Winston, 1961], 189)). We also note that Augustine's "two cities" are mystical, universal entities constituted by all persons across time and space. They are not and never will be concrete, historical phenomena.

[27] Or, what is the same thing, their will. For Augustine, "[l]ove and will are commensurate terms. . ." (Walker, *Moral Foundations,* 85).

mundane order, those who pursue temporal or worldly goods as ends-in-themselves.[28] These two groups, "commingled" and more or less overtly indistinguishable in this life, will be identified and assigned to their respective final destinations—heaven and hell—on Judgment Day. Until that day, they abide together in the temporal community, the earthly citizenry fully at home, the citizenry of God "captives and stranger[s]" in a strange land.[29] According to Augustine, then, there exists what has been called a "fundamental cleavage" within every society that runs along the lines of love ("values" in contemporary terminology).[30] Apart from a common desire for "earthly peace" or the "tranquility of order," members of the two cities are irremediably at odds in their respective evaluations of the goods of existence. In other words, there exists for Augustine an irreducible "pluralism" of values among the members of any society, a pluralism that originates in the very nature of human being, that is, its fallen state. Consequently, and contrary to Cicero, political society cannot be based upon any genuinely common agreement regarding right and wrong, for there can be no such agreement between the earthly men who do not and cannot know true justice (because they do not know God, the source and author of justice), and the heavenly citizenry who do. Augustine denies that political society is or can be based upon a common conception of right, for he believes the two citizenries can never come to terms in this regard.

Although the Two Cities will never share a common conception of right or justice, Augustine nevertheless maintains that their members do have certain goods in common: all persons, whatever their ultimate commitments, require the "necessaries of this life" and at least some measure of temporal peace.[31] Indeed Augustine valorizes the common value of peace to the highest degree: "Peace is a good so great, that even in this earthly and mortal life there is no word we hear with such pleasure, nothing we more strongly desire, or enjoy more thoroughly when it comes."[32] The citizens of the Two Cities may desire peace for different reasons, but they both desire peace. The citizens of Man desire

---

[28] Etienne Gilson, Foreword, St. Augustine, *City of God*, ed and intro, Vernon J. Bourke (New York: Image Books, 1958), 24. Hereinafter cited as *City of God*.
[29] Ibid., XIX: 17, 464.
[30] Walker, *Moral Foundations*, 105.
[31] Augustine, *City of God*, XIX: 17, 465.
[32] Gerhart Niemeyer, cited in Walker, *Moral Foundations*, 105.

peace to gratify their selfish desires and realize their material goals, for even they recognize that lawlessness, anarchy, and perpetual violence will preclude fulfillment of their aims. The citizens of God also require earthly peace and security against violence, for they cannot pursue their love for God without a certain degree of temporal order. Both groups, then, share a common interest in securing earthly peace and this by means of human justice; accordingly, they can agree on the need for government and law.

From the Augustinian perspective, the classical view of politics was faulty, among other reasons, because it posited a common hierarchy of values that does not in fact exist among members of any society. The members of the two cities embrace two irreconcilable scales of values. To impose the scale of the earthly multitude would be an abomination, for the stakes involved, for Augustine, are far too high (eternal salvation and damnation). To impose the higher values of the citizens of God on the multitude is impossible, for those values cannot be achieved by the means of man but only the means of God (his saving grace). If any sort of earthly peace is to be gained, then, government must rest content with providing, as Graham Walker put it, the "least-common-denominator" of human values, which, he says, ". . . reduce to the common interest . . . in the basic goods of this life, none of which is more basic than a modicum of earthly peace."[33]

Such a conception of the proper task of political authority clearly resembles the views later championed by Locke, the Founders, and other modern advocates of limited government. As we have seen, Locke and the Americans agree that the fundamental responsibility of government is to secure certain negative values, namely, Augustine's peace and justice, and the additional value of freedom. Such agreement is not coincidental. Old Whigs such as Locke and the Americans fully subscribed to the Augustinian view restated in the eighteenth century by Edmund Burke: "[t]he great use of government is as a restraint."[34] Indeed, Augustine's conception of government as "Defender of the

---

[33] Walker, *Moral Foundations*, 106; Henry Paolucci, ed, *The Political Writings of St. Augustine* (Washington: Regnery Gateway, 1962), 9.
[34] Edmund Burke, "Thoughts and Details on Scarcity," in *The Works of the Right Honorable Edmund Burke* (London: Oxford University Press, 1907), Vol. VI: 2.

Peace" dominated Christian political thought well into modern times.[35] His emphasis on the irreducible plurality of values (loves) may be viewed in a similar light. Augustine himself recognized two classes of conflicting values—"material" and "spiritual." As Walker explains, however, ". . . in principle, the number of [such] dissonant [classes] is as large as the number of objects that may attract [individuals'] . . . love."[36] It is not necessary to subscribe to Augustinian theology to recognize that individuals, for whatever reason, do in fact serve unique scales of values and ends. As we have seen, the millions of individuals comprised by modern society do not share unanimous desire for particular concrete goods or services. Economic value is always subjective value and thus varies not only among individuals but within the individual depending on circumstance. The only values that *all* persons truly have in common in complex modern societies are those general or abstract values that sustain the social order as a whole. In other words, the truly common good in a pluralistic society consists in the preservation of a general framework of law—Augustine's "earthly peace" and justice—that enables individuals and groups to pursue their own values and goals, restrained only in the means they may employ in such pursuits. Both Augustine and modern proponents of limited government place great significance on the indisputable fact that individuals pursue vastly different and often conflicting values and ends. Both conclude from such a fact that government should be restricted or limited to securing the only value truly shared by all members of society, that is, enforcement of the rule of law as traditionally conceived.

Augustinian Ontology

Augustine's thought leads toward the Western conception of limited government in yet another important manner: the attention he draws to the limited effectiveness of coercion in realizing positive moral or spiritual ends. According to Augustine, the very constitution of human nature precludes the possibility of employing political power to engender the formation of either good and decent individuals or a good and decent

---

[35] A well-known book by medieval author Marsiulius of Padua is titled *Defensor Pacis* (Defender of the Peace). One remnant of this traditional understanding is the American office of "Justice of the Peace."
[36] Walker, *Moral Foundations*, 105.

society. Even persons who may believe that government is justified in imposing a single scale of values on the populace will come to realize the futility of such an approach. Politics, on the Augustinian view, is generally incapable of remedying human ills, personal or social, because the cause of, and cure for, such ills is not material, encompassed within the realm of politics or government, but rather spiritual, encompassed within the realm of religion. We recall that, for Augustine, the need for coercive political rule follows from the human propensity for sin and evil. Sin and evil, he further believes, do not result from material causes but rather what Walker perceptively terms "ontic instability"—a flaw in the nature of human being itself.[37] The "original sin" of Adam and Eve—their willful and perverse rejection of the Eternal Goodness in favor of the goods of the mundane order—is visited on their descendants in the form of a chronic "contraction of being . . . [a] sort of precarious composition of being and non-being."[38] In other words, upon the commission of original sin—man's deliberate aversion from the Divine Goodness—being itself "contracted" toward non-existence and the "bad will" that causes all worldly disorder sprang into play.[39] Man's "chronic deficiency of being" (the absence of God) manifests as willful self-love that intentionally turns away from knowledge and love of its Source toward passionate embrace of things of the flesh.[40]

According to Augustine, human nature before the Fall was good, complete, grounded in its Source. All men since Adam, however, are born in a vitiated state of being, hence all are prone to depravity and sin. The human being does retain a measure of goodness: his nature is not evil but contracted. Consequently, all human beings crave the restoration of their original nature and strive to fill the ontic void, typically by inappropriate material means—the means of man and politics. Such desperate striving is the source of the evils—the violence, deceit, lust for domination and glory, greed, envy, cruelty, selfishness,

---

[37] Ibid., 108.

[38] Ibid. Vernon J. Bourke, cited in Walker, *Moral Foundations*, n48. As Augustine put it, "man did not so fall away as to become absolutely nothing; but being turned towards himself, his being became more contracted than it was when he clave to Him who supremely is. . . . [To experience such a state is] not quite to become a nonentity, but to approximate to that" (Ibid., 4).

[39] Augustine, *City of God*, XIV: 11, 305.

[40] Walker, *Moral Foundations*, 87.

and so on—that call forth the need for political rule. Such perversity originates from man's ontological disorder and not material causes. Politics or government can never cure its cause, which is beyond the jurisdiction of mere human beings, but is limited to palliating its effects. Man's "alienation"—and Augustine, not Marx, was the first philosopher of alienation—is not to be overcome by the means of man but only the means of God, divine grace.[41] Only the suffusion of grace, Augustine insists, can impel the willful turning toward the Source that restores vitiated nature to its original fullness of being. Only conversion toward the Source can reorder the soul and moderate the disposition toward vice and sin.[42] Only the achievement of such an "ordinate" ("rightly ordered") love allows for the realignment of virtue and dissipation of wicked propensities.[43] Political coercion, necessitated, we recall, as punishment and corrective for human sin, would disappear if all men regained the fullness of being attained by reunion with their Source. There is of course no possibility of realizing such a paradise on earth. Augustine is convinced that God only selectively grants to individuals the saving grace that impels the soul's conversion; thus the populace of the City of Man is guaranteed always to outnumber the citizenry of God. Government and law, for Augustine, are permanent elements of historical existence; heaven and earth are mutually exclusive categories.

Augustine's insights into the nature of political authority and the ontological roots of social disorder not only profoundly shaped the distinctive Christian vision of government but long provided sobering counterweight to the extravagant political expectations embodied in classical conceptions of government (and reappearing in various modern political constructs). Throughout the development of Western civilization, such Christian moral realism served to moderate tendencies to idealize or romanticize political rule. Indeed Augustine, and the Christian tradition more generally, cast a profound suspicion on political power as such, clearly perceiving the coerciveness at its core. We have seen that a deep-seated prejudice against arbitrary coercion impelled the American demand for limits on the power of government. Such prejudice was not histrionic or irrational but rather the fruit of centuries

---

[41] Gerhart Niemeyer, *Between Nothingness and Paradise* (Baton Rouge: Louisiana State University Press, 1971), 216.
[42] Cf. the Platonic conception of *periagoge*.
[43] Walker, *Moral Foundations*, 89.

of experience within a political tradition that recognized the essential coerciveness of political rule and its potential danger to human wellbeing. Augustine's recognition as the "father of limited government" is well deserved. Such a uniquely Western conception is profoundly indebted to his insights: the relative unimportance of temporal as compared to eternal values; emphasis on the coerciveness of political authority; the limited effectiveness of political coercion in regard to moral and spiritual development; and the recognition of the plurality of value hierarchies embraced by a people. Indeed, the enduring value of Augustinian insight is indicated not only by its implicit role in shaping the thought of the American Founders but its ongoing support to contemporary efforts to limit the range of political authority as well. The maintenance of constitutional or limited government still depends on prejudice against arbitrary coercion, as well as acknowledgement of both the plurality of human values and impotency of politics to shape the individual soul.

Augustine's most wide-reaching contribution to Western political thought may be the general suspicion he cast on political power as such. He, however, would be the last to claim credit as the source of such a view. Augustine's mistrust of government derived neither from personal idiosyncrasy nor as inheritance of the classical world but rather is of biblical origin. Greece and Rome, for instance, achieved no insights comparable to those expressed in the Book of Samuel. When the children of Israel demand a king like all other nations, Samuel confers with the Lord and tells the Israelites what they can expect if their wish is fulfilled:

> "This will be the manner of the king that shall reign over you. He will take your sons and appoint them for himself, for his chariots, and to be his horsemen, and some shall run before his chariots;
> "And he will appoint him captains over thousands and captains over fifties; and will set them to ear his ground; and to reap his harvest, and to make his instruments of war, and instruments of his chariots;
> "And he will take your daughters to be confectionaries, and to be cooks, and to be bakers;

"And he will take your fields, and your vineyards, and your oliveyards, even the best of them to give to his officers and give them to his servants;

"And he will take the tenth of your seed, and of your vineyards, and give them to his officers, and to his servants;

"And he will take your menservants, and your maidservants, and your goodliest young men, and your asses, and put them to his work;

"He will take the tenth of your sheep; and ye shall be his servants

"And ye shall cry out in that day because of your king which ye shall have chosen you; and the Lord will not hear you in that day.'—I Samuel 8.

Augustine profoundly influenced the development of the Western political tradition, including its characteristic notion of limited government. Such a notion is inseparable from skepticism of political power. Augustine's skepticism, however, was not exclusive or idiosyncratic but rather a distinguishing aspect of biblical faith that informs every consistent philosophy of limited government from Augustine to the American Founders. The chief and revolutionary carrier of such skepticism into the Western political tradition was Christianity. As we shall see, the transformative influence of the Judeo-Christian worldview on Western political order would ultimately extend far beyond that achieved even by the magisterial bishop of Hippo.

The Two Swords

We previously noted that the conception conventionally if misleadingly termed "separation of Church and State" is among the most significant Judeo-Christian contributions to the development of the free society. The Church Fathers, as we recall, interpreted Christ's celebrated dictum "Render unto Caesar the things that are Caesar's, and unto God the things that are God's" as marking a definitive break with pagan culture and establishing henceforth a distinction between political and religious authority. Such a distinction, like the related concept of limited government, is deeply embedded within Western consciousness and more or less presupposed by characteristically Western institutions. For that reason, however, it may be difficult to apprehend its quasi-revolutionary import within the historical context of the Roman Empire. We have seen that the union of political and religious authority was a universal characteristic of pagan or pre-Christian society; political authority was assumed to hold both the right and the duty to order religious practice within society. The Roman Emperor simultaneously held the title of *Pontifex Maximus*, the High Priest of the Roman religion; certain emperors even came to adopt the Hellenistic practice of worshiping the ruler as a god. Rome, as previously noted, was generally tolerant of various religions and granted wide latitude in religious belief, provided certain official cultic practices were observed. The Jewish people were the outstanding exception to this general pattern. The Jews within the Empire were not only tolerated but also granted special privileges that exempted them from the unitary religious-political obligations that fell on other groups.

Such is the historical context in which Christ's pronouncement regarding Caesar and God was received. The statement was probably unremarkable to Roman authorities of the time, who may initially have dismissed Christ as merely one fanatical Jewish rabbi among others.[44] Its implications undoubtedly gained significance as greater numbers of non-Jews converted to Christianity. Most important in this regard, however, was the novel and challenging interpretation eventually placed upon the dictum by the Church Fathers, who, as said, generally interpreted Christ's pronouncement as marking a definitive break with pagan practice. Never again, in the aftermath of Christ's revelation, would the same person or institution be entitled simultaneously to hold ultimate political and religious authority; never again could King simultaneously be Priest. Such all-encompassing power, it was believed, constituted too

---

[44] Certain scholars suggest, however, that from the outset Christ's teachings seemed to Roman ears at least suspicious, if not worse—potentially subversive of political order or even downright revolutionary. For the dictum suggests, of course, that there may exist something that does not belong to Caesar. This was unthinkable on the Roman model of unity between government and religion; everything, spiritual and material, belonged to the realm of the Emperor. Moreover, the emperors of the period claimed to be the highest god on earth, a claim implicitly challenged by Christ's dictum. From the outset Christianity posed at least a potential problem for political rulers. See Brent, *Political History.*

great a temptation for fallen human beings with propensity for prideful self-aggrandizement. The distinction between the political and religious dimensions of social existence would become a central principle of Christian political thought. However much violated in practice, and we shall see that it often was violated, the principle itself was rarely if ever explicitly disavowed and generally considered an essential element of Christian faith.

The Church Fathers' views on the distinction between political and religious authority received substantial development upon Augustine's elaboration of the Two Cities. The Church was readily associated with the City of God and the State with the City of Man. Augustine did not himself draw such an association but rather perceived the Two Cities as abstract trans-historical categories or indexes that can never be substantiated in concrete historical institutions. The City of God comprises all persons throughout history who orient their lives by love of God, the City of Man all those oriented toward worldly values. Obviously "all" persons who have lived on earth cannot simultaneously exist in a concrete human community. Nevertheless, it was probably inevitable that some association between the Two Cities and historically existing states and churches would be made at various points in Western history. Not everyone possesses Augustine's discriminating intellect and mystical insight.

The establishment of Christianity as the official religion of the Roman Empire in the fourth century changed the relationship of early Christians to the state. No longer were Christians persecuted, as had sporadically been the case in the first several centuries of Christian experience. No longer could Christians oppose Roman religious practice; the power of the government was now exercised to support Christianity and not Roman or pagan religion. The new union of Christianity and Empire, however, violated the principled Christian distinction between God and Caesar, which was well established by the fourth century and accepted, in theory, by religious authorities both East and West. Indeed the wedding of Christianity to political power supported not a division of authority but rather the Byzantine concept of Caesaropapism previously discussed. The Eastern or Orthodox Christian Church was firmly ruled by the Roman Emperors, who played an active role in controlling the religious life of society, supporting the clergy with patronage and even defining Church doctrine. It was difficult to maintain institutional fidelity to the distinction between religion and government under such circumstances.

Roman political and religious authorities, as we have seen, encountered a different set of circumstances in the Western territories of the Empire. In the context of church-state relations, the fourth-century imperial union of religion and government encountered Western opposition in the form of various strong clerics who resisted control of Christianity by political authority. Thinkers such as Ambrose of Milan (c. 337/340–397), a mentor of Augustine, and later Pope Gelasius (in office 492-496) would forcefully reassert the Christian distinction between religious and political authority. Among the more famous and historically influential formulations of such resistance is the so-called "Two Powers" or "Two Swords" doctrine elaborated by Gelasius in a letter he wrote to Emperor Anastasius in 494:

> There are two powers, august Emperor, by which this world is chiefly ruled, namely, the sacred authority of the priests and the royal power. Of these that of the priests is the more weighty, since they have to render an account for even the kings of men in the divine judgment. You are also aware, dear son, that while you are permitted honorably to rule over human kind, yet in things divine you bow your head humbly before the leaders of the clergy and await from their hands the means of your salvation. In the reception and proper disposition of the heavenly mysteries you recognize that you should be subordinate rather than superior to the religious order, and that in these matters you depend on their judgment rather than wish to force them to follow your will.
>
> If the ministers of religion, recognizing the supremacy granted you from heaven in matters affecting the public order, obey your laws, lest otherwise they might obstruct the course of secular affairs by irrelevant considerations, with what readiness should you not yield them obedience to whom is assigned the dispensing of the sacred mysteries of religion. Accordingly, just as there is no slight danger in the case of the priests if they refrain from speaking when the service of the divinity requires, so there is no little risk for those who disdain—which God forbid—when they should obey. And if

it is fitting that the hearts of the faithful should submit to all
priests in general who properly administer divine affairs, how
much the more is obedience due to the bishop of that see
which the Most High ordained to be above all others [Rome],
and which is consequently dutifully honored by the devotion
of the whole Church.[45]

The Two Powers doctrine elaborated by Gelasius remained a
fundamental principle of Western political thought for a millennium
and beyond. It played a powerful role in the often contentious relation
between religious and political authority that developed in Western
Christendom over the centuries and reached its head in the so-called
"investiture controversy" of the eleventh century, to which we return
below.

The Christian distinction between religious and political authority was
universally accepted in principle, both in the Eastern and Western
branches of the Christian church, but often violated in practice. As we
have seen, the establishment of Christianity as the official religion of the
Roman Empire led to its violation in the East and the development of
Caesaropapism. In the West, the principle would be challenged by the
historical circumstances encountered by the Latin Church after the fall
of Roman power. Throughout the Dark and early Middle Ages, the
Church in the West was more or less dependent for its survival on
military protection provided by the Germanic kings, many of whom
were regarded by their peoples as divinities. Over time, missionary efforts
successfully converted various Germanic rulers and peoples to
Christianity, at least nominally. Conversion led the tribal peoples to
abandon the conception of the divinity of kingship in favor of the
conception of the sacral office of the Christian ruler. Kings came to
regard themselves as appointed to their positions by God and
acknowledged no superior authority in the Church.

Under the circumstances, the Church not only lent its support to such
conceptions but also formed alliances with contemporary secular rulers,
especially the Merovingian and Carolingian kings descended from the
Franks in Gaul. Over time a new conception of church-state relations

---

[45] Translated in J. H. Robinson, *Readings in European History* (Boston: Ginn,
1905), 72-73.

developed that blurred the distinction between the two realms—the so-called *Sacrum Imperium* ("sacred empire"—*sacerdotium* and *imperium*), later known as the Holy Roman Empire. The *Sacrum Imperium* was conceived as a unified Christian society—Christendom—ruled by two heads, as Gelasius had maintained, but related in a complementary and cooperative manner. Church and state came to be regarded as *mutually* responsible for maintaining and supporting the universal society of Christendom, itself conceived as the *Corpus Christi*, the Body of Christ. As liturgist Dom Guéranger describes the early-medieval concept,

> God assigned [the newly established Holy Empire] the grand mission of propagating the Kingdom of Christ among the barbarian nations of the North, and of upholding, under the direction of the Sovereign Pontiffs, the confederation and unity of Europe. St. Leo III crowned Charlemagne Emperor. Here, then, was a new Caesar, a new Augustus, on the earth; not, indeed, a successor of those ancient Lords of Pagan Rome, but one who was invested with the title and power by the Vicar of Him, who is called, in the Sacred Scriptures, *King of Kings, and Lord of Lords.*[46]

Charlemagne (742/47-814), the most celebrated of the Christian rulers within the *Sacrum Imperium* so conceived, explicitly regarded his personal mission as extending Christianity throughout his realm. The Church supported such efforts, and, as Guéranger observes, on Christmas Day 800 the pope crowned Charlemagne as Holy Roman Emperor, the first ruler to hold the title of Roman Emperor in the West since the fall of Rome in 476.

The Investiture Controversy

Throughout the Dark and early Middle Ages, the Christian distinction between religious and political authority was routinely violated in practice. Under the feudal system as it developed in the West, the king was thought to hold all territory as his possession. Kings typically

---

[46] Dom Guéranger, abbot of Solesmes from 1837-1875, a leading monastic and liturgist of his generation.

parceled out sections of their holdings to personal supporters—warriors and vassals who thereby gained control over local and decentralized fiefdoms. The Church was intricately involved in the feudal system, including its acceptance of land grants from feudal lords to establish monasteries, bishoprics, and other benefices. Bishops and other high church officials often wore two hats during this period, simultaneously holding positions as church official and feudal lord, confounding religious and political authority. Feudal rulers strategically employed land grants and similar devices to strengthen political control over their territories. Such could also be facilitated by appointing their loyal supporters to positions of high office, such as feudal lord in the political sphere and church official in the religious sphere. Feudal rulers claimed and exercised the right, in particular, to choose bishops of the church and also "invest" them with spiritual authority. The practice of simony, selling church offices to the highest bidder, was also widespread during the era.

Over time such political control of authoritative positions within the church hierarchy led to the debasement of its spiritual authority. Simony and political investiture of bishops (and the related problem of clerical marriage) were widely recognized as chief causes of such corruption. Persons selected by the feudal lords for church office were not typically chosen for their spiritual integrity but rather ability to further the political power of the lord. Serious Christians attempted reform of the Church as early as the ninth century. Spiritual reformers were chiefly concentrated in the monasteries of the period, especially the monastery at Cluny, and the demand to end the practices of simony and political investiture of bishops was central to their efforts. During the eleventh century, reform efforts intensified, as did conflict between religious and political authorities, leading to the so-called "crisis of Church and State" that spanned the period 1050-1300.[47] The crisis began with efforts by church leaders to reclaim exclusive authority to appoint members of the church hierarchy, especially bishops—the so-called "Investiture Controversy" or "Papal Revolution" of the eleventh and twelfth centuries. It would extend over the next century and a half as partisans

---

[47] Brian Tierney, *The Crisis of Church and State 1050-1300* (Toronto: University of Toronto Press. 1988). Hereinafter cited as *Crisis of Church and State.*

on both sides of the conflict—royalists and papalists—contended for authority and power. It ended in compromise, as we shall see, but one that the Church could legitimately regard as victory.

Indeed, according to Harold Berman, the successful resistance of medieval religious leaders to control of the Roman church by political authority was a landmark in the history of Western civilization, comparable in significance to the fall of Rome in the West and the later Protestant Reformation.[48] Its significance derives from the pivotal role such resistance played in enabling Latin Christianity to establish itself as an autonomous spiritual authority. As previously noted, independence from political control—symbolized by the papalists' demand for "freedom of the Church" (*Libertas ecclesiae*) and never fully achieved in the East—would prove decisive for the ultimately determinative impact of Christianity on the culture of the West.

The eleventh-century contest between church and state was personified by the conflict between the two highest officials of the era, the Roman Pope, Gregory VII (c. 1015/28-1085, the former monk Hildebrand) and the Holy Roman Emperor, Henry IV (1050-1106), who ruled from territory that would eventually form the nation of Germany. Gregory had absorbed the reform impulse during his early years of monastic life; once selected as Pope, he exerted his new authority to bring long-needed reforms to fruition. He condemned simony and clerical marriage and further demanded an end to the practice of imperial investiture. Henry refused to comply and for understandable reasons: his political power partially rested upon his ability to secure positions of authority, including the spiritual authority of the bishopric, for his loyal followers. The Pope countered Henry's refusal by excommunicating him from the Church. Under contemporary social circumstances, such an action entailed serious consequences for the Emperor. More specifically, under terms of Christian-feudal bonds of political obligation, Henry's excommunication meant that those of his subjects who had previously sworn oaths of allegiance to him as Emperor, such as feudal princes, were thereby dissolved of all such obligation. Various German princes would

---

[48] Harold J. Berman, *Law and Revolution: The Formation of the Western Legal Tradition* (Cambridge: Harvard University Press, 1983). Hereinafter cited as *Law and Revolution*.

certainly use the opportunity provided by excommunication to revolt against the Emperor and assert autonomy within their principalities.

Henry responded to the excommunication order by making his celebrated trip to Canossa in 1077.[49] For three days he stood just beyond the gates of the Pope's residence, reportedly barefoot in the snow and dressed in the hair-shirt of the Christian penitent. Henry came to the Pope not as Emperor but rather repentant Christian asking forgiveness, a petition the spiritual head of the Christian Church could not of course reject. Henry was readmitted to the Church. The drama concluded with compromise between Empire and Papacy, one that restored to the Church internal control over its spiritual offices yet left Henry with residual if diminished authority. The Concordat of Worms (1122) specified that the Emperor would cease investing bishops with spiritual authority but authorized him both to nominate persons for such office and exercise veto power over nominees. He was further authorized to invest bishops with secular authority in the territories they governed. In the language of the day, the emperor was entitled to invest bishops with authority "by the lance" (secular authority) but not "by ring and staff" (the traditional symbols of spiritual authority).

The victory of the Gregorian forces would profoundly shape the subsequent development of Western political and social order. Most important, the liberation of the Latin Church from political control led to establishment of an autonomous religious authority willing and able to exercise countervailing power against political or secular rule. The Gelasian doctrine of the Two Powers was reinvigorated and the longstanding Christian distinction between religious and political authority given institutional efficacy. Not only did the Christian Church assert its right in principle to shape the conscience and religious practice of the populace but also acquired the authority and institutional means to do so. As M. Stanton Evans summarized the significance of such medieval events, the successful resistance of the Church to political control meant that henceforth in Christendom there would exist not only a "law above the King" (the higher law of God) but also a "spiritual force that could construe it, independent of the power that [the king] wielded."[50] Bracton and other medieval jurists forthrightly asserted that

---

[49] In the northern Italian Alps, the region of Emilia Romagna.
[50] Evans, *Theme is Freedom*, 145.

the king is "under God and under law." The tables were turned on the Dark Ages and Byzantine Caesaropapism: political control of religion was supplanted by the moralization of politics and government in line with Christian values and beliefs. The significance of such an achievement, as previously noted, cannot be overstated. The subsequent development of Western political order, including the rise of modern liberal constitutionalism, is profoundly and inextricably linked to the successful institutional division of religious and political authority achieved by the Papal Revolution. The traditional Christian distinction between the Two Swords of religion and government, acknowledged in principle for a millennium, finally attained practical efficacy.

According to Berman, the Papal Revolution led over time to establishment of what has been called the first modern European state, namely, the medieval Papacy. Having achieved internal sovereignty, the Church would develop its own system of law (canon law), courts (ecclesiastical courts), and vast administrative hierarchy (the curia). In the centuries following the Revolution, jurists and canon lawyers developed a complex system of law that demarcated with increasing precision the respective jurisdictional authority of the two spheres of Christian society—the "temporal" and "spiritual," in the language of medieval jurists. Most important, the internal reform of the Church that followed upon the exclusion of political control permitted the achievement of authentic moral and spiritual sovereignty. Free of political control, no longer a mere arm or tool of worldly power, the Christian religion could all the more freely win mind, heart, and soul, win, that is, a genuine and not politically contrived spiritual allegiance and commitment. The independent status of the Christian Church during this "Age of Faith" permitted it to wield influence not by mere coercive power but rather widely acknowledged spiritual and moral authority. By virtue of such authority the biblical message penetrated Western culture with sufficient strength and conviction to shape a unique civilization, a civilization saturated in every respect with Judeo-Christian presuppositions. The characteristic elements of Western order, encompassing government, law, morality, economics, custom, and other cultural expressions, would henceforth develop on a foundation decisively informed by the biblical worldview.

Separation of Church and State

The successful institutional division of religious and political authority achieved by the medieval Church in the West is profoundly related to the rise of modern freedom and corollary demand for limited government. Such a relation follows from the fact that such a distinction establishes intrinsic limits to the coercive power of government and correspondingly enlarges the sphere of individual freedom. The differentiation of the realms of God and Caesar places an entire dimension of human experience—the realm of God—conceptually and institutionally beyond the reach of governmental coercion—the realm of Caesar. As we have seen, such limits on legitimate political authority, long acknowledged in principle, attained institutional efficacy upon the success of the Papal Revolution. The range of the private sphere carved out by the Judeo-Christian distinction between religion and government is clearly perceived by dichotomizing various aspects of personal and social experience traditionally associated in Western society with one or the other of the two spheres:

God ("Church")	*Caesar ('State")*
City of God	City of Man
Religion	Government
Ecclesiastical	Civil
Heaven	Earth
Spiritual	Temporal
Soul	Body
Sacred	Profane
Eternity	Time
Otherworld	This world (*mundus*)
Internal (conscience)	External (outward behavior)
Morality	Legality
Sin	Crime

Members of American society will experience a sense of familiarity with the dichotomies here presented. American moral and political consciousness, like that of the West more generally, has thoroughly assimilated the traditional Christian distinction between the realm of religion and the realm of government, between church and state.

Members of American society know that government is not God. They readily distinguish a person's inner spiritual life, the realm of conscience, from his outward behavior, for instance, lust to murder from an actual act of murder. They distinguish between sin, an offense against God, and crime, an offense against human authority. They understand that not every sin is a crime (for instance, lust or covetousness) and not every crime a sin (assisting a runaway slave in antebellum America). Americans further distinguish between the related but distinct categories of the moral and the legal. They readily recognize that an action may be legal but not moral (pornography) or the reverse, moral but not legal (assisting a Jew escaping Nazi Germany or serving a cup of coffee to a black person in the segregated South). Such distinctions are so deeply embedded within American consciousness and institutions as to seem self-evident. They are far from self-evident, however, and members of various non-Western cultures, both historical and contemporary, might find the concept of two distinct orders within social existence all but incomprehensible. Such distinctions only seem obvious to members of contemporary American society because their culture is rooted in several thousand years of development profoundly impressed by the Judeo-Christian worldview in general and its distinction between the realms of God and Caesar in particular.

The issue is of such importance to comprehending the rise of limited government in the West that further elaboration and exemplification of the basic concepts seems warranted. As we have seen, division of society into distinct realms of religion and government involves various dichotomies such as sin and crime, morality and legality, conscience and behavior, and so on. Such concepts are obviously related but not identical. Sin, for instance, is generally conceived as a broader category than crime; some sins are crimes but not all sins are crimes. Americans would find governmental legislation that criminalized, say, lust, not only unacceptable but also ridiculous. Such is regarded as beyond the legitimate sphere of political authority and competence. Lust is an experience of the inner man, not external behavior or action that government may legitimately prohibit. Murder is another case in point. Most Americans would regard as absurd a law that criminalized the *desire* to murder another human being. Not only has government no authority to enact such a law—no constitutional right to do so—but no competence in this dimension of human experience. The *desire* to murder another person cannot be affected by the coercive penalties of human law; the very notion is preposterous to the American mind, steeped as it is in Judeo-Christian and even Augustinian presuppositions. The desire to murder can only be affected, to employ the language of Locke, by "the inward persuasion of the mind," a persuasion, he insists, utterly immune to threats or application of coercive force.[51] The persuasion of the mind is a matter of inner experience and conviction— a matter of religion and the spirit—and thus beyond the reach of coercion, whether exercised by private individuals or the public force of law The early Christian martyrs, among many other examples, testify to the impotence of coercive violence to touch the inner man.

Locke was not the first philosopher to recognize the impotency of political coercion with respect to the spiritual life of man. We have discussed Augustine's views on the limited efficacy of coercive rule. Governmental coercion, suggest Augustine, Aquinas, and other Christian philosophers, is only competent to control "externals." Coercion may succeed in controlling the outward behavior of a human being, which, indeed, is precisely the purpose of secular law. A human or positive law establishes certain consequences of action (external behavior) intended to influence the governed to act as the lawmaker wishes and not as the governed himself may wish to act. A law against murder, for instance, establishes consequences for the outward (external) act of murder, consequences intended to make a would-be murderer think twice before killing an innocent person. Human law, under jurisdiction of temporal government, legitimately punishes such outward or external behavior; the Western tradition has always regarded law prohibiting the act of murder as an entirely proper exercise of governmental authority. Such legitimacy, however, extends *only* to such outward behavior, never to the inner desire that impels an act of murder. The desire to murder, in contrast to the act of murder, falls under jurisdiction not of political but rather spiritual authority, the realm of God and religion. Moreover, the reason government is encouraged to enact and enforce such a law is not to "make men good," to shape their conscience or their souls. The American Founders, as we recall, rejected the Platonic (pagan) conception of statecraft as soulcraft, a rejection

---

[51] John Locke, *A Letter Concerning Toleration* (Indianapolis: Hackett Publishing, 1983), 219.

grounded in Judeo-Christian presuppositions regarding the distinct jurisdiction of religious and political authority. The justification for extending the *sin* of murder to the *crime* of murder is not spiritual formation, the province of religion, but rather the mundane fact that human society could not be preserved if wanton acts of murder were permitted to occur without consequence.

Such a conclusion applies not only to murder but various other moral violations traditionally and simultaneously regarded as crimes. Moreover, it raises a more general question: how to determine which of the broad class of moral violations customarily regarded as sins should also be regarded as crimes. Upon what basis should sin—an offense again God—be extended to the category of crime—an offense against human authority? The traditional answer to this question, articulated by Aquinas, among others, is the conclusion just stated: certain moral rules (prohibiting sin) are indispensable to the preservation of mundane society and thus must be enforced not only by divine authority in eternity but also human authority here on earth. Such moral violations (sins) cannot be exclusively entrusted to the realm of religion and conscience because mundane society could not exist in peace and prosperity if certain moral rules were not also enforced by coercive human sanction (crimes). The previously mentioned moral prohibition of murder is a classic example of a sin that is also and legitimately considered a crime. With respect to religion, murder is a sin that will be punished by God. Wanton murder, however, is so destructive of security in this world that it must also be punished by human authority. Society could not endure if people were permitted to murder with impunity; thus governments universally, and legitimately, enact laws against murder. Stealing, rape, and other such sins are similarly, and legitimately, prohibited by human law, that is, properly regarded as crimes. Society could not be preserved, let alone flourish, if people could steal and rape with impunity.

A sin may properly become a crime, then, when the violation of a particular moral or religious rule would have consequences not only for the individual's relationship with God but also the preservation of human society. The relevant question is whether a particular rule, believed to derive from divine authority, is so essential to the preservation of society that it simply must be enforced in this world, in time, by human authority as well as divine authority in eternity. If the answer is yes, the sin may legitimately be made a crime. If not, the moral violation should remain within the realm of religion and conscience, subject only to consequences established by God and immune to coercive sanction by human government. Governmental authority is limited to temporal jurisdiction.

The inextricable link between the traditional American conviction of the necessity for limited government and the Judeo-Christian distinction between God and Caesar may be further highlighted by considering the nature of political rule in societies that have not, and do not, explicitly distinguish between the spheres of religion and government. Such, indeed, is the case for the vast majority of societies known to history. Western civilization is distinguished from other civilizations precisely by its unique success not only in conceptualizing but also institutionalizing the two realms of social existence, the achievement, as we have seen, of the Papal Revolution of the eleventh and twelfth centuries. The overwhelming majority of historical societies have not and do not explicitly recognize a division between religious and political authority let only enjoy established institutions instantiating and enforcing such a division.

Societies that do not practice separation of church and state can be subdivided into one of two classes, Caesaropapism and theocracy, neither of which conceives, let alone institutionalizes, firm jurisdictional boundaries between religion and government. Caesaropapism, as we have seen, involves political control of religion, such as practiced in the Eastern Roman Empire and the ancient world more generally. Theocracy (Greek, "the rule of god"), conversely, involves religious control of government; various contemporary Islamic states are representative. Saudi Arabian and Iranian religious authorities, for example, do not view the Koran (the Holy Book of the Islamic faith) simply as a guide for Moslem believers but demand its enforcement as law of the land by political authorities, who also regard such religious enforcement as properly within their purview. A theocratic society makes no conceptual distinction between religion and government; government is held responsible for enforcing not only what Americans would regard as secular law but also religious law. Such is analogous to holding the American government responsible for enforcing not only civil and criminal law but also Biblical law. Societies that unite religion

45

and government, such as modern Iran and those of the ancient world, charge government with the joint responsibility for establishing spiritual and temporal order, for placing both conscience and behavior under control of human authority, either political authority (Caesaropapism) or religious authority (theocracy). Such societies of course do not recognize the various conceptual dichotomies characteristic of Western or Judeo-Christian consciousness. The absence of a distinction between God and Caesar leads to conflation not only of church and state, religion and government, but also conscience and behavior, morality and legality, sin and crime. The moral is identified with the legal; a sin is also and invariably a crime.

Societies that do not distinguish between religion and government are totalitarian in the most literal sense of the world; their governments routinely exercise total control over every dimension of human existence, acknowledging no moral limits to political power. To the traditional American mind, committed to the principle of limited government, failure to respect the proper boundaries of religion and government, whether Caesaropapist or theocratic, thus constitutes far-reaching and illegitimate abuse of political power. The American tradition emphatically denies government the right to interfere with, let alone coercively enforce, the religious or spiritual life of the people. Within that tradition, on the contrary, an entire dimension of experience—the spiritual dimension of God, historically represented by the Church—is regarded as "off-limits" to political control. Government is restricted to exercising control over the temporal dimension of existence, over "external" and mundane concerns or crimes relating to existence in time, in this world. Political authority is forbidden to intervene in the inner or spiritual life of the individual, forbidden to coerce his conscience or religious belief, to interfere with his relation to God, to insert itself into religious matters involving conscience, morality, and eternity. It is forbidden to attempt "statecraft as soulcraft" or, in the popular American expression, to "legislate morality." Spiritual formation is beyond its purview.

All such conventional American assumptions regarding the legitimate reach of political power are incomprehensible in societies that fail to separate church and state, as in pagan and modern theocratic societies. Such limitation of government, by contrast, is a defining and central characteristic not only of the liberal tradition in general but its American expression in particular, which expressly and emphatically denies both the authority and competence of government to intervene in matters of religion. Authority and competence in the spiritual realm—"that which belongs to God"—are reserved to religion and the church. The proper realm of government—"that which belongs to Caesar"—is confined or limited to temporal and worldly concerns, largely dealing with the preservation of society in time. Government may legitimately exercise control only over those aspects of existence previously enumerated under the head of Caesar. The strength and depth of such fundamental American convictions are evident throughout the course of American history. Such is evident, among numerous other indications, in both the first natural right claimed by the American colonists—the right of conscience—and the very first clauses of the First Amendment to the U.S. Constitution, which absolutely forbid the federal government from either establishing religion or interfering with its free exercise. It is evident in the traditional American distinction between sin and crime, the moral and legal, a distinction, moreover, and as we shall see, implicit in the characteristically American conception of "civil disobedience." Such distinctions and convictions were not novel American constructions but rather outgrowths of a cultural soil prepared for centuries by the civilization from which America was born, Western or Judeo-Christian civilization, saturated in every respect with the presuppositions of biblical faith. Among the most significant of such presuppositions is the intrinsic division of authority between the realms of God and Caesar and the intrinsic limits posed by such a division on the legitimate reach of political power.

The Christian revelation of a spiritual destiny beyond this world, as we have seen, simultaneously delimited and devalued the general authority and competence of temporal government. The implications and institutional expressions of the biblical worldview, however, would only gradually unfold over the course of centuries. The halting development of limited government, inspired by the underlying distinction between religious and political authority, was checkered with progress and regression. Nevertheless, the Christian distinction between God and Caesar, the spiritual and temporal dimensions of social existence, would lead over time to ever-more precise specification of the limits to political authority that would become characteristic of Western political culture. What would ultimately become the American understanding of the limits to government demanded by rights of religion and conscience was not explicitly formulated until the early-modern period, pointedly emerging from the conflict previously discussed in another context—the conflict within Christendom engendered by the Protestant Reformation. Locke would again provide the Americans with the leading concept: religion and the church, he said, must be understood as *voluntary* societies which, as such, renders them beyond reach of the coercive arm of government. Locke of course was himself heir to the longstanding Western distinction between religious and political authority, but the greater precision of his formulation marked a substantial contribution to its development.

Indeed his characterization of the Church as a voluntary society became foundational to later American constitutional thought regarding the proper limits of both governmental and religious authority. Many Americans of the founding era would, like Locke, emphasize the voluntariness of religious belief and practice, which places religion beyond the jurisdiction of coercive secular government, a topic to which we return in the final chapter. The American Founders, moreover, made their own historic contribution to the development of the quintessentially Western distinction between God and Caesar. They were the first people in history explicitly to embed that traditional Christian distinction within the very framework of constitutional order. The first clauses of the First Amendment of the Bill of Rights of the United States Constitution unequivocally establish an institutional division between the realms of religion and government, expressly limiting the reach of federal governmental power with respect to religion.

The Higher Law

The traditional Western distinction between God and Caesar, as we have seen, implies various other conceptual distinctions, including that between sin and crime. On the Judeo-Christian view, the two categories are related but not identical. Not every sin is also a crime and, conversely, not every crime is also a sin; not every offense against human authority is also regarded as an offense against God. To further explore the importance of such a distinction for American political order, we turn to yet another significant concept crucially bound to the Western ideal of limited government, namely, the concept of higher or natural law.

We previously encountered the higher or natural law in discussions of the Romans, Locke, and the American founders.[52] Locke and Jefferson appeal to the "Laws of Nature" and "Nature's God," self-evident rules of right and wrong that originate in a source higher than human preference or will. In so doing, they carried forward a well-established tradition of moral and political reflection. The idea of the natural or higher law, as we have seen, is of ancient lineage and appears in diverse forms throughout the development of the Western tradition. The Old Testament of the Hebrews unequivocally declares the objective reality of law and justice that derive from a Source superior to human being. Various scholars have attributed the first appearance of the idea of natural law in Western literature to Sophocles' celebrated play *Antigone*.[53] Stoic philosophy, as we recall, transmitted the tradition of natural law to the Romans, receiving its most eloquent and enduring definition in the hands of Cicero. Christianity absorbed and further developed the natural-law tradition, especially the influential medieval formulation contributed by the "Angelic Doctor," Thomas Aquinas.

The concept of the natural law would receive somewhat different interpretations within pagan and Judeo-Christian civilizations, but the essence of the idea remained more or less constant for millennia. The term always refers in some manner to an unchanging and objective moral law, valid for all times and places, independent of and superior to human will. Such law is "natural" both because it consists of rules inherent to human nature and is accessible to human beings independent of "supernatural" revelation.[54] The natural law can be known by every human being regardless of personal religious belief or training because every human being is endowed with reason, the means by which the

---

[52] The terms are often used interchangeably. The "higher law" is the term preferred within the Protestant tradition, the "natural law" within the Roman Catholic tradition.

[53] Russell Kirk, *The Roots of American Order* (Wilmington, DE: Intercollege Studies Institute, 2003). Hereinafter cited as *Roots of American Order*.

[54] Brian Tierney, "Natural Law and Natural Rights," in John Witte, Jr. and Frank S Alexander, eds, *Christianity and Law* (Cambridge: Cambridge University Press, 2008), 89.

individual discerns the natural law. Man, suggested the ancient Greeks, is the "rational animal."[55] All men are created in God's image, says the Bible, which means all men are endowed with reason and free will. The natural law thus transcends culture and particular religious commitment and can be recognized by every human being simply by virtue of his nature as a rational creature. Such is the tradition inherited by Locke and which informs his conviction that "[The] state of nature has a law of nature to govern it, which obliges every one: and reason, which is that law, teaches all mankind, who will but consult it, that being all equal and independent, no one ought to harm another in his life, health, liberty, or possessions."[56] It is the tradition that informs Jefferson's conviction that the "Laws of Nature and of Nature's God" justify American resistance to British power.

Cicero's celebrated formulation of the natural law has previously been cited. The decisive influence of Christianity on the development of Western legal and political institutions, however, meant that the Christian elaboration of the traditional doctrine of natural law would also prove decisive. Medieval Christendom was characterized by passionate interest in both theology and law, reflected in its establishment of the first universities in the Western world. The oldest university in the West, which specialized in the study of law, was founded at Bologna in 1088. The second oldest, the University of Paris, was founded in the mid-eleventh century and officially recognized as a university sometime between 1150 and 1170. It specialized in the second great medieval interest, theology. The period was marked by vibrant civilizational growth and expansion: increase in population, expansion of trade and commerce, development of cities, and so on. The Papal Revolution of the eleventh century, as we have seen, had secured the independence of Latin Christianity from political control, leading over time to tremendous growth in the influence and prestige of the Roman Church. Similar growth was experienced in the secular realm; the territories of Europe were slowly consolidating into the European nations of the modern world. Such civilization development called forth the need for more precise clarification of the law, including more precise

---

[55] A phrase coined by medieval Scholastics to represent the Aristotelian emphasis on the rational principle inherent to all mankind.

[56] John Locke, *Second Treatise of Government*, ed and intro C.B. Macpherson (Indianapolis: Hackett Publishing, 1980 [1690]), 9.

specification of the respective jurisdictional authority held by the two putatively complementary "powers" of medieval society, spiritual and temporal, Church and State. Over the centuries, medieval jurists and canon lawyers would address such issues with skill and vigor.

The task of medieval jurists was facilitated by the eleventh century's discovery and resurrection of Roman law, which became the bedrock upon which medieval law was built. Most important was the discovery of the *Corpus iuris civilis*, the codification of late imperial law compiled by the Emperor Justinian in the sixth century. Major developments also arose within the sphere of canon law, the rules governing the Church and application of Christian doctrine to the faithful. The two bodies of law, Roman and canon, formed the medieval common law, the *jus commune* of Western Europe.[57] The social success of Christianity, and especially the authority acquired by the Church upon securing freedom from political control, assured, moreover, that all law, secular as well as canon, would develop under the influence of Christian moral precepts— the higher law of God.

The most important philosophical elaboration of law within Christendom was provided, as mentioned, by Aquinas. Aquinas identified four kinds of law: the hierarchically ordered eternal, divine, natural, and human law. At the apex of the hierarchy is the eternal law, the comprehensive law that involves God's all-encompassing and providential plan for creation. The divine law comprises the law revealed by God to humanity in those Scriptural passages that deal explicitly with law. The natural law, in Aquinas's well-known formulation, represents man's "participation in the eternal law."[58] The human being participates in the eternal law by virtue of his reason, one of the "parts" of human being made in the image and likeness of God; such "participation" is called the natural law.[59] Natural law, in other words, comprises certain human moral inclinations originating in the Being or nature of God, His intrinsic lawfulness, goodness, and justice.

---

[57] Including specializations such as royal, urban, mercantile, manorial, feudal law, and so on. Berman, *Law and Revolution*.

[58] Aquinas, *Summa Theologica*, Q 91, Second Article, in *On Law, Morality, and Politics*, 2nd ed, trans, Richard J. Regan (Indianapolis: Hackett Publishing Company, Inc., 2002), 18. Hereinafter cited as *Law, Morality, and Politics*.

[59] I am indebted to Thomas E. Lordan for his exposition of the natural law. Private correspondence, 2013.

Man's natural inclination toward right and aversion toward wrong serve as inherent guides toward fulfillment of his uniquely human nature, which he can recognize as such by virtue of that nature (a rational creature made in the image of a rational God). The natural law so conceived, as noted, has at times been associated with the laws "written on the heart" referred to in Romans 2: 12-16.[60] The fourth kind of law, human law, completes Aquinas's hierarchy. Human law (sometimes referred to as "positive" or "man-made" law) comprises legislation, edicts, regulations, decrees, and so forth enacted by human authority, legal or political, that is, "law" as generally conceived by the popular mind.

The hierarchical arrangement of the four types of law means, of course, that certain types of law are superior to others; there is "higher" law and lower or inferior law. The higher law comprises the law of God, eternal, divine, and natural; the "lower" law, indeed the lowest form of law, is comprised of human law.[61] Moreover, for Aquinas as for Aristotle, what is superior or higher necessarily governs that which is inferior or lower. With respect to law this means that the higher law of God necessarily governs the lower law of man. More particularly, it means that a human law is valid *if and only if* it conforms to the higher law of God. A human or positive law that violates or contradicts the higher moral law is illegitimate or invalid; it is not a true law. Aquinas did not originate such a conception. His contribution was to provide a philosophical elaboration of the relation between the law of God and the law of man that was more or less traditional for his era. A thousand years earlier Augustine had succinctly pronounced a conclusion identical to that carefully expounded by Aquinas: "an unjust law," said Augustine, "is no

---

[60] Romans 2: 12-16. 12. "For all who have sinned without the law will also perish without the law, and all who have sinned under the law will be judged by the law. For it is not the hearers of the law who are righteous before God, but the doers of the law who will be justified. For when Gentiles, who do not have the law, by nature do what the law requires, they are a law to themselves, even though they do not have the law. They show that the work of the law is written on their hearts, while their conscience also bears witness, and their conflicting thoughts accuse or even excuse them on that day when, according to my gospel, God judges the secrets of men by Christ Jesus."

[61] Both human and divine law may be regarded as forms of "positive" law. What distinguishes them is their source, human and divine, respectively.

law at all."[62] Such an unequivocal judgment derived from Augustine's implicit adherence to the view that Aquinas would make explicit: a human law, to be just, must be in conformity with the higher law of God. Further implied in Augustine's pronouncement is the traditional belief that law, by definition, secures justice (*jus*), just as a king, by definition, is an authority who secures justice. A human rule, command, decree or edict that itself violates justice is not law, just as a king who violates justice is not a true king. A king who engages in acts of injustice by those very acts "un-kings" himself and becomes a mere tyrant. True law, like a true king, secures justice, and this can only be achieved, for Augustine as for Aquinas, if in conformity with true or higher justice, the justice of God embodied in His law. A human law is valid law, true law, law proper, *if and only if* it conforms to the higher law of God: "An unjust law is no law at all."

The significance of the conception of the higher law for the development of limited government and the free society cannot be overstated. Such a conception imposes intrinsic and stringent moral limits on the action of government. Political authorities, like all members of society, are forbidden to engage in actions that violate the higher law of God and, moreover, any such unlawful actions do not bind the Christian conscience (they are not true law). The profound influence of Christianity on the formation of modern Western legal and political institutions thus ensured their development within a framework of biblical morality. The Romans, as we recall, were the first people in history explicitly to incorporate the concept of the natural law (*jus naturale*) into legal reasoning. Roman jurists, however, unlike their Christian counterparts, did not conceive the natural law as superior law on the basis of which the validity of human or positive law might be challenged. The Roman concept of natural law remained more or less descriptive and not functional in this sense. Christian thinkers would develop the concept of the higher or natural law in another direction. In time it was not only identified with the eternal and objective moral law of God that took precedence over all forms of strictly human law but also regarded as a basis for challenging and even resisting human law perceived to violate the higher law of God. If "an unjust law is no law at

---

[62] Augustine, *On Free Choice of the Will* (Indianapolis: Hackett Publishing Company, 1993), Book 1, § 5, 8.

all," then it cannot be binding on the Christian conscience. Neither Roman nor any other civilization developed such a potentially revolutionary conception.

The Christian interpretation of the higher law would further impress the development of Western political order, including its characteristic conception of limited government, by its insistence that every human being, including each and every political ruler, is bound by the higher moral law originating in God. Medieval thinkers, as we have seen, unequivocally pronounced the king to be "under God and under law." Centuries earlier, long before the achievement of formal institutional division of religion and government, forceful Christian clerics such as St. Ambrose declared that political rulers, as "sons of the Church," were as much bound by the higher law of God as their subjects. We have discussed the fifth-century doctrine of the Two Powers, in which Gelasius not only conceptually distinguished spiritual and worldly authority but further asserted the inherent superiority of spiritual authority to the mundane power of secular rulers.

Indeed the political significance of the Christian conception of the overarching higher law of God emerges long before the fourth and fifth centuries. It is bound up with the very birth of Christianity and shaped Christian political experience and attitudes from the outset. Christianity was born in tension with political rule. Not only did Roman authority crucify Christ but, as we have seen, the Christian revelation, in contrast to the expectations embodied in the Roman state, radically devalued the worldly sphere in general and political sphere in particular. The experience of sporadic persecution during the centuries following the death of Christ further deepened Christian suspicion of political rule. From the beginning, moreover, the newfound faith of many Christian converts engendered an existential dilemma with significant political consequences—the previously discussed dual allegiance henceforth required of believers. On the one hand, Christians were exhorted to "obey the powers that be," to be good citizens, keep a low profile, and refrain from actions that might antagonize Roman authorities or the pagan population more generally. Christians were undoubtedly aware of the suspicion with which they were often regarded. As Edward Gibbon observed, "By embracing the faith of the Gospel the Christians incurred the supposed guilt of an unnatural and unpardonable offence. They dissolved the sacred ties of custom and education, violated the religious institutions of their country, and presumptuously despised whatever their fathers had believed as true, or had reverenced as sacred."[63]

On the other hand, the spread of Christianity meant that increasing numbers of Christian-Roman citizens found themselves bound by an obligation they regarded as infinitely superior to mere obedience to secular rule, let alone conventional public opinion. The foremost duty of a Christian is of course obedience to the salvific higher law of God. In the case of conflict between the two authorities—Caesar and God—the latter must take precedence; nothing less than eternal salvation or damnation is at stake. Such a conflict, moreover, was not a mere theoretical possibility but, at times, a concrete reality that demanded existential response. Both Roman law and public opinion, as we have seen, called for participation in Rome's traditional public or civic religion. Christians generally refused such participation, arousing hostility and even localized persecution of the new sect. We also recall that the Roman Empire came to adopt the Hellenistic practice of worshiping the king or emperor as a god or quasi-divine being of some sort, undoubtedly posing intense conflict of allegiance to the Christian mind. For Christians, only God is divine. The created order is good but bears no trace of divinity; indeed the worship of a secular ruler or any other earthly phenomenon, however nominal, is explicitly condemned as idolatry. The law of the Roman state, however, required precisely such an act of worship (*adoratio*). What is a Christian to do? That is the question raised by the revelation of God's higher law, and the Christian response would profoundly shape the development of Western moral, legal, and political traditions for two thousand years.

Civil Disobedience

Most persons are familiar with accounts of early Christian martyrs who maintained allegiance to God in the face of conflicting Roman authority, among the more dramatic historical responses of Christian faith to the tension between God and Caesar. The significance of such tension, however, extends far beyond ancient acts of martyrdom and, indeed, shapes Christian and American attitudes toward political power to the

---

[63] Edward Gibbon, *Decline and Fall of the Roman Empire*, Amazon Digital Services, Volume 2, Chapter XVI, Part I.

present day. Such is pointedly illustrated by the uniquely American conception known as *civil disobedience*, a term coined by Henry David Thoreau in 1848 and without precise counterpart in other languages, Western or non-Western.[64] Civil disobedience is a characteristically American conception whose influence, however, has extended far beyond the immediate orbit of American society. Mahatma Gandhi, who led the twentieth-century struggle for Indian independence from British rule, was inspired by Thoreau's seminal essay, "On the Duty of Civil Disobedience," and the concept also played a role in the Nuremberg Trials of Nazi war criminals in the aftermath of World War II. In the United States, the tactic of civil disobedience was adopted by Martin Luther King, who led the struggle to achieve full-bodied civil rights for African-Americans in the second half of the twentieth century. Moreover, while the term is peculiarly American, the experience it describes is ancient, wedded as it is, and as we shall see, to the ancient notion of a moral law superior to the law of man. Antigone may legitimately be regarded as having engaged in a form of civil disobedience, as may those Christian martyrs whose higher allegiance to God impelled them to violate the law of Rome.

Civil disobedience may be defined as deliberate and nonviolent resistance to a human law that is considered unjust. The lawbreaker who deliberately violates the human law simultaneously affirms the validity of the rule of law by peacefully submitting to the consequences of his illegal act. He does not challenge the right of the authorities to arrest him or attempt in other ways to avoid legal or man-made punishment for breaking the law. The purpose of civil disobedience, according to Thoreau, is not to antagonize authority but rather avoid personal participation in injustice. When the laws are unjust, he says, the proper place for a just person is jail. Civil disobedience is employed primarily for the sake of personal rectitude but also as a means to elevate the moral consciousness of society. The hope is that such an act of peaceful protest against perceived legal injustice will move the conscience of its members, leading ultimately to repeal or revision of the unjust law.

---

[64] The term was coined by Henry David Thoreau (1817-1862, "On the Duty of Civil Disobedience" (London: Forgotten Books, 2008). It describes his refusal to pay the state poll tax implemented by the American government to prosecute war in Mexico and enforce the Fugitive Slave Law.

Our principal interest concerns the grounds upon which an individual may legitimately challenge the justice of a human law. Every act of civil disobedience is necessarily informed by certain definite if implicit moral presuppositions. Such assumptions are perhaps most readily perceived by contrasting the two chief philosophies of law that have guided Western jurisprudence over the centuries, generally referred to as *natural law* and *legal positivism*. The tradition of natural or higher law has been previously discussed. On such a view, as we have seen, a human law is considered valid *if and only if* in conformity with the higher law of God. On such a standard, Augustine could flatly and unequivocally declare that "an unjust law is no law at all" and thus not morally binding on the Christian conscience, a conviction that retained its force, implicitly or explicitly, throughout the development of Western civilization. We have seen, however, that the eighteenth and nineteenth centuries witnessed a sustained attack on biblical religion conducted by various antitheistic forces. The consequences of the modern "revolt against God" included not only the rise of the militant ideological movements but, equally important if less dramatic, evisceration of the ancient tradition of the natural or higher law, dependent as it is on traditional religious presuppositions. A competing philosophy of law, generally referred to as legal positivism and dramatically at odds with natural-law jurisprudence, gained ascendancy. Contrary to the school of natural law, legal positivism asserts that a law is a true law *if and only if* duly authorized by the proper constitutional authority in a given society, for instance, a representative assembly such as the United States Congress. Law proper is confined to law that has received such legal and political (human) sanction. Legal positivism thus eliminates at a stroke all other possible kinds of law, most pointedly, the kinds of law that constitute the ground and standard of the Judeo-Christian tradition of higher law (the eternal, divine, and natural law believed to have their source in God, and not man). According to legal positivism, the only true or actual law is man-made, human, or positive law.

The rise of legal positivism raises significant issues with respect to American constitutional order, arising, as we shall see, from the interdependence of traditional American political and legal institutions and traditional religious conceptions of the higher law. Legal positivism eliminates a theological basis for law and assigns its source exclusively to human agents. In so doing, it eliminates the concept of an autonomous sphere of morality distinct from, and superior to, the legal enactments of government, in other words, eliminates the very concept of higher law. The consequences of legal positivism, moreover, extend far beyond the dismantling of the higher-law tradition. Such a philosophy collapses *in toto* the characteristically Western distinction between the realms of God and Caesar and the entire set of dichotomies that follow from such a distinction. In assigning the source of law to human rather than divine government, for instance, legal positivism eliminates the traditional dichotomy between the "moral" and the "legal." The elimination of the concept of higher law (morality) superior to human law (legality) leads, explicitly or implicitly, to the identification of morality and legality, to the conflation of what is morally right with the rules enacted by human authority. As we have seen, the traditional Western dichotomy between the realms of God and Caesar, by contrast, simultaneously differentiates morality from legality, the former belonging within the province of God, the latter of Caesar. On such a view, morality and legality are far from identical, just as sin is far from identical to crime and inner conscience to external behavior. All such distinctions collapse under the philosophy of legal positivism. The ascendancy of legal positivism is not an autonomous development but rather a consequence of the so-called "death of God" famously announced by Nietzsche at the close of the nineteenth century and to which we return in the following chapter. In the context of legal and moral philosophy, the rejection of the transcendent God of the Bible would lead human government to assume simultaneous authorship of morality and law, to become, in effect if not in name, the new god, in Nietzsche's well-known phrase, the "new Idol."[65]

We are now prepared to return to our earlier topic, the moral basis of civil disobedience. We are exploring the grounds upon which a person may legitimately challenge the justice of a law enacted by legal or constitutional authority in a given society, such as state and federal legislatures. On the view of legal positivism, which regards law as valid or just, by definition, so long as it has been enacted by a proper constitutional authority, no such grounds exist. There is no basis on which to condemn or resist as unjust any legal enactment of government;

---

[65] Friedrich Nietzsche, 'The New Idol," in *Thus Spoke Zarathustra,* (NY: Penguin Classics, 1961).

justice is secured, by definition, so long as a law is enacted in accordance with proper constitutional procedure. A government informed by the philosophy of legal positivism thus implicitly or explicitly assumes the right to define justice and, indeed, morality more generally. Justice of course is a moral concept. Legal positivism abandons the concept of higher moral law, higher justice, and restricts law to that which has been legally enacted by human authority. Such a philosophy of law thereby, in effect if not intention, grants human beings exclusive authority to define not only law but morality and justice as well. In defining what is legal, political authorities necessarily and simultaneously define what is right and what is wrong; there is no authoritative higher moral law on the grounds of which to challenge such authorities. It cannot be otherwise in a society that embraces the philosophy of legal positivism.

The situation is quite otherwise, however, in a society that adheres to the traditional Western understanding of law. As we have seen, from Cicero through Augustine through Aquinas, Locke and the American Founders, that tradition insisted that human law, to be legitimate, must be in conformity with the higher law—objective rules of right and wrong established not by human authority but rather by God or Nature (whose governing principles are thought to be themselves imprinted by God). Such a traditional view of law is a necessary condition not only of civil disobedience but, indeed, any possible criticism of the justice of any legal enactment. We recall in this context that one characteristic attribute of justice within the Western tradition is *isonomia* or equal justice under law, the equality of each person before the human law. Judeo-Christian civilization of course also conceives the equality of man before God; to paraphrase the conventional expression, God, like law, is no respecter of persons. Equality before both God and law means that *all* persons, private and public, citizens and government officials, are bound alike by the law, both higher law and human law. We have discussed the profound Christian conviction that the king, like everyone else, is "under God and under law." On the traditional view, human government is not regarded as competent to "make," invent, or construct law, justice, or morality. As previously discussed in the context of the Lockean social contract, it merely declares, adjudicates, and enforces the *given* moral law that governs all human beings, public officials and private citizens alike. According to Madison and his contemporaries, as we recall, the purpose of government is to *secure* justice, not define it. Justice, as historically

59

conceived in the West, is not defined by man but rather by a source beyond human or legislative preference. A human enactment or "law" that violates the given and objective rules of right and wrong—the justice established by the higher law—is therefore "no law at all" and not binding on the human conscience.

Such were the traditional grounds upon which Thoreau took his stand by engaging in an act of civil disobedience, deliberately violating the human law enacted by the government of his day. His particular concern involved law that supported and enforced the institution of slavery in the first half of the nineteenth century. His act of civil disobedience took the form of refusal to pay a state poll tax, a tax, as he recognized, that financed a government complicit in the egregious injustice of human slavery. No just person, he argued, could in conscience pay a tax that served such injustice; to obey an unjust law is itself to participate in injustice. Thus a person who desires to be just is morally obliged to violate an unjust law. He has a "duty," Thoreau insists, to engage in civil disobedience; he has a duty to honor his individual conscience. Conscience must take precedence if in conflict with human law; the individual is first and foremost a human being and only secondarily a citizen.

The American founders justified their decision to separate from England on similar grounds. The English government, they believed, had violated the Laws of Nature and of Nature's God, in other words, had violated the objective standard of justice. The Americans, like Thoreau, took their stand upon the firm ground of the higher law, the law above the king, the objective rules of right and wrong valid for all times and all places, the eternal rules of morality, as Cicero said, that can never be rescinded by mere men. The enduring strength of the tradition of the higher law in the United States, as well as its relation to civil disobedience, is further evidenced by Martin Luther King's celebrated *Letter from Birmingham Jail.* King of course was a Christian minister. It is thus not surprising that in defending the tactic of civil disobedience, which he famously employed toward securing the rights of all Americans, he went straight to the source: the Judeo-Christian conception of the higher law. King explicitly cites Aquinas and various biblical sources in the opening sections of his *Letter.* He and his supporters regarded the laws that enforced segregation in various southern communities as unjust, a violation of God's higher law. As such, "they are no laws at all," in the words of both Augustine and King. Individuals are duty-bound, as Thoreau counseled, to disobey such purported "laws," lest they themselves participate in injustice. The proper place for a just person in a society governed by unjust laws, for King as for Thoreau, is prison. Henry Thoreau peacefully submitted to confinement in a Concord cell; Martin Luther King peacefully submitted to confinement in a Birmingham cell.

The decline of the traditional conception of the higher or natural law has had, and continues to have, immense moral and political consequences for Western society. A classic illustration of such consequences is provided by Germany under Hitler and National Socialism. Germany was foremost among European nations in embracing the philosophy of legal positivism in the nineteenth century. By the early twentieth century, the German people, including the educated elite of lawyers, judges, and others in positions of authority, had thoroughly assimilated its presuppositions.[66] A law was considered valid and binding *if and only if* it had been enacted by the appropriate constitutional or governmental authority. Hitler came to power as *Reichschancellor* through perfectly legal and constitutional means and sustained in power through various national (legal) plebiscites. His decrees and edicts were similarly enacted in accord with proper legal procedure, approved by the German parliament (*Reichstag*) and courts. Laws such as the commitment of disabled children to state institutions, prohibition of marriage between Jews and Germans, and, later, deportation of Jews, homosexuals, and gypsies, among others, were enforced by judges and obeyed by the majority of the German people, traditionally among the most law-abiding citizens in the world. The widespread influence of legal positivism largely eliminated any moral basis for resistance to Nazi laws and legislation, however subversive of the constitution or traditional morality. They had been legally enacted and thus, by definition, must be regarded as morally permissible; legal positivism, as we have seen, eliminates any and all conception of an autonomous moral code superior to legal enactment.

In the aftermath of World War II, various Nazi war criminals were prosecuted in the famous Nuremberg Trials of the late 1940s. One of

---

[66] One of the foremost and influential theorists of legal positivism is the German scholar Hans Kelsen (1881-1973).

the defenses mounted on their behalf went straight to the heart of legal positivism. The defendants, said the defense team, were good German citizens and soldiers. As such, they did their duty, which was to follow orders and obey the law; they were not criminals but rather law-abiding citizens. The defense spoke the truth—the "truth" of legal positivism. At the time, however, the conscience of the West was still in touch with the older tradition of the higher law, and the prosecution relied on natural-law theory to advance its case. Some defendants were convicted on the grounds that every human being is morally obliged to disobey orders so wantonly unjust as to lead to the murder of millions upon millions of innocent people. Further, the defendants' status as human beings, they were told, takes precedence over national or political affiliation. Accordingly, they were obliged to honor the higher moral law when it so clearly conflicted with mere legality; they were obliged, in other words, to engage in civil disobedience. The prosecution implicitly reminded the audience that "there is a law above the King," above Hitler and military commanders, above judges, courts, and representative assemblies, above all human opinion. The role of legal positivism in contributing to the horrors of the Third Reich was clearly recognized and natural-law theory resurrected, however briefly.

The Constitution as Higher Law

The decline of the higher-law tradition has profound significance for American political and social order. The traditional Western and Anglo-American conception of morality and justice—objective, given, and eternal rules of conduct binding on all persons, rulers and ruled alike— lies at the very foundation of American political order. Such moral convictions are presupposed by and embodied in both the general framework of American constitutionalism and its particular institutions. The abandonment or even evisceration of the Western moral heritage necessarily threatens traditional American order at its root. Such a threat is not merely hypothetical but clearly evidenced by the historical and ongoing transformation of American government away from the limited Constitution of the Framers and toward the exercise of increasingly unlimited power. Such a development, as we shall see, proceeded in tandem with the decline of the tradition of higher law. Moreover, it is not surprising that the depreciation of traditional morality, comprised by deontological rules generally regarded as both objective and absolute, has been accompanied by the corresponding rise of various forms of consequentialist and subjectivist ethics and a radical moral relativism, all which pose further challenge to the viability of traditional American constitutionalism. Neither the rejection of higher law nor the embrace of moral consequentialism, subjectivism, and relativism, however, are autonomous, incidental, or random developments. Such moral perspectives and propensities are rather particular manifestations of a more general and overarching modern development—the historical and ongoing evisceration of traditional Western or Judeo-Christian religious convictions.

The United States Constitution has long been recognized and represented as a secular embodiment of the Judeo-Christian conception of higher law, most notably by Edward S. Corwin in his classic work, *The Higher Law Background of American Constitutional Law.*[67] The parallel between traditional Judeo-Christian conceptions of law and the fundamental law of the U.S. Constitution is striking and obvious. The higher moral law, as we have seen, is conceived as originating in a source higher than man and regarded as both objective, independent of subjective human preference or desire, and absolute, unconditionally binding in any and all circumstances. The traditional moral law is a law *given* to man, one to which he is expected to align his actions and which he himself cannot change at will. *Thou shalt not kill* forbids taking an innocent person's life in all circumstances whatsoever; the prohibition against killing is not dependent on time, place, culture, socioeconomic status, ethnicity, and so on.[68] The U.S. Constitution, crafted by persons steeped in such traditional conceptions, embodies all such attributes of the higher law. The fundamental law of the land is conceived, like the higher moral law, as both objective and absolute. Government is bound by the law of the Constitution regardless of its subjective preferences, and, moreover, obliged to honor the Constitution absolutely or

---

[67] Edward S. Corwin, *The Higher Law Background of American Constitutional Law* (Indianapolis: Liberty Fund, 2008).

[68] Exceptions to the general prohibition against stealing have been treated by Christian scholars such as Aquinas (*Summa Theologica*, Q66, Seventh Article, *Law, Morality, and Politics*, 139-140) and recognized in the branch of law known as "equity," which treats those unusual cases in which a strict application of the law would be unjust.

unconditionally, under any and all circumstances, independent of time, place, social conditions, and so on. Further, just as the higher moral law is *given* to man, so the law of the Constitution is *given* to government. Just as individual persons are expected to align their actions with a higher law they cannot change at will, so government is expected to align its actions with a higher law it cannot change at will. The parallel between the higher moral law and higher law of the Constitution further involves their mutual conception of the hierarchical status of law. As we have seen, traditional Judeo-Christian philosophy of law conceives a hierarchical relation among its various levels, that is, certain kinds of law (eternal, divine, natural) are regarded as superior to and controlling on lower or inferior kinds (human law). In the same manner, the fundamental law of the U.S. Constitution is regarded as superior to and controlling on inferior kinds of law, such as congressional legislation, statutory law, executive orders, bureaucratic regulations, certain kinds of state law, and so.[69]

It should not be surprising that the U.S. Constitution bears such close resemblance to the traditional Judeo-Christian conception of higher law. The American Founders were heirs to centuries of Western reflection on the nature of law. They were heirs to a developed moral, legal, and religious tradition saturated with the conception of a higher moral law binding on all persons, private and public alike. It is probably not coincidental that the most widely read book of the revolutionary era should prove to be Deuteronomy. Nor does coincidence adequately explain why the amendments that constitute the Bill of Rights are ten in number and why many are cast in the form *thou shalt not* ("Congress shall make no law. . ."). The American Founders, as we have seen, carried forward various Judeo-Christian assumptions, values, and beliefs into the modern world. Such included not only the previously discussed Augustinian view of human nature but also the Christian understanding of higher law. Such a conception, and the biblical worldview from which it derives, is everywhere implicit in the constitutional order they designed. Neither the purpose nor substance of their constitutional construction can be adequately comprehended apart from the moral and

---

[69] Strictly speaking, says Hayek, the U.S. Constitution is not a "law" but rather a "superstructure erected to secure the maintenance of the law. . ." (*nomos*). Convention, however, generally describes the Constitution as "fundamental law." Hayek, *Rules and Order*, 134.

religious presuppositions that informed their efforts, including and especially the implicit embrace of the tradition of higher law. American order is rooted in centuries of experience within a civilization profoundly shaped by Judeo-Christian presuppositions regarding the nature of law, as well as existence more generally.[70]

Indeed, the United States of America was *born* taking its stand for the higher moral law over and against human law. There is no understanding the birth of America, its revolt against England, without recognizing the moral and religious roots from which such resistance grew. We have previously discussed in another context the well-known slogan of the American Revolution, "no taxation without representation." The slogan, while familiar, does not quite capture the essential grounds of American resistance to British rule. Indeed it readily yields the false impression that American resistance to British demands for additional taxes sprung from vulgar—pecuniary—motives. While such demands no doubt entailed pernicious financial consequences for many colonists, colonial resistance was ultimately motivated not by economic but rather moral concerns. The War for Independence was impelled, above all, by concern for justice and, moreover, explicitly defended on that ground—the ground of Higher Law and Justice, the "Laws of Nature and of Nature's God." As Francis Scott Key would later immortalize the revolutionary motives of American patriots, . . . *Then conquer we must, when our cause it is just, and this be our motto: 'In God is our trust'.*

The moral conviction impelling the American Revolution is clearly evidenced by a brief survey of significant pre-revolutionary events. In the aftermath of the French and Indian War (1754-1763) the British government sought to replenish a Treasury depleted by costs of the war, fought, in part, for control of the North American colonies. Parliament thus explored means of obtaining additional tax revenue, including more vigorous enforcement of existing colonial taxes and imposition of additional and novel taxes on the American colonies. Of particular importance was the novel imposition of what the colonists called "internal" taxes, in distinction to the customary "external" taxes imposed in accord with British mercantile policy. An "external" tax, such as the tax on sugar, was levied on goods imported into the colonies, paid

---

[70] Kirk, *Roots of American Order.*

directly by importers and only indirectly by colonial consumers. An "internal" tax, by contrast, was levied directly upon the property and goods of individual colonists, for instance, the tax imposed by the Stamp Act of 1765, which required colonists to purchase special watermarked paper for newspapers and legal documents. The Americans regarded such policy as an innovation, without precedent in colonial experience. They had never previously been directly taxed by the British government but rather accustomed to levying such "internal" taxes on themselves, through the several colonial assemblies. In line with traditional Western political conceptions inherited by the colonists, they argued against the novel British policy by re-asserting the longstanding principle of consent of the governed, more particularly, that taxation requires consent granted through colonial representative assemblies. The colonists had elected no representatives to the British Parliament and thus, they argued, had not granted relevant consent to "internal" or direct taxation. The British countered with the assertion that the colonists were indeed represented in Parliament, "virtually" if not actually, and, for the first time, mandated direct taxation of the colonies.

The colonists refused to acknowledge the justice of such policy. An individual whose personal resources can be taken without his consent, they reasoned, is, in effect, little different from a slave. Recurring to history and precedent, they insisted that taxation requires actual consent of the governed: "No Taxation without Representation!" The Americans rose up in arms, at first figuratively and, later, literally. The defense of their right to resist British policy was initially grounded on traditional principles of English law and liberty. We are Englishmen, proclaimed the colonists, entitled to the rights and liberties guaranteed to all English subjects as well as governance on English principles, including consent of the governed. England had no right, on its own political principles and traditions, to tax the colonists without their consent. In response to colonial protest, the British repealed the Stamp Act in 1766. At the same time, however, they further fanned the flames of colonial resistance by refusing to acknowledge the validity of the colonists' claims and, moreover, accompanying the repeal with the so-called Declaratory Act, which asserted Parliament's authority to legislate for the colonies "in all cases whatsoever."[71] The British asserted, in other words, the doctrine that came to be known as "Parliamentary Sovereignty." In response to such British recalcitrance, the Americans would shift the grounds of their resistance, a tactic for which their heirs must be forever grateful. For in so doing the colonists came to elaborate what is arguably the greatest of the many American contributions to liberty and the free society: the conviction that the political order of a free people is grounded in, and established upon, the fixed foundation of the Higher Law, the immutable "Laws of Nature and of Nature's God," the "law above the King."

The English colonists who first arrived in America in the early 1600s carried with them the traditional constitutional principles of their homeland. These included the aforementioned historical rights and liberties of Englishmen initially asserted against the innovative British policy of direct colonial taxation. Parliament responded, as mentioned, by denying their claims in favor of the novel constitutional doctrine of Parliamentary Sovereignty.[72] The colonists, said the British, must recognize that English constitutional principles had changed over the hundred and more years since establishment of the American colonies. The Glorious Revolution of 1688, which established constitutional limits on the power of the British Crown, had further involved the transfer of political sovereignty from Crown to Parliament. Parliament, the colonists were informed, is now the locus of sovereignty, ultimate political authority beyond which there is no other. Accordingly, Parliament is the final arbiter of the legitimacy of the laws it enacts and these include the decision to lay direct taxes on the colonies in America. There is no appeal beyond Parliament; Parliament is sovereign. The English constitution, it might be said, had "evolved" over time. Colonial conceptions and expectations were outdated; the Americans were living in the past.

---

[71] Declaratory Act of 1766: ". . . the king's Majesty, by and with the advice and consent of the Lords Spiritual and Temporal, and Commons, of Great Britain, in Parliament assembled, had, hath, and of right ought to have, full power and authority to make laws and statutes of sufficient force and validity to bind the colonies and people of America, subjects of the crown of Great Britain, in all cases whatsoever. . . ."

[72] David Ammerman, "The British Constitution and the American Revolution: A Failure of Precedent," 17 *William and Mary Law Review* 473 (1976).

Such was more or less the English response to the colonists' defense of their historical rights and liberties, a response that would profoundly alter the course of human events. To defend what they continued to regard as their legitimate rights and liberties, British disavowal notwithstanding, including the right to be taxed only upon their own consent, the colonists turned away from English law and custom and toward a law superior to Parliament and Crown. They turned to the Higher Law, the "law above the King," to the medieval tradition of law carried from England by their forebears and which the Americans, unlike the English, had never abandoned. Among other sources, the colonists turned to the natural-law defense of the right to resist arbitrary government elaborated by Locke in the previous century. Locke's argument in the *Second Treatise* seemed tailor-made for colonial purposes. The Americans regarded their situation as analogous to that which had engendered Locke's defense of the right of resistance during the English constitutional crisis of the seventeenth century. The novel British theory of Parliamentary Sovereignty seemed scarcely distinguishable from the claim of Monarchical Sovereignty asserted by the Stuart kings; the locus of "absolute sovereignty" had merely shifted from Crown to Parliament. To the colonial mind, the claims of both King and Parliament, their mutual demands for unconditional obedience to their respective laws, appeared as mere assertions of arbitrary power. Indeed the Americans would ultimately reject *in toto* the very concept of absolute sovereignty. It should not be forgotten that the first settlers fled England precisely to escape what they regarded as oppressive and tyrannical government. They were undoubtedly familiar not only with Lockean resistance theory but also the extensive resistance literature developed during the religious conflicts of Post-Reformation Europe and the English Civil War.[73] Traditional European resistance theory would achieve a renaissance in the New World.

---

[73] Representative works include George Garnett, ed, *Vindiciae, contra tyrannos: or, Concerning the Legitimate Power of a Prince over the People, and of the People over a Prince* (Cambridge: Cambridge University Press, 2003); Rev. Samuel Rutherford, *Rex, Lex, or, the Law and the Prince: A Dispute for the Just Prerogative of King and People* (1644). See Quentin Skinner, *Foundations of Modern Political Thought*, Volume II: *The Age of Reformation* (Cambridge: Cambridge University Press, 1978).

The Declaration of Independence unequivocally grounds American resistance to British rule in the Higher Law. It pointedly expresses the colonists' belief that the English government had violated eternal and objective rules of morality and justice that originate not from human authority but an authority higher than man. The English conception of rights and liberties may have changed, but that did not and cannot change the actual status of individual rights and liberties. Such are not granted by government and thus cannot be rescinded by government. Individual rights and liberties are not the gift of England but rather of "Nature's God"; all human beings are "endowed by their Creator with certain unalienable rights. . . ." English political doctrine may have changed but the eternal laws of justice, the "Laws of Nature," do not and cannot change; such are perpetual and immutable, grounded in God and Nature, in a law above the King. Although the colonists themselves did not explicitly employ the language of Cicero or Augustine or Aquinas, the convictions and insights of their forebears saturate the American perspective. The colonists might readily have invoked the Augustinian conviction that "an unjust law," such as taxation without consent, "is no law at all." They might explicitly have invoked Aquinas's hierarchy of law, demanding that all human law conform to the Higher Law of God. Such traditional views, however implicit, are foundational to American political thought of the founding era. The Americans stood in a stream of tradition, flowing over the course of millennia, that denied the possibility of imposing moral obligation by mere exercise of political power. Indeed, far from imposing moral duty on the governed, acts of injustice, exercises of arbitrary power, both demand and justify resistance. As the colonial slogan summarized the central conviction, "rebellion to tyrants is obedience to God."[74]

The American colonists, as we have seen, rejected the very core of the British argument, that is, the very concept of absolute sovereignty, whether situated in Crown or Parliament. A free society has no place for an *absolute* sovereign of any kind, king, president, members of Parliament or Congress, judges, or anyone else. The Lockean/American social contract, as we have seen, rather regards all political obligation as

---

[74] "Rebellion to Tyrants is Obedience to God" is the motto imprinted on Benjamin Franklin's draft proposal for the first Great Seal of the new United States. Both Franklin and Jefferson wanted the slogan to be the motto of the United States.

conditional, never absolute. Nor does traditional American political thought recognize the concept of *personal* sovereignty, that is, ultimate authority of some *person* over other persons. The only "sovereign" entity or ultimate authority recognized within the political order of a free people is law—*impersonal* general rules equally applicable to all persons. Such an ideal, as previously discussed, is historically summarized in the Anglo-American conceptions of "a government of laws, not of men" and the rule of law more generally. In a free society, *lex, rex*: law is sovereign.[75] Moreover, as we further recall, the rule of law emphatically does *not* mean the rule of any and all legislation passed by a representative assembly, as advocated by legal positivism. The American Founders were not legal positivists but rather passionate champions of the opposing legal philosophy, the tradition of natural law. Human law or legislation is valid *if and only if* in accord with the higher law, the moral law established by God and the secular higher law established by the U.S. Constitution. The Americans staked their claim to liberty and justice on the traditional Western convictions that "the king is under God and under law" and "an unjust law is no law at all." They expected each and every agent and act of government to accord with eternal and objective rules of right and wrong, rules embodied in the equally fixed and objective law of the Constitution. As Madison repeatedly emphasized, the very purpose of government is to secure justice, conceived not as an arbitrary or subjective human construction but rather an objective and determinate moral virtue rooted in God or Nature.

The American Founders, then, believed in the objectivity of the moral law, in the objectivity of justice, in immutable rules of right and wrong given to man independently of his subjective preferences or desires. Man's task is to align himself with the higher law, and all human actions may be judged in its light. Such were the grounds upon which the Americans defended their unalienable natural rights against the British and justified resistance to British rule. American constitutional order is inextricably entwined with the traditional conception of the higher law from its inception. Not only are its political history and institutions largely unintelligible without recognition of their implicit moral foundation but the stability and vitality of traditional American

---

[75] Hayek. *Rules and Order*, 91-93; *Law, Legislation, and Liberty*, Vol. 2, *The Mirage of Social Justice* (Chicago: University of Chicago Press, 1976), 61.

constitutionalism is inevitably dependent upon the stability of its foundation. American constitutionalism presupposes an enduring commitment to an objective and enduring moral standard that transcends human will. The interdependence of such traditional moral and religious convictions and free government raises crucial issues for contemporary American society, for it is not clear that the majority of the American people continue to embrace the conception of a higher moral law that underlies and sustains their political and legal institutions.

The widespread failure to recognize the significance of higher law with respect to American political order cannot be blamed on undue complexity of American constitutional design. The moral paradigm implicit in the Founders' construction, on the contrary, is relatively straightforward. God, the author of Nature, is the source of the Laws of Nature, the eternal and objective moral law. The Creator endowed each and every individual with certain natural and unalienable rights, that is, moral entitlement to particular manners of treatment. Human beings agree to establish government in order to obtain greater security for their unalienable rights. Government is assigned the responsibility of securing such rights and granted the resources requisite to that task. If, however, government should fail to honor its obligation, or worse yet, itself violate the rights it is established to secure, then the people have the right, and the duty, to abolish such government and create another better designed to secure the safety of their rights. The basic theory is not inordinately complex but its very simplicity veils certain profound presuppositions: belief in a Creator (God, the author of Nature); belief that God has created a kind of being—human being—whose very nature entitles it to special treatment (unalienable rights); belief in an objective and immutable moral order given to man; belief that the purpose of government is to secure individual natural rights; and, finally, the belief that a government that fails to do so is illegitimate and may justifiably be resisted.

It is difficult to gauge the extent to which such assumptions continue to be shared among members of contemporary American society. The key element, that from which all else follows, is the existence of a Creator who is the author of the moral law and who endows human beings with rights. As will be discussed more fully in a following chapter, such an assumption has been widely challenged in the modern era, along with the biblical worldview from which it derives. The decline of traditional religious conviction is of special concern to those who would preserve limited government and the free society. Both uniquely Western achievements, paradigmatically expressed in the American constitutional framework, stand or fall with preservation or abandonment of the religious presuppositions that impelled their development.

The Value of the Person

We conclude the discussion of the Judeo-Christian conceptions that implicitly inform the Founders' constitutional construction with what is arguably the most significant of all such conceptions, namely, the profound value of the human person. Members of contemporary American society, as we have seen, are heir to millennia of cultural development profoundly impressed with the spiritual assumptions comprised by the biblical worldview. The formative influence of such presuppositions on Western consciousness readily enables members of American society to take its characteristic values and institutions for granted. An American citizen may be forgiven, for instance, for assuming the universal and self-evident appeal of such political values as individual freedom and limited government. Such values, however, like various other Western values (justice, peace, toleration, and so on), have neither been held as conscious ideals nor provided institutional protection within the overwhelming majority of societies over the course of history. Such characteristically American values, as has been discussed, are rather unique outgrowths of a unique cultural and religious tradition, the Western or Judeo-Christian tradition.

Such is emphatically the case with respect to what would ultimately become the core value of Western civilization—that which from all else follows: the inherent and profound worth of the individual person. Over the course of centuries, Western society would come to assume the sanctity of human life in general and the individual person in particular. From the outset, American political ideals assumed that human life is precious and, as Locke said, to be preserved. They assumed that each and every individual is morally entitled to exist, that is, possesses an unalienable right to life. They assumed that every individual is entitled to be treated justly and fairly, and to live in peace. They assumed that every individual has a right to be free, to pursue his self-chosen values and purposes and not compelled to realize goals imposed by others.

Throughout their history, members of American society have taken for granted that each and every individual possesses such rights; such conceptions, as Jefferson observed, have generally seemed "self-evident" to the American people.

Such is not to say, of course, that such ideals and convictions have invariably been honored in practice. The egregious institution of chattel slavery comes immediately and inevitably to mind, certainly in the American context. Failure to honor one's ideals and convictions, however, does not invalidate them but merely highlights the obvious and inevitable imperfection and fallibility of human being, American as all other. The existence of slavery in the American experience did not follow from lack of conviction with respect to the aforementioned ideals but rather from a human flaw that has plagued the experience of mankind throughout the course of history: racism. When the slave-owner Jefferson pronounced that "all men are created equal" he was not engaging in hypocrisy but revealing a deep-seated prejudice that excluded non-white peoples from the category of humanity. Hypocrisy and racism are both evils, but distinct evils. In this regard, modern American history seems to be characterized by the curious phenomenon of simultaneous progress and decline. The decline involves the evisceration of traditional moral beliefs and the rise of moral relativism and subjectivism. The progress involves the historic and ongoing transcendence of racist convictions and practice, however imperfectly achieved. For the first time in history, the American people, having largely if not universally overcome the historical challenge of racism, have the opportunity to fully realize the promise of their founding principles and ideals: All men are created equal and endowed by their Creator with unalienable rights. All men.

Leaving aside the imperfect realization of traditional American ideals and principles in practice, we return to the issue at hand: the source of the characteristically Western belief in the value of the human person. Such a value is far from self-evident and far from the universal conviction of mankind, even within the pre-Christian West. It is rather yet another fruit of the biblical worldview, as clearly evidenced by comparison of the Roman and Christian conceptions of the "person." The word derives from the Latin *persona,* itself derived from the Etruscan *phersu* or "mask" and associated with the Etruscan and Roman theatre. In the earliest Roman usage, *persona* could mean mask or role, the character played by the actor. By the first century B.C. the word had several different but related meanings. *Persona* was employed as a technical term for the various roles an individual played in society, for instance, his role as a father and his role as a citizen. Eventually *persona* became a definite legal category, connected with the legal right to have a name. As Marcel Mauss explains, "the Roman citizen had a right to the *nomen*, the *progenomen* and the *cognomen* that his gens assigned to him. . . . Thus to be a persona meant to have access to one's name, one's status, . . . [which further] meant that one had the right to have property, to do business, and to be a member of the senate."[76] "Personhood" continued largely to refer to legal standing as late as the sixth century A.D. The term persona also appears in Stoic moral philosophy. In *De Officiis*, Cicero discusses the four *"persona"* that make an entity human, the most important of which is reason, thereby relating *persona* to moral consciousness.[77] The classical meanings of *persona*, then, were largely bound up with legal status, ownership, and rationality.

Christianity did not significantly alter the formal definition of the person. The sixth-century Christian philosopher Boethius (480-534) defined the "person" as "an individual substance of a rational nature" ("*Naturæ rationalis individua substantia*"), a definition accepted by Aquinas, with revisions.[78] The concept of the person as developed within Christendom, however, while preserving classical attributes such as legal status and possession of reason, historically carried far greater significance than the *persona* of the Romans. Christian civilization retained the classical definition of the person but radically revised the *value* of the person. *Persona* becomes much more than a legal status or rational attribute related to moral consciousness. The human person becomes a soul, a spiritual being of unspeakable significance. A new and unique conception of the human person emerges under the Christian dispensation, a conception central to the Western vision of existence.

---

[76] Marcel Mauss, *The Category of the Person: Anthropology, Philosophy, History,* eds, M. Carrithers, S. Collins, S. Lukes (Cambridge: Cambridge University Press, 1985), 16. Hereinafter cited as *Category of the Person.*

[77] The other three are individuality; the historical factors that form the individual; and the individual's own will.

[78] Cited in Robert Sokolowski, "The Human Person and Political Life," in *Christian Faith & Human Understanding* (Washington DC: CUA Press, 2006), 181.

The significance of the Christian valorization or re-evaluation of the human person is seldom appreciated, and this for several reasons. First, we have seen that members of Western society generally take that value for granted. Heirs of Judeo-Christian civilization generally hold the value of the human person as a tacit presupposition or kind of self-evident truth that requires no defense or justification. Second, the implications of the new faith for the status of personhood unfolded but slowly and over time. Christianity did not instantaneously transform human consciousness or human society. The history of Western development, like that of all civilizations, is marked by progress and regression, in this case, by movements toward the recognition of the inherent worth of every person and tragic steps backward in the direction of callous disregard for the person. Despite such checkered and uneven progress, the fact remains that Christianity would ultimately engender a radical revision of classical or pagan values, including and especially the value of the person.

On the biblical view, human life is precious indeed. Every person is regarded as a divine work of art, made in God's image, endowed with reason and free will. Every human person shares to some extent in the nature of God himself, his rationality, creativity, goodness, and justice.[79] The person is more than mere matter, more than an accidental by-product of blind chemical and biological forces. He possesses an immortal soul engaged in the most profound of possible quests—the gaining of eternal life. The life of every human person represents the unfolding of a spiritual destiny, the stakes of which could not be higher. Human life matters; it has purpose, significance, and meaning. Such applies, moreover, not only to human life en masse, "humanity" as a whole, but, more important, to the individual person. The life of the individual matters; the life of every individual matters. The significance of the individual person is inherent to Christianity, the religion of the individual *par excellence*. On the Christian view, the quest for eternal salvation cannot be pursued collectively—Christianity recognizes no form of "collective salvation"—but only personally, through individual

---

[79] "Every man is truly a human person and, subsequently, is an individual substance of rational nature with an eternal destiny that is loved personally by the Creator." Hector Zagal, "Aquinas on Slavery: An Aristotelian Puzzle," *Instituto Universitario Virtual Santo Tomás* (2003). *Fundación Balmesiana – Universitat Abat Oliba CEU.* Hereinafter cited as "Aquinas on Slavery."

faith and moral action, a conception immeasurably strengthened by the Protestant Reformation. Moreover, the God of the Bible, as is said, is no respecter of persons; the locus of His concern is not only the individual as such but *each* and *every* individual. Every human life is of equal substantive worth. Such traditional religious convictions may seem trite or outdated to modern sophisticates, but the fact remains that such Christian convictions would revolutionize human consciousness. In so doing, they engendered a civilization—Western civilization—that ultimately, and for the first time in history, established political and legal institutions charged with the responsibility of securing the rights of the individual, securing to the human person, this being of unutterable worth charged with the most profound of all possible missions, the moral treatment to which he is entitled by virtue of his very being.

We have discussed the contrasting conceptions of the person held by Roman and Christian civilization. Rome, however, was not alone in holding a relatively shallow conception of personhood; such a view was all but universal within ancient or classical civilization. Indeed human life in pre-Christian society was often, so to say, cheap. Slavery was ubiquitous, from Mesopotamia to Egypt to Greece to Rome, and everywhere beyond. It is estimated that 50% of Roman subjects were slaves, *nonpersona*, without personhood and thus status or rights. Early Christianity did not frontally challenge the Roman institution of slavery; to do so would have been suicidal for the small and suspect religious cult. But Christian teaching ameliorated the lot of the legal slave by teaching that true slavery and true freedom are not legal but rather spiritual phenomena. True slavery is slavery to lower passions, bondage to sin. True freedom is gained by mastery of sinful propensities, through the grace of God. Thus a legal slave who strove to avoid sin could be considered spiritually superior to a legal master who did not. As Augustine said, "[he] that is kind is free, though he is a slave; he that is evil is a slave, though he be a king. . . . Beyond question it is a happier thing to be the slave of a man than of a lust; for even this very lust of ruling, to mention no others, lays waste men's hearts with the most ruthless dominion."[80] Augustine further emphasized that legal slavery, while legitimate, is contrary to the intention of God, who intended all persons to be free from the dominion of other men. Augustine rejects

---

[80] Augustine, *City of Goa*, Book XIX: 15, 460-462.

the Aristotelian conception that certain human beings are "slaves by nature"; the institution of slavery is not natural but rather a result of sin.[81] As Augustine put it, "God said, "Let him have dominion over the fish of the sea and the winged things of the heavens and all the crawling things which crawl upon the earth" [Gn 1: 26]. He did not will that the rational being, having been made according to his own image, dominate any except the irrational beings; he did not will that man dominate man, but that man dominate the beasts."[82]

Christianity continued over the centuries to regard slavery as a legitimate institution in certain circumstances. Nevertheless, by the later Middle Ages, as Christian convictions were assimilated by ever greater numbers of people, legal slavery in the West would all but disappear. Although revived in the early-modern period, with tragic consequences in America and elsewhere, it should not be forgotten that the movement to abolish legal slavery was also a product of the Christian conscience. During the Middle Ages the Roman Church repeatedly prohibited the practice or at least the export of Christian slaves to non-Christian lands.[83] Persons who fought against Spanish subjection of the Indian population in South America, like later abolitionists in the United States, were inspired by Christian convictions, perceiving slavery as a violation of God's higher law. The same is true, as we have seen, of the later civil rights movement led by Martin Luther King.

The gradual decline of the institution of slavery in the West was related to the Christian re-evaluation of the status of the individual person. The Roman *persona* became a human person, a new status accorded to each and every individual, each conceived as a child of God, possessing an immortal soul. The novel and indeed revolutionary Christian

---

[81] Aquinas, however, would support, in a qualified manner, Aristotle's conviction that some men are "slaves by nature." See Zagal, "Aquinas on Slavery."

[82] Augustine, *City of God,* Bk. XIX: 15, 460-461. "Since not at all for need's sake was the class of slaves introduced, else even along with Adam had a slave been formed; but it is the penalty of sin and punishment of disobedience. But when Christ came, He put an end to this. . . . So that it is not necessary to have a slave: or if it be at all necessary, let it be about one only, or at the most two." St. John Chrysostom, "Homily 40 on I Corinthians."

[83] The Council of Koblenz (922), the Council of London (1102), and the Council of Armagh (1171).

conception of the person dissolved class, ethnic, gender, and other distinctions: "There is neither Jew nor Greek, slave nor free, male nor female, for you are all one in Christ Jesus" (Galatians 3: 28). The poor, the rich, the outcasts and the powerful, slaves and masters, are of equal and unutterable worth, embarked on a unique and profound spiritual journey. Culture, status, economic position, ethnic identity, all became irrelevant in light of Christian universalism. As Hector Zagal summarized the Christian view, "[e]very man is truly a human person and, subsequently, is an individual substance of rational nature with an eternal destiny that is loved personally by the Creator."[84] Moreover, as Mauss observes, "[o]ur own notion of the human person is still basically the Christian one."[85]

Christianity was the school in which Western consciousness was decisively shaped. Classical moral virtues—courage, moderation, wisdom, and justice—were not overturned but imbued with a new spirit of faith, of hope, of love. Christian spirituality would develop the interiority of human consciousness, the inward and introspective movement of mind and soul. In contrast to the Christian *person*, antique man, the human being of Greece and Rome, seems relatively brittle, deprived of psychological substance and subtlety. The Greek *psyche* seems relatively shallow in comparison to the rich depth of the Christian soul and intricacy of the Christian conscience. It is not coincidental that art forms such as the autobiography and the novel were unknown to the classical world. The first autobiography to appear in Western letters is that of Augustine. His *Confessions* (397-398 A.D.) seems to enter a realm of consciousness unknown to pagan literature, to touch upon depths of being that eluded even the saintly Marcus Aurelius. Indeed the conscience of the Christian would become one of the great spiritual forces in history, rising to ever more profound significance with the Protestant Reformation. Martin Luther (1483-1546) defended his radical challenge to the religious powers-that-be by planting his flag firmly on the ground of conscience: "Here I stand," he explained, "I can do no other. God help me. Amen!"[86] The first natural right claimed by

---

[84] Zagal "Aquinas on Slavery: An Aristotelian Puzzle."
[85] Mauss, *The Category of the Person*, 19.
[86] Martin Luther, Diet of Worms April 1521.

the American colonists, as we have seen, was the right of conscience. Several hundred years later Thoreau stood the same ground.

Ethical thought within pagan culture generally valorized the virtue of self-assertion, whether the magnanimity of the great-souled man of the Greek imagination or the desire for glory and dominion characteristic of late Rome. Christianity, by contrast, taught Western man humility and gentleness of spirit, kindness and compassion (virtues famously castigated by Nietzsche as "slave morality"[87]). In contrast to self-assertion, Judeo-Christian ethics emphasized the virtue of *self-restraint* ("thou shalt not"). We have discussed the significance of the negative or inhibitory rules characteristic of traditional biblical morality, in particular, their formative influence on the development of Western legal and political values and institutions. As we have seen, law as traditionally conceived in the West consists of a body of negative general rules that aim to prevent one person from harming another or the government from harming the citizens. Such a conception is an outgrowth of biblical morality. Traditional Judeo-Christian morality does entail certain positive obligations ("remember the Sabbath day, to keep it holy"; "honor thy father and thy mother"; "love thy neighbor as thyself"), but the bulk of its moral obligations, especially those that deal with treatment of other human beings, are met not by positive action but rather negative self-restraint. The majority of the Decalogue consists precisely of general negative rules that forbid one individual to harm another; traditional Western social morality is largely a morality of self-restraint or self-inhibition. Moral development so conceived involves progress in controlling or curbing the self, in refraining from certain actions. The New Testament enlarges on such morality but does not abolish it. Traditional Judeo-Christian social morality is preponderantly a negative morality and, moreover, the implicit moral and religious basis of the negative Lockean rights to life, liberty, and property enshrined in the American Declaration.

The inseparability of the moral, legal, and political dimensions of social order is reflected in the inseparable relation among traditional Judeo-Christian morality, the rule of law, and the rise of the free society, including its characteristic conception of individual rights and the limits

---

[87] Friedrich Nietzsche, *On the Genealogy of Morals* (Mineoloa, NY: Dover Publications, 2003 [1887]).

these place on the reach of legitimate governmental power. We have seen that traditional individual rights (life, liberty, property, conscience) are negative rights that engender corresponding negative obligations on the part of other persons, obligations that largely derive from the negative rules of Judeo-Christian social morality. The moral obligations entailed by the rights of other individuals can only be met by individuals willing to exercise the Judeo-Christian virtue of self-restraint. A free society on the American model requires that each individual restrain himself from harming another individual's life, liberty, and property. Each person is obliged to restrain himself from murder (the right to life), from exercising arbitrary coercion (the right to liberty), and from stealing (the right to property). As we have seen, the correspondence between traditional Judeo-Christian social morality and traditional Anglo-American conceptions of right and duty is not coincidental. Such correspondence follows from the fact that the laws of any society, as well as related conceptions such as rights, develop from the moral substratum of that society. In the case of Western civilization, the moral substratum that informed the development of Western law in general and the moral and legal framework of the free society in particular is intricately linked to the negative rules of the Judeo-Christian Decalogue.

The free society as historically achieved in the United States is an outgrowth of Western or Judeo-Christian civilization. For that reason, as previously observed, the modern offensive against liberal society advanced by the ideological movements of the era necessarily involved a similar offensive against the spiritual vision that generated and sustains that civilization, namely, biblical religion. Judeo-Christian belief and practice has thus been a central target of self-avowed communists, fascists, and fellow travelers over the past several centuries. The free society, limited government, individual rights, and the capitalist economic order represent earthly fruits of the biblical worldview. Those who seek to replace the free society with some form of unlimited government and its economic corollary, a centralized, planned, or "managed" economy, well understand that the destruction of Western liberal order requires destruction at the root, that is, destruction or evisceration of the religious worldview that, historically and existentially, gave birth to free government. We turn now to explore the modern "rebellion against God" and its relation to modern social and political developments in greater depth.[88]

---

[88] Albert Camus, *The Rebel: An Essay on Man in Revolt* (New York: Vintage, 1992 [reissue]).

TWELVE

POLITICAL RELIGION AND THE DEATH OF GOD

Let me say . . . that this conception of the state, that it is merely a police force, is, to my mind, a wholly erroneous conception; . . . the state is something far higher and more godlike than this . . . If we could only invest it in our thought with its true divine character, we should need no other agency for the unification of society.   —*Washington Gladden*

'On earth there is nothing greater than I: it is I who am the regulating finger of God'.—thus roareth the monster.   —*Friedrich Nietzsche*

The most significant political development in the United States over the past century has been the gradual but incessant growth of government and corresponding transformation of American constitutional order. Several related trends have contributed to such a development. The growth of government is partly due to the ever-wider embrace of socialist or quasi-socialist ideals among the American electorate, including the pursuit of social justice and correlative belief that government possesses the right and responsibility to override the market process through various forms of economic intervention. It is also a consequence of the greater demands placed upon government by the American people. The modern corruption of language bemoaned by Orwell and others has played a role as well, resulting in significant changes in the meaning of various concepts central to American moral and political discourse—law, rights, justice, equality, tolerance, and others—and corresponding degeneration of constitutionalism and the rule of law. Such factors, like the rise of moral consequentialism, subjectivism, and relativism, are not isolated phenomena but rather particular manifestations of a more general and far-reaching change in Western and American culture, namely, change in religious belief and practice.

We have previously discussed the fact that every culture is ultimately informed by the implicit and explicit presuppositions, beliefs, and values—the worldview—held by its members, including and especially assumptions regarding the nature and purpose of existence embodied in religion, broadly conceived. The word cult, as we recall, originally referred to religious association or practice, pointedly indicating the inextricable link between religious belief and culture. We have also explored the formative influence of biblical religion on Western civilization. The unique civilization that emerged in the West—Christendom—received its characteristic identity through the profound impress of biblically based assumptions, values, belief, and practice. As we have seen, the United States Constitution, to take but one of innumerable instances, is incomprehensible without recognition of the Judeo-Christian worldview that tacitly informs its substance. The biblical presuppositions underlying the Constitution were taken for granted throughout much of American history. As the Illinois Supreme Court remarked in 1883, ". . . [o]ur laws and our institutions must necessarily be based upon and embody the teachings of the Redeemer of Mankind. It is impossible that it should be otherwise. And in this sense and to this extent, our civilization and our institutions are emphatically Christian. . . ."[89] As President Calvin Coolidge further observed, "[the] foundations of our society and our government rest so much on the teachings of the Bible that it would be difficult to support them if faith in these teachings would cease to be practically universal in our country."[90] Similar historical observations could be repeated almost endlessly. The characteristic values and institutions of Western civilization, and most emphatically its American expression, were definitively shaped by the Judeo-Christian vision of existence. They are both a product of, and implicitly dependent upon, the unique spiritual foundation comprised by the biblical worldview. *The Death of God*

---

[89] Illinois Supreme Court, *Richmond v. Moore,* 107 Ill. 429, 1883 WL 10319 (Ill.), 47 Am. Rep. 445.
[90] Cited in Lee Hallman, *A Patriot's Devotional* (Author House, 2015)

The Judeo-Christian worldview that decisively informed the development of Western civilization, as we have seen, has encountered profound challenge over the past several centuries. The French Revolution of 1789 represented in part a militant revolt against the religious traditions of the West, a revolt carried forward with growing intensity in the nineteenth century. Indeed, by the end of that century the celebrated German philosopher Friedrich Nietzsche could famously announce: "God is dead . . . And we have killed him," thereby providing postmodern or post-Christian Western society with its defining symbol—the "death of god."[91] We have discussed the socialist assault on traditional liberal society that rose to prominence in the nineteenth century, an assault accompanied by simultaneous attack on biblical religion, most prominently, Christianity. Reformers as diverse as Rousseau, Mill, and Marx recognized that traditional Christian commitments posed insurmountable barriers to achievement of their goals. Fabian socialists in England and their Progressive counterparts in the United States were similarly concerned to weaken or redefine traditional Christian commitments and for similar reasons. The ascendancy of the socialist moral ideal over the course of the nineteenth century also influenced internal developments within certain Christian denominations in the direction of socialist ethics, mostly notably, the Social Gospel movement.[92]

The explicit and implicit attack on Christianity was accompanied, moreover, by construction of various novel "religions" or quasi-religions intended to serve as replacements for biblical faith. Nineteenth-century critics of classical-liberal society well understood the importance of

---

[91] "God is dead. God remains dead. And we have killed him. How shall we comfort ourselves, the murderers of all murderers? What was holiest and mightiest of all that the world has yet owned has bled to death under our knives: who will wipe this blood off us? What water is there for us to clean ourselves? What festivals of atonement, what sacred games shall we have to invent? Is not the greatness of this deed too great for us? Must we ourselves not become gods simply to appear worthy of it?" Friedrich Nietzsche, *Thus Spoke Zarathustra: A Book for Everyone and No One*, R.J. Hollingdale, ed and trans (London: Penguin Classics, (1961 [1883]).

[92] Charles D. Cashdollar, *The Transformation of Theology (1830-1890)* (Princeton: Princeton University Press, 1989). Hereinafter cited as *Transformation of Theology*.

religion to culture. Many such thinkers were particularly cognizant of the role played by religion in establishing bonds of social cohesion or unity. They recognized that the demise of Christianity, regarded by its critics as both justified and salutary, would nevertheless create a spiritual void for the millions upon millions of Christianized peoples comprised by Western society. They further recognized that such spiritual disorientation would threaten the existential sense of meaning and purpose requisite to social order. Accordingly, such thinkers concluded, mere evisceration or elimination of Christianity, however necessary and beneficial, was insufficient. The religious void produced by the eighteenth century's critical attacks on Christianity must be filled by the propagation of new and different religious or quasi-religious aspirations. Thinkers such as Comte in France and J. S. Mill in England, among others, occupied themselves with the construction of precisely such a religious replacement for Christianity—the Religion of Humanity, the proximate forebear of contemporary Secular Humanism. The socialism of Marx and fellow travelers would serve an identical quasi-religious purpose.[93]

The nineteenth century, then, witnessed powerful challenges to traditional biblical faith, its reinterpretation in the direction of socialist ethics, and construction of various forms of "secular" or "political religion" intended to supplant Judeo-Christian aspirations, beliefs, and values in the minds of the masses.[94] Modern political religion comprises forms as varied as classic communism, socialism, and fascism, the Social Gospel, the Religion of Humanity or Secular Humanism, and others. The particular secular or political religions vary in form but are united in inspiration, substance, and purpose. The aim of all such constructions is the reorientation of religious devotion away from its traditional locus—the *transcendent* God of the Western tradition—and toward one or another *immanent*, intra-worldly, or mundane entity. In the case of Marx, the transcendent God is supplanted by the immanent communist society of the future. The realization of communism, like the Christian *eschaton*, is characterized as the "end of history"—the goal toward which

---

[93] Richard H. Crossman, ed, *The God That Failed* (New York: Columbia University Press, 2001) (hereinafter cited as *God That Failed*).

[94] See Linda C. Raeder, *John Stuart Mill and the Religion of Humanity* (Columbia, MO: University of Missouri Press, 2002). Hereinafter cited as *Religion of Humanity*.

history is ineluctably moving and toward which all spiritual and material efforts are to be directed. Comte, Mill, and fellow travelers conceive the replacement for the Judeo-Christian God as the intra-worldly abstraction proposed by Comte—the so-called "Great Being of Humanity."[95] In this case, religious aspirations are to be reoriented away from the transcendent God and toward this-worldly "service to Humanity," a service, said Mill, which henceforth will supplant biblical ethics as the very "law of our lives." The German-Nazi version aimed to reorient religious devotion away from the God of the Bible and toward the realization, in this world, of the millennial reign of the Third Reich. Nietzsche, who witnessed the emergence and propagation of various such quasi-religious constructions, clearly perceived their significance: such representations symbolize not only the "death of God" but also the implicit transfer of divine status from God to Man. He perceived, more particularly, that the "death of God," in effect and in practice, entailed the transfer of divine status from God to the "state."[96] The state, government, the wielders of political power, said Nietzsche, had become the "New Idol," the worldly replacement for God: "'On earth there is nothing greater than I: it is I who am the regulating finger of God'.— thus roareth the monster."[97]

The most significant aspect of such efforts to replace biblical with secular or political religion—"a religion without a God," in the words of Mill—has been their success.[98] Christianity was significantly weakened, relegated to the private sphere of mere subjective preference, or rejected outright. The de-Christianization of the West has advanced more thoroughly in Europe than America, but American society has not been immune to modern and postmodern developments. The spiritual

---

[95] John Stuart Mill, *Auguste Comte and Positivism* (Ann Arbor: University of Michigan Press, 1968 [1865]), 136-137. Hereinafter cited as ACP.

[96] Henri de Lubac, *The Drama of Atheist Humanism* (San Francisco: Ignatius Press, 1995). Hereinafter cited as *Drama*.

[97] Nietzsche exclaims: "The state? What is that? Well then! Now open your ears, for now I shall speak to you of the death of peoples. , [t]he state is the coldest of all cold monsters. Coldly it lies, too; and this lie creeps from its mouth: "I, the state, am the people. . . . On earth there is nothing greater than I: it is I who am the regulating finger of God."—thus roareth the monster." Nietzsche, "The New Idol" in *Thus Spoke Zarathustra* (1883).

[98] Mill, *ACP*, 133.

vacuum created by the "death of God" was filled on both continents by the modern ideological movements and their descendants and fellow travelers. Communism, socialism, fascism, English Fabianism, Social Gospel, and contemporary movements such as liberal Progressivism, radical environmentalism, Liberation Theology, and others served, and serve, for many adherents as quasi-religious substitutes for traditional faith, that is, as political religions. The moral ethos that typically accompanies the various modern forms of political religion similarly assumes various forms, including utilitarianism, naturalism, Marxian egalitarianism, Comtean altruism and positivism, secular humanism, postmodern perspectivism, and others. Such post-Christian moral constructions, like the modern political religions, vary in form but are united by a common and characteristic attribute, namely, rejection of a theological *source* of morality. All post-Christian moral constructs regard human beings, in one way or another, as the exclusive authors of right and wrong. As one disciple of secular humanism succinctly expressed the essence of post-theological, secular, or naturalistic ethics, "Man is his own rule and his own end."[99]

We have said that the most important aspect of the novel religious and moral constructions accompanying the "death of God" has been their social success. Marx's particular construction was so influential as to have become more or less synonymous with the twentieth century, the Age of Ideology. Unadulterated Marxism was undoubtedly too strong a brew for American tastes. Its underlying anti-theological ethos was nevertheless conveyed to the United States in somewhat less virulent forms, including secular humanism and other varieties of nontheistic, naturalistic, and "social" ethics, embraced chiefly but not exclusively by its political, intellectual, and cultural elite. It is rarely recognized or acknowledged, however, that secular humanism (the Religion of Humanity), along with similar non-theological ethical constructs, was expressly conceived by its founders and advocates as a rival to Christianity, which was explicitly and rightly regarded as the chief competitor of the new Humanitarian faith.[100] It is not coincidental that

---

[99] J. Wesley Robb, *The Reverent Skeptic: A Critical Inquiry into the Religion of Secular Humanism* (New York: Philosophical Library, 1979.
[100] Raeder, *Religion of Humanity.*

every religion but traditional biblical religion is tolerated in the contemporary American public square, including the public schools.

The modern and postmodern transformation of Western religious and moral beliefs—the replacement of biblical with secular or political religion and relocation of the source of morality from God to Man—has had, and continues to have, immense repercussions for Western and American society. Religion of course touches upon the most profound of existential questions and fulfills perhaps the most essential of human needs—the individual's need to find meaning and purpose in existence. Contrary to the assertions of nihilism, no human being can live without meaning and without purpose. Man by nature is not only a rational and social being, as the Western tradition long recognized, but also a religious being. No human being can avoid the fundamental existential questions: Who am I? Where did I come from? What am I doing here? Where am I going? Every society known to history, from ancient Sumer to modern America, has sought answers to such questions, answers embodied in its religion. The very term (from the Latin *religare*—to fasten or bind*)* points clearly to the human need for connection with the source of existence.[101] We have seen that it is impossible not to embrace a religion in this broad sense. Atheism too purports to answer the fundamental religious questions—where did I come from, where I am going? However unsatisfactory its response ("nowhere") may appear to persons of traditional religious views, its denial of God nevertheless aims to guide the human quest for existential comprehension.

That said, however, it is clear that not all religions are created equal. Religious truth of course involves the greatest and thorniest of all possible quests for knowledge. Ultimate Truth regarding man's relation to God must ever remain a perennial quest and not the absolute possession of any human being. Despite such irremediable ignorance on the part of every human being, the Western mind has nevertheless believed it possible to differentiate religion according to the degree to which it captures or fails to capture the higher truth of existence. A particular religion may be true or false, more true than false or more false than true, a judgment which depends on the degree to which it embodies the truth of reality. Of particular relevance in this regard is the

---

[101] There is some dispute regarding the etymology of the term but this is the sense favored by Christian thinkers such as Augustine.

distinction made by scholars such as Eric Voegelin (1901-1985) between transcendent and immanent (cosmological) religion. The early Greek philosophers are generally credited with the philosophical differentiation of existence into two dimensions: the "intelligible" realm—the transcendent realm of existence "Beyond" (*epekeina*) or above this world—and the "sensible" realm—the immanent realm of existence "within" the world. The great world-historical religions, Judaism, Christianity, and Islam, all conceive God as Being who simultaneously transcends and dwells within the immanent world, who, in the language of the Greeks, exists beyond and within the mundane realm of normal worldly experience.

The biblical worldview embodies such a differentiation in the most profound sense. We have previously discussed the political significance of the dual allegiance implicit in the Judeo-Christian worldview (God and Caesar) and the dual jurisdictional authority that ultimately developed within Christendom (church and state). More generally, however, the Christian revelation deepened the experience of transcendence and immanence first apprehended and articulated by Greek philosophers. Christianity more fully elaborated the transcendent nature of God and eternity, inevitably bringing into greater relief the relatively more limited significance of experience in time, "within" this world, and ultimately leading to the existential transformation of Christian consciousness. Christian man had to learn to maneuver simultaneously in two dimensions of experience, this world (*mundus*) and the other world (the Beyond). Religious experience always involves existential contact with the higher reality of God, a reality experienced by Christian consciousness as transcendent, beyond this world. The experience of transcendent Being, however, can be problematic for human consciousness. The problem is that religious seekers who have gained experience of the transcendent reality of God must nevertheless and simultaneously continue to exist *within* the immanent or mundane world. Newly Christianized consciousness had to learn to balance existence-in-time with existence-out-of-time. To avoid potential disorientation and destabilization, Christian man had to learn to negotiate what Voegelin, following Plato, calls the "tension" of life in the *metaxy*—the "in-between."[102]

Such metaphysical discursions may seem far removed from the topic under discussion—the rise of political religion in modern Western society. According to Voegelin, however, they are profoundly implicated in that development. We have seen that biblical religion was widely and successfully challenged in the eighteenth and nineteenth centuries, a challenge, indeed, that continues to the present day. The result was the weakening or reinterpretation of traditional faith in the transcendent God of the Bible. The religious yearning of Western man, however, did not die alongside the "death of God." Many persons responded to the existential despair inevitably created by the loss of God by turning toward the substitute meaning and purpose promised by one form or another of political religion. Early adherents to the new socialist faith, for instance, amply testify to the quasi-religious fulfillment they experienced from their newfound pursuit of "heaven-on-earth"—the earthly paradise promised by socialism and communism.[103] Western religious devotion has traditionally been oriented toward a God *beyond* this world in the hope and expectation of ultimate fulfillment *beyond* time, in eternity. Political religion captures that devotion and expectation and reorients it away from the transcendent Beyond and toward this world, toward mundane or intra-worldly phenomena, in the case of socialism and communism, toward achieving the future Kingdom of God on earth.

Many advantages were promised to potential converts. For one thing, human beings would no longer have to cling to mere faith, to mere hope for ultimate fulfillment in eternity. Their yearning for justice, for instance, would no longer have to await divine judgment but could rather be fulfilled in this world. Socialism promised the achievement of justice, not in a perhaps fanciful "beyond" in eternity but rather here and now. Indeed it promised total justice—social justice—on earth and in

---

[102] Eric Voegelin, "Reason: The Classic Experience," in *Published Essays, 1966-1985 1990*), vol. 12 of *The Collected Works of Eric Voegelin*, ed. Ellis Sandoz (Baton Rouge: Louisiana State University Press, 1990), 289-90; *Order and History, Volume IV: The Ecumenic Age*, vol. 17 of *The Collected Works of Eric Voegelin*, ed. Michael Franz (Columbia, MO: University of Missouri Press, 2000), 408.

[103] Crossman, *God that Failed.*

time and by strictly human means. Nor would believers have to await death to experience spiritual transfiguration, as promised by Christianity. The political religions promised spiritual rebirth, transformation, transfiguration, here and now, on earth and in time. Human nature itself would be transformed under the socialist dispensation. In line with the Marxian theory of consciousness, as we recall, the establishment of socialist relations of production promised the eventual emergence of a new type of human being—Socialist Man, unselfish, cooperative, devoted to the common good. Goodness, equality, justice, the amelioration of all human suffering—heaven-on-earth—were said to be within human reach, in this world, in time, no longer relegated to a (possibly illusory) future state in eternity. All that is required to realize Heaven-on-Earth is the transformation of social, economic, and political reality by human will and action. The Kingdom of God is at hand: "Workers of the world unite!! You have nothing to lose but your chains!"[104]

The socialist evangel spoke directly to the religious needs and spiritual yearning of those persons whose faith in the traditional God of the West had been weakened or shattered by the modern assault on Christianity. Many of them replaced the loss of existential meaning and purpose that accompanied the "death of God" with the quasi-religious pursuit of the socialist heaven-on-earth. The Christian yearning for salvation was reinterpreted in political and temporal terms. Various "secular messiahs," from the St. Simonians to Hitler, Stalin, and others, arose to lead the masses to the Promised Land. The pursuit of political salvation undoubtedly provided existential comfort for the individuals it consumed. Their lives were no longer empty, without meaning or direction. Although religious devotion could no longer be oriented toward its traditional object, the transcendent God of the Bible, now "dead," it could be redirected toward an eminently worthy entity, toward a purpose larger than mere self, a political purpose. The Christian promise of individual or personal salvation was supplanted by the collective salvation promised by political religion. Salvation would lie not in unity with a moribund God but rather with Man, the "Great Being of Humanity," a unity to be achieved by collective realization of

---

[104] Karl Marx, *The Communist Manifesto,* in Robert C. Tucker, *The Marx-Engels Reader,* 2nd ed (New York: W.W. Norton & Company, 1978).

quasi-religious socialist ideals. More formally stated, modern political religion represents a corruption of the Christian *eschaton*. The "vertical" transcendence *beyond* the world promised by Christian faith is replaced by promise of a "horizontal" transcendence *within* this world, achieved by pursuit and realization of the final end of history, the Communist Paradise of the future. Transfiguration and salvation are relocated from eternity to time, from the transcendent Beyond to the immanent world. In Voegelin's celebrated phrase, all forms of modern political religion represent an "immanentization of the *eschaton*."

The Balance of Consciousness

By measure of respect for human life, the twentieth century was an era of unprecedented horror. From the Russian Revolution through the two World Wars to the Chinese Cultural Revolution and Cambodian killing fields, millions upon millions of persons were oppressed, enslaved, or slaughtered by revolution, war, and explicit policy of their own governments. Such widespread disorder demands explanation. One of the more persuasive and profound explorations of the political convulsions that plagued the Age of Ideology and Totalitarianism was offered by Voegelin. He argues that the ideological movements bound up with the modern catastrophe were neither random and inexplicable outbursts nor solely products of particular material and historical conditions. Such phenomena are instead bound up with the nature of modernity itself, in particular, with the religious developments under discussion. Voegelin argues that the ideological constructions that accompanied the "death of God" should be understood as the extreme manifestation of a general form of spiritual or psychic disorientation prevailing in the modern Western world. The crisis of modernity, he says, is in essence a spiritual crisis rooted in a deformation of the truth of reality.[105]

Voegelin, as mentioned, characterizes human existence as always and everywhere "existence-in-tension," existence in the "in-between" reality

---

[105] Portions of this section first appeared in Linda C. Raeder, "Voegelin on Gnosticism, Modernity, and the Balance of Consciousness," *Political Science Reviewer,* Vol. XXXVI, 2007. I would like to thank the publisher for permission to use the material in this book. Hereinafter cited as "Balance of Consciousness."

which Plato termed the *metaxy* and which is constituted by a simultaneous tension toward mundane, worldly, existence and its transcendent divine ground beyond this world. Human consciousness finds itself embedded within a mysterious, participatory reality "halfway between God and man." The experience of human consciousness comprises a simultaneous pull toward the existential poles of transcendence and immanence (*beyond* and *within* the world), the poles of immorality and mortality, knowledge and ignorance, perfection and imperfection, timelessness and time, spirit and matter, existence and non-existence, life and death, truth and its deformation. [106] Reality is a comprehensive whole that consists of both transcendent and mundane dimensions, of mutual participation of the divine and the human.

A "healthy," "balanced," or "well-ordered" consciousness, Voegelin maintains, is one that accepts the "tensional structure of existence" and mediates successfully between its opposing poles.[107] "Diseased" or "unbalanced" or "disordered" consciousness, on the other hand, may be defined as a mode of experience wherein one or the other of the existential poles whose tension constitutes the "in-between" reality of human existence has collapsed. It is existence within a truncated or deformed reality characterized by the eclipse of one or the other of its two inseparable dimensions. Disordered consciousness, then, may take one of two main forms, depending upon which existential dimension—the immanent or the transcendent—recedes from experience. The first possibility is the case wherein intense consciousness of transcendent reality (religious experience) serves to eclipse mundane reality. Voegelin terms such a condition one of "metastatic faith"—the belief in the imminent arrival of divine presence on earth in such a manner that worldly existence is transfigured. The second possible response to the tension inherent in human existence, and the one more problematic in the modern era, is the eclipse of the transcendent pole of existence by the illegitimate expansion of immanent to total reality. This world, the mundane world of time and space, is represented as Reality *in toto*; the transcendent dimension is obscured or denied. According to Voegelin, such is the existential response that underlies the various ideological

---

[106] Plato, cited in Eric Voegelin, "Reason: The Classic Experience," in *Anamnesis,* trans. and ed. Gerhart Niemeyer (Columbia, MO: The University of Missouri Press, 1978), 103.

[107] Voegelin, "Reason," 100.

constructions and other peculiarly modern and postmodern political and social movements.

Voegelin conceives the phenomenon of imbalanced consciousness as intimately related to humanity's spiritual advance from what he calls the "compact" spiritual experience of the ancient cosmological empires to the "differentiated" experiences bound up with classical philosophy and Christianity. The inhabitants of the cosmological empires, such as ancient Egypt, Persia, and Syria, experienced the Divine Source as an intra-cosmic entity and, accordingly, dwelled within a divinized "world full of gods." Their world was experienced as a microcosm that reflected the divine order of the cosmos, an order mediated through the political ruler to the people and the realm. Cosmological man did not yet differentiate or separate the divine and the immanent. He had not yet discovered either the soul or the transcendent Ground of Being, experiences which could dissociate the cosmos and the Ground into radically immanent and radically transcendent realms. Tension between the "truth of society" and the "truth of the soul" was undoubtedly experienced even in the compact societies. [108] Such tension, however, could not become socially disruptive so long as the cosmological order was experienced as all-embracing and so long as the existential reality of the soul and the transcendent divine source remained undifferentiated.

The problem of unbalanced consciousness—the problem, as Michael Franz explains, "of maintaining a balance between openness to transcendent experience and sober attentiveness to the necessities of mundane existence"—is thus bound up with the "theophanic events" wherein the transcendent God revealed himself to man, beginning with the revelation of the "I Am" to the Hebrews.[109] Indeed, the prophet Isaiah is for Voegelin the prototypical bearer of metastatic faith—the "faith that the very structure of pragmatic existence in society and history is soon to undergo a decisive transformation."[110] Isaiah counseled the King to lay down his arms and trust that God would defeat his enemies.

---

[108] The conventional self-interpretation of a society as it regards its existential role as representative of a higher truth; and universal humanity's existence under God, the discovery that the human psyche immediately participates in the Divine Source of order, respectively.

[109] Michael Franz, *Eric Voegelin and the Politics of Spiritual Revolt: The Roots of Modern Ideology* (Baton Rouge: Louisiana State University Press, 1992), 30.

[110] Ibid. 32.

Isaiah's experience of the transcendent God was so intense as to eclipse the reality of political existence in time. He became convinced that divine intervention would transform the very structure of mundane reality in such a way as to ensure the victory of the Chosen People over their worldly enemies. Isaiah's experience of participation in divine transcendent reality was so strong that, according to Voegelin, he "tried the impossible—to make the `leap in being' a leap out of existence into a divinely transfigured world beyond the laws of mundane existence."[111] Voegelin further argues that such a "prophetic conception of a change in the constitution of being," bound up as it with the existential discovery of the "truth of transfigured reality," lies at the root of the ideological consciousness that he regards as one of the main sources of disorder in the modern era.[112]

The classical philosophers also struggled with the problem of existential balance deriving from the discovery of spiritual order. The discoveries they made—of the transcendent nature of the divine source (the Platonic *epekeina* or Beyond) and of the psyche, the "human spiritual soul" that is the "sensorium of transcendence" —were epochal events in mankind's advance from spiritual dimness to spiritual clarity. Plato discovered that openness of the psyche toward divine reality may permit certain transcendent experiences that shape the order of soul and society. He discovered the transcendent Ground of Being that is the source of personal, social, and historical order. Voegelin contends, however, that Plato, unlike Isaiah, managed to maintain a balance of consciousness in the face of the theophanic event. He did not permit his transcendent experiences to disturb his awareness of the autonomous structure of mundane reality, of the enduring reality of existence in the cosmos-of-begetting-and-perishing. Although Plato glimpsed a realm of enduring perfection, he remained lucidly aware of both the "improbability" of its establishment in time and the inevitable decline of such a perfect order if it were somehow to come into being. Platonic

---

[111] Ibid. 34.
[112] Ibid. Thomas J. J. Altizer, "A New History and a New But Ancient God," in Ellis Sandoz, ed, *Eric Voegelins Thought: A Critical Appraisal* (Durham: Duke University Press, 1982), 184.

philosophy thus represents for Voegelin a model of "noetic control," of healthy, balanced existence within the enduring tensions of the *metaxy*.

Although the Platonic discovery was an advance from compactness to differentiation, it was, according to Voegelin, but a step on the spiritual path that found its end in the epiphany of Christ. Christianity, for Voegelin, represents the "maximal differentiation" of the relation between God and man. The "leap in being" that accompanied the epiphany of Christ fully differentiated the transcendent nature of the divine source and the truth of transfigured reality. The effect was not only to heighten the tension of existence in the *metaxy* but also potentially destabilize the balance of consciousness, as previously mentioned. It is perhaps difficult for modern man to re-experience the "shock" felt by those who first experienced the revelation of the transcendent God and the concomitant "withdrawal of Divinity from the world." The newly de-divinized cosmos, in contrast to the "world full of gods" experienced within cosmological society, must have "seemed to be left an empty shell, void of meaning, [indeed,] void of reality."[113] Christianity, Voegelin observes, further "reordered human existence in society . . . through the experience of man's destination, by the grace of the world-transcendent god, towards eternal life in beatific vision."[114] In light of such experiences, as we have seen, the value, meaning, and significance of mundane existence could only appear diminished or limited.[115] In Voegelinian terms, the Christian revelation challenged the existential balance of consciousness. The modern ideological movements, which he regards as manifestations of existential imbalance and disorientation, are thus intimately bound up with the Christian experience. It is not accidental that such movements arose within Western civilization, within Christendom.

Gnosticism and Modernity

---

[113] William C. Havard, "Voegelin's Diagnosis of the Western Crisis," *Denver Quarterly* X (1975), 129-30.

[114] Eric Voegelin, *The New Science of Politics: An Introduction* (Chicago: The University of Chicago Press, 1952), 107.

[115] We have previously discussed the Christian devaluation of the political realm.

From the seventh century B.C. onward the ancient Near East was racked by a series of military conquests that profoundly disoriented the inhabitants of the various cosmological empires. A widespread sense of meaningless and psychic disorientation was engendered by the slaughter, enslavement, and forced intermingling of peoples and cultures, inevitably undermining faith in the traditional cosmological order. Various responses arose in the attempt to comprehend the meaning of existence within such a troubled world, among the more important of which were Stoicism, Christianity, and Gnosticism.

To the Gnostics of the era, the world appeared neither as the "well-ordered" cosmos of the Greeks nor as the Judeo-Christian world that God created *ex nihilo* and "found good." On the Gnostic view, by contrast, the world appeared as a "prison from which [man must] escape, . . . an alien place into which man has strayed and from which he must find his way back home to the other world of his origins."[116] The fundamental experience of the ancient Gnostics was of an alien, disorganized, chaotic, and meaningless world. God was experienced as an absolutely transcendent entity utterly divorced from mundane existence, the existing world as false, devoid of reality, as "existent nothingness." Not surprisingly, the central theme of the diverse Gnostic thinkers was the "destruction of [such an abhorrent] old world and the passage to [a] new."[117] A new world, one that offers salvation from an old world felt to be wrong in its very constitution, could be gained, they taught, through personal effort and a privileged *gnosis* (knowledge) of the means of escape.

According to Voegelin, the ancient Gnostic speculations engendered in response to the disorder of the "ecumenic age" are significant because the experiences and beliefs they symbolize have re-emerged in modernity with such force as to decisively have shaped the character of that era. The history of modernity, he argues, is the history of a struggle between two different representations of the truth of existence: the representation of the truth of the soul and of man's relationship to God as manifested in classical philosophy and Christianity, on the one hand, and, on the other, the "new truth" propounded by modern gnostic thinkers—the

---

[116] Eric Voegelin, *Science, Politics, and Gnosticism*m (Chicago: Henry Regnery Company, 19678), 9.
[117] Ibid. 10.

alleged truth of the radical immanence of existence and the promise of revolutionary transfiguration of man and society in time. [118] Greek philosophy, as we have seen, discovered the truth of transcendent divinity, a truth decisively differentiated by the epiphany of Christ. The Christian revelation particularly effected an "uncompromising [and] radical de-divinization of the world" and a concomitant dissociation of previously unified spiritual and temporal power, as previously discussed. [119] Henceforth the transcendent spiritual destiny of man was to be existentially represented by the Church and the de-divinized temporal sphere of political power by the Empire, a "double representation of man in society" which endured through the Middle Ages and beyond. [120]

Voegelin maintains that the philosophic and Christian truth of man in society was challenged during the late Middle Ages by the rise of various gnostic spiritual movements. Such would prove to be the seedbed of the modern ideological consciousness that ultimately effected the "re-divinization" of political society in the name of a new truth of existence (cf. Nietzsche's "New Idol"). The medieval movements, according to Voegelin, were an outgrowth of a division within the early Christian community that stemmed from varying interpretations of the Revelation of St. John. The Revelation had aroused chiliastic expectations among certain early Christians, and they impatiently awaited Christ's imminent Second Coming. Augustine had sought to dash such expectations by re-interpreting John. Christ's thousand-year reign on earth, he declared, had already begun with the Incarnation; thus "there would be no divinization of society beyond the pneumatic presence of Christ and his

---

[118] Voegelin uses the term "gnosticism" in an unconventional and very broad sense. It is his term for certain disorders of the spirit arising from "pneumapathological" or imbalanced consciousness. It is more or less synonymous with other terms Voegelin employs to symbolize the phenomenon of spiritual disorder: "activist dreaming, egophantic revolt, metastatic faith, activist mysticism, demonic mendacity, Prometheanism, parousiasm, political religion, social Satanism, magic pneumatism, and eristics" (Franz, 17).

[119] Voegelin, New Science, 100.

[120] Gregor Sebba, "History, Modernity, and Gnosticism," in Peter J. Opitz and Gregor Sebba, eds, The Philosophy of Order: Essays on History, Consciousness and Politics (Stuttgart: Ernst Klett, 1981), 231.

Church."[121] According to the Augustinian philosophy of history, the period following the epiphany of Christ was the last of six historical phases, the *saeculum senescens*—a time of waiting for the end of history to be brought about through eschatological events. Augustine, moreover, had drawn a further distinction between profane and sacred history; the latter, in turn, was embedded in a transcendental history of the *civitas dei*, the City of God. Only transcendental history, including the sacred history of the epiphany of Christ and the establishment of the Church, had direction toward eschatological fulfillment. Profane history had no such direction or, indeed, meaning of any sort; it was merely a waiting for the end in a radically "de-divinized" world.

The End of History

The twelfth century, as previously noted, was a time of civilizational expansion and growth. Population increased, trade and settlement expanded, urban culture and intellectual life flourished. In the midst of such expansive vitality, Augustine's conception of a "senile" age seemed incongruous, and, at this critical juncture, a new construction of history emerged to challenge the Augustinian interpretation. The Calabrian monk Joachim of Flora (1135-1202) created a speculative history that satisfied the desire to endow mundane existence with a meaning which Christianity, and especially the Augustinian conception of history, had denied it. He did so by relocating the end of transcendental history— the Christian *eschaton*, the ultimate transfiguration in God out of time— within historical existence. Joachim's project, according to Voegelin, was the "first Western attempt at an immanentization of the meaning of history."[122] What begins with Joachim is a conception of Western society "as a civilizational course that comes into view as a whole because it is moving intelligibly toward an end."[123] Thus begins the modern attempt to find a Final End of mundane history that would substitute for the end of history in the transcendent Christian sense.

Joachim modeled his novel conception of history on the Trinity, dividing the course of history into three ages—the Age of the Father, the

---

[121] Ibid.
[122] Voegelin, *New Science*, 119.
[123] Ibid. 128.

Son, and the Holy Spirit. The Age of the Father was said to span the beginning of creation to the time of Christ; the Age of the Son began with Christ and ended in Joachim's time; the Age of the Holy Spirit was about to dawn (Joachim predicted it would begin in 1260) and would last indefinitely. According to Voegelin, Joachim's construction is significant because the three-age symbolism he created rules not only the modern ideological constructions of history but also the "self-interpretation of modern [Western] society" and thus the structure of its politics to the present day. Joachitic history, which allowed immanent history to end with the End of sacred history (transfiguration in God), says Voegelin, was "fallacious, but not un-Christian." In the several centuries following Joachim's construction, the novel historical expectations he raised remained more or less within the Christian orbit; the anticipated increase of fulfillment in history was to come about through a new eruption of transcendent spirit. Over time, however, the process of "fallacious immanentization" begun by Joachim became more and more radical and the relation to transcendence ever more tenuous. By the eighteenth century, the increase of meaning in history would be conceived as a radically intra-mundane phenomenon; the transcendent pole that sustains the balance of existential consciousness collapsed. The result, according to Voegelin, is the spiritual and temporal disorder and disorientation of the so-called "modern" age.[124]

Voegelin further argues that the various manifestations of such spiritual disorder (he cites Marxism, National Socialism, fascism, positivism, progressivism, psychoanalysis, and modern liberalism) are united by a common attribute, namely, a radical "will to immanentization." All such constructions involve a closure toward the transcendent dimension of human experience. We previously noted another such common attribute —the rejection of a theological source of morality; the demand for a "purely human" ethics, as Mill put it, clearly manifests the Voegelinian "will to immanentization."[125] Indeed, the most extreme modern ideologies go a step further. Their proponents

---

[124] Voegelin maintains that the symbol of a "modern age" was created precisely to denote the "epoch marked by the decisive victory of the gnostics over the forces of Western tradition in the struggle for existential representation" (New Science, 134).

[125] J. S. Mill, "On Liberty," ed, Elizabeth Rapaport (Indianapolis: Hackett Publishing Company, Inc., 1976), 48.

not only aim to obscure the transcendent ground of existence but further seek to transform the nature of being itself. As Voegelin explains, the aim is to "abolish the constitution of being, with its origin in divine, transcendent being, and to replace it with a world-immanent order of being."[126] In other words, and as previously discussed, the radical ideological constructions anticipate the transfiguration of human nature through human action in history, in particular, the spiritual rebirth anticipated by establishment of a terrestrial paradise endowed with the meaning and salvific qualities of the Christian *eschaton*. The Christian conception of man's ultimate transfiguration in God is brought "down to earth," transformed into the promise of human transfiguration in time accomplished through strictly human and immanent action. The transcendent Christian end of history is transformed into a mundane "End of History" to be concretely realized in the immanent future, within the world. The ideologists carried the process begun by Joachim to its limit; the transcendent dimension of reality was fully absorbed into mundane existence. Karl Marx is of course characteristic.

Gnostic Symbolism

Voegelin contends, then, that the modern ideological constructions are productions of "speculative gnostics" who share certain basic beliefs, existential motivations, and aims with their ancient forebears. These include:

1. Dissatisfaction with present existence.
2. Belief that such dissatisfaction is caused by the intrinsically poor organization of the world. If something is not right, the reason is to be found in the evil of the world.
3. Belief that salvation from the wickedness of the world is possible.
4. Belief that the order of being will be changed in an historical solution, that a good world will evolve over time.
5. Belief that a change in the order of being can be realized through human action, that "self-salvation," salvation through man's own effort, is possible.
6. Construction of a formula for personal- and world-salvation based

---

[126] Voegelin, *New Science,* 121.

upon knowledge of how to alter being. The gnostic thinker typically presents himself as a prophet proclaiming knowledge regarding the salvation of mankind.

The ancient and modern gnostics, then, share certain characteristic traits, but they also differ in certain respects. Most important, the moderns typically assume an aggressive, activist stance toward the putative evil of existent reality; the ancients, by contrast, were relatively quietist. Despite their disparate stances, Voegelin maintains that the experiential motivations and aims of ancient and modern gnostics are nevertheless of a piece. All gnostics experience the world "as a place of total chaos which would be transformed into a world of perfected, durable order by divine or human intervention. . . ."[127] All gnostics aim to alter the constitution of being through human effort in order to escape a world experienced as alien and evil and to do so by applying their special gnosis to that task. All of them falsely extrapolate their experience of the "Beyond" to the "Beginning," claiming knowledge of the nature and meaning of human existence and of history-as-a-whole that they do not and cannot actually possess. Modern gnostic ideologues also differ from their ancient counterparts in that the modern "revolt against reality" is directed against a world shaped by the Christian differentiation of spiritual truth. Accordingly, their constructions must be understood in light of the Christian background that informed their development.

Indeed, Voegelin maintains, the various modern ideologies may be said to "derive" from Christianity in that they represent immanentized transformations of Christian experience and symbolism, a derivation evidenced by their structural congruence with traditional Christian doctrine. First, all the modern ideologists adopted and transformed the Christian idea of perfection. For the Christian, life on earth is shaped by the expectation and aim of realizing a "supernatural [fulfillment] through grace in death."[128] The Christian idea of supernatural perfection thus consists of two components: a *teleological* (*telos*, final end or purpose) movement toward a final *axiological* goal (the state of ultimate perfection or "highest value"). We have seen that the ideological

---

[127] William C. Harvard, "Notes on Voegelin's Contributions to Political Theory," in Ellis Sandoz, ed, *Eric Voegelin's Thought: A Critical Appraisal* (Durham, NC: Duke University Press, 1982), 97-98.

[128]Voegelin, *New Science*, 105.

constructs immanentize the Christian *eschaton* by aiming to produce a final state of perfection within historical existence (axiological), a perfect society to be created through implementation of the ideologue's particular program or system (teleological). The ideological constructions differ, however, according to their varying emphases on the teleological and axiological elements of the Christian conception from which they derive. Accordingly, Voegelin classifies the various immanentist constructions under several heads:

1. *Teleological immanentization.* When the teleological component of the idea of perfection is immanentized, the main emphasis of the system lies on the forward movement toward the goal of perfection in this world. According to Voegelin, the eighteenth century ideal of "progress" is of this type, as is liberal progressivism in general. The emphasis is on movement; typically there is little clarity about the final state to be realized ("Change, change, change!").

2. *Axiological immanentization.* Here the emphasis is placed on the state of perfection in the world. Generally the thinker paints a detailed picture of the proposed perfect society while giving short shrift to the means by which it is to be realized. All formulations of "ideal societies" fall into this category. Thomas More's *Utopia* is a classic example.

3. *Activist Mysticism.* In this form of immanentization, the teleological and axiological types are combined. Here the thinker typically provides a more or less clear picture of the final state to be achieved as well as `knowledge" of the means by which it is to be brought into existence. Comte's final state of industrial society under rule of managers and positivists is one example; Marx's communist society to be ushered in by the proletarian revolution is another.

The second set of Christian symbols transformed by the modern ideological speculators derives from the Joachitic conception of history previously discussed. Joachim created and bequeathed to modern man a complex of four symbols.[129] The first is that of the "Third Realm"—the third "world-historical phase that is at the same time the last, the age of fulfillment." Such symbolism reappears at a later date in various forms: the now-familiar distinction among ancient, medieval, and modern

---

[129] Ibid. 111-13.

historical periods; the Comtean periodization of history into the theological, metaphysical, and positivist states of man; Marx's division of history into primitive communism, bourgeois class society, and the final realm of the classless Communist society; the Third Reich symbolism adopted by the Nazis; and so forth. The second symbol derived from Joachitic trinitarian eschatology was the symbol of the leader, the *dux*, who "appears at the beginning of each new era and establishes it through his appearance." This symbol also reemerges in various guises throughout the ensuing centuries: the belief that St. Francis of Assisi would usher in the new Age of the Holy Spirit; the self-styled paracletes imbued with the spirit of God who led the various sectarian movements of the Renaissance and Reformation; Machiavelli's Prince; the charismatic leaders of the national-socialist and fascist movements. The third symbol created by Joachim and adopted by the ideological thinkers was that of the prophet, the precursor of each of the three ages. This symbol was transformed over time from the still-Christian conception of Joachim's era into the secular intellectual who knows the program for salvation from the evils of the world, who can predict the future course of world history and knows the meaning of that history (e.g., Comte, Hegel, Mill, Marx). The final symbol bequeathed by Joachim to the modern world was the "community of spiritually autonomous persons." Joachim believed that the Age of the Holy Spirit would witness highly spiritualized individuals existing in community without the mediation and support of institutions and organizations; he had in mind the monks. Such a notion reappears in later times, for instance, as the Marxian and anarchist notion of the "withering away" of the state and the radical-democratic conception of a society of "autonomous" men.

Gnostic Experience

"The substance of history," Voegelin maintains, "is to be found on the level of experiences, not on the level of ideas."[130] Accordingly, the logic of modern political developments, especially the rise of the ideological mass movements, is only apparent in light of the existential consciousness that engendered them. Such phenomena must be traced

---

[130] Ibid. 125.

to their source in the experiences and motivations of their founders and followers, above all, the aforementioned "will to immanentization." The existential drive for immanentization, according to Voegelin, arises from a desire to assuage the tension of existence in the *metaxy* and to do so by eliminating one source of such tension—man's experience of the transcendent. We recall that for Voegelin human existence is existence-in-tension within the participatory reality constituted by the simultaneous pull toward both mundane existence and its transcendent divine ground. By definition, a healthy or well-ordered consciousness is one that successfully mediates between the existential poles of immanence and transcendence; a disordered consciousness does not so succeed. Modern ideological consciousness obscures or denies the transcendent dimension of reality (closure toward the divine ground) and may thus be regarded as a form of imbalanced or disordered consciousness in the Voegelinian sense.

Although there is no one "cause" of such a disturbed relation to reality, of "pneumopathological" or spiritually disordered consciousness, Voegelin's analysis highlights certain existential characteristics common to the various ideological constructions. In all cases of ideological consciousness, he suggests, the lust for power has grown immense. In his words, the will to power of the thinker "has triumphed over the humility of subordination to the constitution of being." The principal aim of the ideological thinker, he says, is to "destroy the order of being, which is experienced as defective and unjust and through man's creative power to replace it with a perfect and just order." In order to destroy such a "defective" order, it must be conceived as susceptible of human intervention. Such a requirement rules out the created order of the Judeo-Christian God, which of course is impervious to human manipulation. The order of being must be conceived as under man's control, in other words, its "givenness . . . must be obliterated."[131] The acquisition of human control thus requires the "retroactive" destruction of the God whose existence would prevent man from fashioning the order of being to his liking. Consequently, the first and most important task of the ideological thinker, as Nietzsche succinctly put it, is to "murder God." The radical "will to immanentization" and the passion to abolish transcendent reality emerge from an unbounded desire for

---

[131] Voegelin, *Science, Politics, and Gnosticism*, 107, 53.

power over being, the pneumopathological wish and need to *be* God. According to the "logic" of the disordered soul, such a wish can be realized by destroying God; in some quasi-magical fashion, he "who murders god will himself become god." Thus, says Voegelin, the "murder of God is of the very essence of the gnostic recreation of the order of being."[132] He further acknowledges, however, that full comprehension of the modern ideological passion to murder God is, in the final analysis, inaccessible to the human mind. As Voegelin put it, "[b]eyond the psychology of the will to power we are confronted with the inscrutable fact that grace is granted or denied."[133] The search for an ultimate explanation of the emergence of the modern would-be gods founders on the ultimate mystery of man's relation to God.

Existential Resistance, Ideology, and the Drive for Certainty

Voegelin further emphasizes that the modern ideological thinkers do not necessarily *deny* the truth of reality but rather *resist* such truth. They may in fact be spiritually sensitive persons with an acute sense of transcendence.[134] The defiant modern gnostics who created the ideological systems, like the philosophers and prophets who created the symbolism of philosophy and Christianity, experience a reality that has eschatological direction, one that is moving beyond its present structure. Moreover, they know reality moves not only into an historical future but also toward a transcendent Beyond. Ideological concepts such as "transcendence into the future" clearly point to the distinction they intend to obscure (an existence that "comes to an end in time without coming to [a] final End out-of-time"[135]). The question is why the ideological resisters defy a truth which with they do not actually disagree. A related question concerns the experiential sources that have made resistance to the truth of reality a recurring force in history.

---

[132] Ibid. 55.

[133] Ibid. 31.

[134] J. S. Mill is a case in point. He vigorously denied the charge of atheism, insisting in no uncertain terms that the Religion of Humanity he championed but not only a real religion but better than any previous religion.

[135] Eric Voegelin, Volume Five, *In Search of Order* (Baton Rouge: Louisiana State University Press, 1987), 34.

The existential resisters, says Voegelin, are dissatisfied with the lack of order they experience in personal and social existence. Such dissatisfaction is readily understandable. Human existence is afflicted with many miseries—hunger, arduous work, disease, early death, injustice—and painfully disoriented by rapid change (such as engendered by the modern scientific and industrial revolutions and the rise of capitalism). Ideological resisters, like many other persons, suffer from present disorder. More important, however, they further suffer from the discrepancy between that disorder and the higher, truer order which they also apprehend yet which seems beyond the possibility of realization. They are "disappointed with the slowness of the [transfiguring] movement in reality toward the order they experience as the true order demanded by the Beyond" and, moreover, morally outraged at the human misery entailed by such "slowness." Such experiences can lead to the conviction that something is "fundamentally wrong with reality itself." At such a point, the resister to disorder becomes a revolutionary who seeks to overturn the structure of reality itself. The "Beyond is no longer experienced as an effective ordering force," and the ideologist constructs a system that will replace the defective force.[136] The tension of existence in the *metaxy* dissolves.

According to Voegelin, there further exists an even deeper stratum of ideological resistance, one originating in the very structure of consciousness and especially its imaginative capacity. Imagination, for Voegelin, is the capacity that permits human beings to symbolize, articulate, and otherwise express their participatory experience within the "*metaxy* of divine-human movements and counter-movements." It is the capacity that makes a human being a "creative partner in the movement of reality toward its truth."[137] Such a creative imaginative force, however, can go awry if the creative *partner* forgets he is a *partner* and begins to regard himself as "the sole creator of truth." Underlying the ideologist's illusory belief that he can create a new reality merely through creating a new symbol or image is precisely such an "imaginative expansion of participatory into sole power."[138] The imaginative capacity

---

[136] Ibid. 36-37.
[137] Ibid. 26, 37.
[138] Ibid. 38.

of human beings means that they can confuse their personal images of reality with reality itself.

The ideological thinker, as we have seen, aims to abolish existential reality and the constitution of being in order to deliver man from various perceived evils. The control of being, however, does not actually lie within his grasp; reality is not actually susceptible of human manipulation. Accordingly, as Voegelin puts it, "nonrecognition of reality is the first principle" of the ideological constructions.[139] In order to make his pathological constructions seem plausible, the thinker must imaginatively construct what Voegelin, following Robert Musil, calls a "second Reality," a transfigured "dream world" that replaces the First Reality he finds so unsatisfactory. The Second Reality will resemble the First Reality in many respects (otherwise it would be too patently absurd), yet the ideological constructor necessarily eliminates from his model certain inconvenient features of reality.[140] The ideologists vary in regard to which elements of reality are omitted. Such may include the primary experience of the cosmos (the begetting and perishing of all existent forms), as in all constructions that anticipate the "End of History"; the need for institutional constraints and incentives as in Marx; the human penchant for possession, as in More's *Utopia*, and so on. The point is that every ideological thinker constructs an imaginary dream-world that eliminates essential elements of reality as we know it.

The construction of ideological systems or programs does not, of course, permit actual control over being or reality but nevertheless provides a measure of gratification to those who pursue it. The ideological constructors, Voegelin maintains, gain the "fantasy satisfaction" of certain psychic needs, in particular, the need for "a stronger certainty about the meaning of human existence."[141] Ideologues and their followers are comforted by the increased sense of certainty that accompanies their newfound knowledge; the pretense of knowing the future course of events provides a seemingly firmer, if illusory, basis for action. Voegelin maintains, then, that ideological thinkers are ultimately impelled to action by the inherent *uncertainty* of human existence, an

---

[139] Voegelin, *New Science*, 169.

[140] For instance, Marx's communist paradise; Comte's positivist industrial society; the thousand-year rule of the Aryan masters, the eternally peaceful order of liberal constitutionalism, and so forth.

[141] Voegelin, *New Science*, 107.

existence wherein assurance of meaning and purpose is only to be gained by faith-engendered experiences. The painful uncertainty of human existence is assuaged by the construction of Second Realities and philosophies of history that envision an everlasting realm of bliss in time.

Christianity and the Ideological Movements

We have seen that, according to Voegelin, the modern ideological movements are bound up with the heightened spiritual tension engendered by the Christian differentiation of reality. In particular, Christianity's further differentiation of the truth of the soul and clarification of man's relation to a transcendent God exacerbated the existential uncertainty that the ideological constructions serve to assuage. The Christian faith, on Voegelin's view, requires tremendous spiritual strength, providing, as it does, no assurance of the meaning or value of personal existence other than that attained by faith itself. It does not provide massively *certain* knowledge of the nature of being, of God, or the meaning of mundane events but only the hard truth that the "order of reality is essentially mysterious."[142] A faith whose very "essence is uncertainty," Voegelin suggests, may generate a chronic and intolerable anxiety among those who long for greater reassurance. [143] The fact that the Christian differentiation of the truth of the soul is "more accurate" may provide scant consolation to those who crave a more certain guarantee of meaning and purpose.

Voegelin further maintains that Christianity's widespread social success in the West brought many people into the Christian orbit who did not possess the spiritual stamina to endure the strain of existence demanded by a faith characterized by essential uncertainty. The result, he says, was that "great masses of Christianized men who were not strong enough for the heroic adventure of faith became susceptible to ideas that could give them a greater degree of certainty about the meaning of their existence than Christian faith." The reality of being as known by Christianity, he says, is difficult to bear; and many persons took flight into alternative spiritual constructs that permitted a seemingly "firmer

---

[142] Ibid. 68.
[143] Ibid. 122-23.

grip on God" than afforded by Christian faith.[144] The modern flight into such alternate constructs, moreover, was not an entirely novel development; similar responses have appeared throughout history wherever the truth of the transcendent God had been differentiated. As Voegelin explains, the "temptation to fall from spiritual height that brings uncertainty into final clarity down to a more solid certainty of world-immanent, sensible, fulfillment seems to be a general human problem."[145] The Israelitic differentiation of the transcendent God is a case in point. Individuals who could not endure the demands placed upon the Chosen People fell back upon the still culturally viable polytheism of the surrounding society. In the late Middle Ages, the socially available spiritual alternative to a difficult Christianity was the "living culture" of the various underground gnostic movements, which, according to Voegelin, provided "experiential alternatives sufficiently close to the experience of faith but far enough from it to remedy the uncertainty of strict faith."[146]

More particularly, the "experiential alternatives" offered by the gnostic spiritual movements, the forebears of modern ideology, consisted of various attempts to "expand the soul to the point where god is drawn into the existence of man."[147] In other words, the aim of such efforts was self-divinization. As Voegelin explains, the aim was to "divinize [the person who undergoes the experience] by substituting more massive modes of participation in divinity for faith in the Christian sense."[148] Voegelin identifies three such kinds of experiences, intellectual, emotional, and volitional. The intellectual variant typically takes the form of a "speculative penetration" of the mystery of creation and existence; the Hegelian system is representative. The emotional variant assumes the form of an "indwelling of divine substance in the human soul," as in the experiences of the paracletic sectarian leaders. The third type, the volitional, manifests itself as an "activist redemption of man and society," classically illustrated by Comte and Marx. According to Voegelin, such existential self-divinization constitutes the "active core" of the immanentist eschatology that impelled the modern re-divinization

---

[144] Ibid. 124.
[145] Voegelin, *Science, Politics, and Gnosticism*, 114.
[146] Voegelin, *New Science*, 124.
[147] Ibid. 124.
[148] Ibid.

of state and society, a process unfolding "from medieval immanentism through humanism, enlightenment, progressivism, liberalism, positivism, and Marxism."[149]

The example of Marx well illustrates the existential dynamics involved in the process of self-divinization. Marx, following Feuerbach, insisted that God was a "projection" of man's highest and best qualities into some illusory Beyond; man's task is to draw his projection of God back into himself. In so doing, man becomes conscious that he himself *is* god; man is transfigured into a kind of Nietzschean *Übermensch* ("superman"). According to Voegelin, Marxian transfiguration represents the extreme form of a "less radical medieval experience, which drew the spirit of God into man, while leaving God himself in his transcendence." The modern supermen of Comte, Marx, and Nietzsche did not emerge from a cloud but rather represent the end of the road to radical "secularization" marked over previous centuries by such figures as the "godded man" of the English Reformation mystics and similar constructs.[150] "Modern secularism," Voegelin concludes, "should be understood as the radicalization of . . . earlier forms of [medieval and] paracletic immanentism, because the experiential divinization of man is more radical in the secularist case."[151] He perceives historical continuity between medieval and modern gnostic movements and continuity of experiential dynamic within all forms of gnostic consciousness.

We have seen that the overarching goal of the modern ideologues is to abolish the tensions of historical existence by obscuring or denying the transcendent dimension of existence. To that end, the truth of the open soul in tension toward the divine, as well as its symbolic representations--philosophy and Christianity--must be abolished. Such a strategy accounts for the marked hostility to both classical philosophy and Christianity that characterizes the peculiarly modern and postmodern strains of Western civilization. On Voegelin's view, however, Christianity is not altogether blameless in this regard. Over time, he maintains, it came to embrace an excessive doctrinization and dogmatism that served to eclipse the experiential foundation of Christian truth. The ossification of that truth in formalistic and literalistic

---

[149] Ibid.
[150] Ibid. 126.
[151] Ibid.

theological and metaphysical doctrine led Christian symbols to become opaque; the existential truth they were intended to express became increasingly obscure. According to Voegelin, the erosion of the existential meaning behind Christian symbols is implicated in the rise of the modern ideological movements insofar as it "permitted gnostic symbols of reality to take over the representational function among the nation states of the Western world."[152]

Indeed the rise of gnostic consciousness has led to a gradual transformation of the meaning of the principal symbols by which Western civilization had ordered itself for a millennium. The Christian person, whose spiritual qualities we have discussed at length, became a mere "man," a world-immanent being who governs the universe through intellect and will, through science and pragmatic action. The highest-order goods of the Western tradition—the life of contemplative reason expressed in philosophy and the life of the spirit symbolized by the Church—were attacked as "false and anachronistic." Under the influence of the scientistic and positivistic "science" that stems from gnostic consciousness, the "real" contracted to that which is immanent and objectively measurable; man's spiritual needs were no longer regarded as grounded in the truth of reality or being. On Voegelin's view, the resulting experiential impoverishment partially accounts for the mass appeal of the modern political religions and corresponding re-sacralization of the state: "Men can allow the world to so expand that the world and the God behind it disappear. But they cannot thereby solve the problem of their existence, for it endures in every soul. Thus when the God behind the world is unseen, the contents of the world emerge as new gods."[153] We have previously discussed the modern emergence of the New Idol.

For Voegelin, however, the most devastating consequence of the modern gnostic victory is the "radical expurgation of a whole range of experiences previously open to man"—the symbolic experiences of transcendence through which the human being gains his sense of order, meaning, and immortality. Indeed, the loss of such experiences was both cause and effect of the rise of revolutionary gnostic consciousness. The

---

[152] Eric Voegelin, *Political Religions,* trans. T. J. DiNapoli and E. S. Easterly III (Lewiston, NY: The Edwin Mellen Press, 1986), 50-51.
[153] Ibid.

ossification of existential truth into dogma served to eclipse the living truth such dogma was meant to protect, creating an existential void to be filled by the gnostic promise. The radical immanentization that ensued served in turn to further suppress those intimations of order and meaning rooted in participation in the divine ground. Those who embraced the gnostic vision experienced a world deprived of any relation to transcendent being. The ensuing sense of confinement fanned the flames of revolt against the limits of such a closed existence and fueled the revolutionary drive to realize the impossible goal of intramundane perfection embodied in the modern political religions. The nightmare of the past century was created by disoriented souls railing against the prison-like confines of a closed or truncated reality.

The "unprecedented destructiveness" of the twentieth century was accompanied, paradoxically, by significant social achievement: growth in population accompanied by advances in material well-being, longevity, and literacy, much of which made possible by the development of science and technology. The contemporary age, Voegelin says, represents the curious phenomenon of a civilization that is "declining" and "advancing" at the same time. His analysis of modernity suggests that the simultaneous material growth and spiritual decline of Western civilization is related to the process of radical immanentization or "secularization" under discussion. As he explains, "gnostic speculation overcame the uncertainty of faith by receding from transcendence and endowing man and his intramundane range of action with the meaning of eschatological fulfillment; . . . as this immanentization progressed experientially, civilizational activity became a mystical work of self-salvation."[154] The modern "recession from transcendence" permitted the release of tremendous spiritual energy for the pursuit of worldly achievement; in building civilization, man felt himself to be earning salvation itself. Insofar, however, as civilizational pursuits became a diversion from or substitute for genuine spirituality, the life of the spirit was vitiated. Insofar as intramundane activity "absorbed into itself the eternal destiny of man," the transcendent experiences that constitute the ultimate source of both personal and social order tended to disappear or become unintelligible. "The price of

---

[154] Ibid. 129.

progress," Voegelin pessimistically concludes, "is the death of the spirit."[155]

Despite such a gloomy conclusion, however, Voegelin also leaves grounds for hope: Truth, in the end, must prevail. As he says, "[t]he closure of the soul in modern gnosticism can repress the truth of the soul . . . but it cannot remove the soul and its transcendence from the structure of reality." The flight from reality cannot last forever. Moreover, the eschatological interpretation of history results in a false picture of reality (the order of concrete human societies is not in fact an *eschaton*); and errors with regard to the structure of reality have practical consequences. One would think that the totalitarian nightmare of the twentieth century and eventual collapse of the former Soviet Union would give pause to even the most zealous ideologues. Tragically, however, that does not seem to be the case. Marxism, socialism, and efforts to remove Christianity from the public sphere, indeed, even from the private sphere, are alive and well in contemporary Western society, including American society. Moreover, the ideological constructs identified by Voegelin are not the only manifestations of the radical immanentization or secularization he decried. Other socially influential paradigms and perspectives, both historical and contemporary, have contributed, and continue to contribute, to erosion of the spiritual foundation of Western and American order. We turn now to an examination of the most important of such cultural, intellectual, and academic trends.

---

[155] Ibid. 131.

THIRTEEN

THE TRANSFORMATION OF AMERICAN SOCIETY

The truth does not cease to exist because it is ignored.   —*George Orwell*

The modern ideological movements—communism, socialism, fascism, and related constructs—were driven by persons who desired fundamental transformation of Western society. Movement leaders well understood that the "change" they demanded required transformation not only of established political, economic, and legal institutions but also the values, beliefs, and traditions that constitute their ground. Carriers of the ideological impulse understood, in particular, that the radical expansion of governmental power central to their vision was unlikely to be achieved in a society saturated with traditional religious commitments. Western Christianity is fundamentally at odds with totalitarian or unlimited government of any form. Indeed Christian thought and practice in the West led to development of precisely the opposite concept—limited government, limited as temporal government inevitably appears in light of the eternal life anticipated by the Christian faithful. The Judeo-Christian conception of moral law— an objective and higher law rooted in divine authority—establishes further intrinsic limits to the power of government, as does the historical Christian differentiation between the related but distinct realms of God and Caesar. Government is conceived not as the source of law or rights but rather administrator of a pre-existing moral law that binds ruler and ruled alike, and its authority is confined to its legitimate sphere. Traditional Christianity, moreover, turns a granite face to the lure of worldly or political salvation—the explicit or implicit promise of modern secular messiahs of all stripes—and rather condemns worship or divinization of the state as idolatry. It regards salvation as individual or

115

personal salvation through the grace of God, not collective salvation through the secular state. For such reasons and others, modern ideologues aimed their guns, figuratively if not literally, directly at biblical religion. Such a strategy is true of Comte, Marx, Stalin, Hitler, Castro, and others.

The attack on the Judeo-Christian tradition, however, was not restricted to the more virulent expressions of the ideological impulse, such as communism and Nazism, but joined by sympathizers and fellow travelers of various stripes. English movements such as Fabian socialism, positivism, and the "advanced liberalism" of J. S. Mill, as well as American counterparts such as Progressivism and Social Gospel, shared many goals with their more radical brethren, as well as the assumptions, beliefs, and motivations that informed them. The chief differences between the two camps concerned strategy, not substance. The main such strategic division was the preference of Anglo-American variants for democratic gradualism over violent revolution. A second difference relates to the degree of socialization or collectivization advocated by either camp. Classic Marxism advocated overthrow of the free society in toto—limited government, capitalism, private property, rule of law, customary morality—and its replacement with totalitarian communism. The Anglo-American variants aimed to replace the free society not with outright communism but rather a managed or planned economy ordered by political elites or "experts" believed to possess knowledge unavailable to the common man. The classic communist and socialist vision has been explored in other chapters.[156] The present chapter examines its ideological cousins and fellow travelers, the less virulent but equally influential Anglo-American expressions of the modern and postmodern collectivist impulse.

I.   *Progressivism, Social Gospel, Secular Humanism*

The chief carrier of nonviolent collectivist aspirations in the American context was the so-called Progressive Movement that rose to prominence at the turn of the twentieth century. Early Progressivism had broad

---

[156] Linda C. Raeder, *Freedom and American Society*, Volume II, *Freedom and Economic Order* (Palm Beach: Sanctuary Cove Publishing, 2017), Chapters 8, 9, and 10; Volume III, Chapter 12.

political appeal, encompassing both Republicans and Democrats, both Theodore Roosevelt and Woodrow Wilson. Its central belief, shared by partisans of all stripes, was that "Progress" entailed an ongoing adaptation of existing social institutions to time and circumstance. History, argued the Progressives, does not stand still and neither should the institutional structure of society. Social institutions, most pointedly, should evolve in accord with historical change. Only thus may a society achieve the "living" institutional and interpretive frameworks essential to its Progress. Progressives were particularly concerned to adapt American political principles and practice to the flux of history. Traditional conceptions embodied in the vision of the Founders, especially the concept of a government limited to securing the unalienable rights of the individual, were said to be outdated and unhistorical. Progress was said to require novel constitutional constructions better adapted to prevailing historical circumstances. More particularly, Progressives generally argued that contemporary circumstances called for greater centralization and rationalization of government, which meant, among other things, its direction by unelected administrative elites more or less immune to the pressure of politics. The Progressive view of government, however, was not confined to specific prescriptions or even general principles but, in line with its overarching philosophy, elastic and flexible. As R. J. Pestritto observed, Progressives championed an evolving conception of government, "one whose ends and scope would change to take on any and all social and economic ills."[157]

Such an expansionist view of legitimate governmental power led Progressives to chafe at the limits on federal power established by the United States Constitution. Federalism, separation of powers, negative rights, and other constitutional restraints on government were said to stand in the way of Progress. Progressives understood, however, that efforts to move beyond the Founders' Constitution would encounter resistance among an American populace historically devoted to both their memory and their principles. They further understood the intimate relation between American political institutions, particularly limited government and the rule of law, and traditional American religious

---

[157] R. J. Pestritto, *Woodrow Wilson and the Roots of Modern Liberalism* (Lanham, MD: Rowman & Littlefield Publishers, Inc., 2005).

convictions. They well recognized that the American people since the Founding regarded themselves as "endowed by their Creator with certain unalienable rights" and that the Creator in question was generally regarded as the transcendent God of the Bible. The realization of the Progressive aim—the gradual removal of limits on the power of government in the name of greater administrative rationality—thus required simultaneous attack on three pillars of traditional American order—reverence for the Founding Fathers, the U.S. Constitution, and the Christian faith.

Many early Progressives were schooled in the philosophy of American Pragmatism. Pragmatism typically embraces a form of ethical consequentialism, evaluating meaning, truth, or value on the basis of practical consequences and not a priori axioms or principles. Pragmatism, somewhat like Utilitarianism and Socialism, regards right and wrong, good and evil, truth or untruth as determined not by fixed and permanent standards but rather outcomes, which are necessarily contingent on particular and ever-changing circumstance. The ever-changing circumstances of human history thus lead to changing conceptions of right and wrong. If society is not to be mired in the past, if it is to progress, its moral standards must adapt to the movement of history. On such a view, particular moral conceptions can never be regarded as absolute but only relative to their time and place. Indeed American Progressivism is wedded to a radically relativistic perspective not only with respect to morality but any and all social and cultural phenomena, moral, legal, political, economic, and religious. Progressivism, like its contemporary cousins, Postmodernism and Multiculturalism, challenges the existence of universal, absolute, and immutable Truth that transcends history. On the Progressive view, the only truth accessible to human beings is relative historical truth: what is true in one society or era may or may not be true for other societies shaped by different circumstances or existing in different periods of time. Truth, like every aspect of historical existence, can and does evolve or Progress over time.

On such a view, the allegedly "self-evident Truth" proclaimed in the Declaration of Independence, like the moral Truth proclaimed by Christianity, appear not as absolute but merely relative "truths." Indeed such traditional "truths" appear as little more than quaint historical relics, certainly not binding, universal, and eternal axioms valid for all human beings in all times and places. Progressives acknowledge that the U.S. Constitution may have been culturally appropriate to its time, reflecting widespread beliefs held in an earlier stage of historical development. The same holds true for Christianity and other historical expressions of religious belief. History, however, has moved on and so must morality, religion, law, and government. Thus emerges the Progressive concept of the "Living Constitution."[158] The clever phrase symbolizes the idea that the U.S. Constitution—the fundamental law and framework of American political order—must be progressively adapted to the forward march of history. To do otherwise, to cling to the outmoded and antiquated eighteenth-century conceptions of the Founders, is to defy the movement of history, to defy Progress. It is to saddle members of contemporary society with the archaic beliefs of a former age and thus preclude a truly representative government "of the people, by the people, for the people.: Progress requires movement beyond such putatively historically obsolete conceptions as limited constitutional government, individualism, negative natural rights, free-market capitalism, traditional morality, and justice as the rule of law. Such can only be achieved by throwing off the dead weight of the Founders' Constitution that binds the American people to such obsolete values and institutions. Progress requires a "Living," changing, growing, evolving Constitution, not a petrified and lifeless relic of times long past.

Social Gospel

Progress so conceived further requires movement beyond traditional Christianity. The particularly religious dimension of Progressivism was largely elaborated by its spiritual arm, the Social Gospel movement of the era. Representative leaders included Christian ministers such Walter Rauschenbusch and Washington Gladden, as well as Richard T. Ely, American economist and founder of the Christian Social Union.[159] Such

---

[158] The term originally derives from the title of a 1927 book of that name by Prof. Howard McBain, while early efforts at developing the concept in modern form have been credited to figures including Oliver Wendell Holmes, Louis D. Brandeis, and Woodrow Wilson.

[159] Richard Theodore Ely (1854–1943) was an American economist, author, and leader of the Progressive movement, which called for more government intervention to reform the alleged injustices of capitalism, especially regarding

Progressive Social-Gospelers assumed the task of revising or adapting Christianity and Judeo-Christian morality to the changing circumstances of history. Many Social Gospel ministers and theologians, like their Progressive counterparts, had received graduate training at contemporary universities in Germany, where they were exposed to the dominant philosophy of the day, so-called German Idealism. Among other teachings, German Idealism held that the "state" (government) possesses an independent reality separate and distinct from the people who compose it. Rauschenbusch and other Social Gospelers would interpret such a concept to mean that society is a "social organism." Progressives such as Woodrow Wilson and others also applied an organic metaphor to society, as reflected in the concept of the "Living" (growing, organic) Constitution.

In all instances, the organic conception of society and government led not only to emphasis on change, evolution, and growth but also elevation of the collective—the putatively organic social whole—over the individual (a mere part). As Arthur Ekirch explains, both Social Gospelers and Progressives were convinced that "[s]ociety in the future would have to be based more and more on an explicit subordination of the individual to a collectivist, or nationalized, political and social order."[160] Subordination of the individual was regarded as essential to progress and reform. Such a view of course utterly contradicts traditional American conceptions regarding the relation between the individual and government. American social-contract theory conceives society as constituted by individuals endowed with unalienable natural rights and not a living "organism" independent of and superior to the individuals it comprises. The traditional American view presupposes the individual as the exclusive bearer of moral agency and society as a merely nominal abstraction. Moreover, it further regards government ("the state") as a more or less utilitarian organization established by individuals to secure

---

factory conditions, compulsory education, child labor, and labor unions. Ely is best remembered as a founder and the first Secretary of the American Economic Association, as a founder of the Christian Social Union, and as the author of a series of widely-read books on the organized labor movement, socialism, and other social questions.

[160] Arthur Ekirch, *The Decline of American Liberalism* (Oakland, CA: Independent Institute, 2009).

their rights, certainly not an autonomous or self-subsistent entity superior to the people it is meant to serve.

Progressives and Social Gospelers also embraced other aspects of German Idealist philosophy, including the Hegelian philosophy of history.[161] Hegel, like Marx and various other nineteenth-century thinkers, maintained that History is moving by inexorable laws toward a final goal, the "End of History," a path, in Hegel's version, directed by the so-called "cunning of reason."[162] Throughout the autonomous movement of History toward its goal, Hegel further maintained, the highest ethical force in society is embodied in government or the state. As Jon Ray explains, for Hegel, "the State is the essential reality and embodies all of human progress. And we are free only when we are all merged into a common will within the State." As Hegel himself put it, the "state" represents nothing less than the "march of God through the World" and "the Divine Idea as it exists on earth." Accordingly, he concludes, "we must . . . worship the State as the manifestation of the Divine on Earth."[163]

Such views stand of course in the starkest possible opposition not only to the traditional Anglo-American conception of government but also the religious conceptions that implicitly inform it. Americans of the founding era certainly did not regard government as "the Divine Idea . . . . on earth." On the traditional American view, informed as it is by conventional Judeo-Christian presuppositions, no aspect of the created order is divine. Divinity is an attribute of God alone, and rulers, as Augustine admonished, must remember that they too are men. Indeed to regard the state or government as "divine" is to commit the sin of idolatry.

---

[161] Their experience in Germany led both Progressives and Social Gospelers not only to embrace Idealist philosophy but also its practical application. They particularly admired Bismarck's novel social-welfare policy, which employed government resources to provide guaranteed welfare benefits such as social security and health care to the citizens.

[162] Georg Wilhelm Friedrich Hegel (1770-1831). *Lectures on the Philosophy of History*, originally given as lectures at the University of Berlin in 1821, 1824, 1827, and 1831.

[163] G. W. F. Hegel, *Philosophy of History*, in Jacob Loewenberg, ed, (New York: C. Scribner's Sons, 1929), 388-89, 443-44.

The efforts of Progressive Social Gospelers to revise or adapt Christianity to the movement of history clearly manifest the radical relativism presupposed by such efforts. Nowhere is such relativism more evident than in their attempt to divinize government or the state in the Hegelian manner.[164] As the Social Gospel minister Washington Gladden put it,

> Let me say . . . that this conception of the state, that it is merely a police force, is, to my mind, a wholly erroneous conception; . . . *the state is something far higher and more godlike than this . . .* [I]f we could only invest it in our thought with its true divine character, we should need no other agency for the unification of society (emphasis added).[165]

In the context of traditional American conceptions of both government and religion, as well as Gladden's status as a Christian minister, such a remark is nothing less than stunning. His comments obviously constitute a veiled attack on traditional American political principles. The political thought of the Founders does in fact lead to a view of government as more or less a "police force," as suggested by the traditional metaphor of the "night watchman." They are also utterly incompatible with biblical religion, however latitudinarian or heterodox. Christianity of course forbids the imputation of a "true divine character" to government, or any intramundane entity, but rather condemned such practice as pagan idolatry from the outset. Gladden's statement is representative not of traditional American or Judeo-Christian thought but rather the modern impulse toward re-divinization or re-sacralization of the state, the erection, as Nietzsche put it, of the "New Idol." It represents, not orthodox Christianity, which radically de-divinized the realm of government and politics, but rather the corruption of certain variants of modern Christianity and their transformation into yet another form of political religion. Traditional Christianity, again, condemns in no uncertain terms the attribution of divinity to any aspect

---

[164] Redivinization is probably the more apt turn, as the modern divinization of the state resembles the pre-Christian or pagan conception that attributed divinity to political rule.

[165] Cited in Edmund A. Opitz, *The Libertarian Theology of Freedom* (Tampa: Hallberg Publishing Corporation, 1999), 16-17. Hereinafter cited as *LTF*.

of the created order, precisely the move advanced by Hegel and Social Gospelers such as Gladden.

Such views cannot be reconciled with Christianity, a fact soon apprehended by traditional Christians of the era. The rise of the Social Gospel provoked orthodox American Protestants to reassert the "fundamentals" of Christianity over and against the degenerate socialization of the Christian faith, represented by both the Social Gospel and its fellow traveler, the so-called Christian Socialism that arose in the same period. Such developments, in other words, prompted the rise of what today is known as Christian Fundamentalism. Its early adherents clearly recognized the merely nominal character of the putatively "Christian" Social Gospel.[166] American Social Gospelers and other Progressives thoroughly absorbed the socialistic, and antitheistic, moral vision that rose to prominence in nineteenth-century Europe.

The socialist aspirations of the Social Gospel movement are of course evident in its very name. They are also evident in the attempts of Social Gospel thinkers to reconstruct the image of Christ, indeed, to reconstruct Him in their own image. The era witnessed the publication of various books portraying Jesus Christ as a socialist and asserting the identity of Christian and socialist ethics.[167] As Charles Cashdollar explains in *The Transformation of Theology, 1830-1890*, Christianity in the nineteenth century found itself in a kind of dialectical confrontation

---

[166] The movement became active in the 1910s after the release of *The Fundamentals*, a ten-volume set of essays, apologetic and polemic, written by conservative Protestant theologians to defend what they regarded as Protestant orthodoxy.

[167] For instance, *In His Steps* (1897) and *The Reformer* (1902), by the Congregational minister Charles Sheldon, who coined the motto "What would Jesus do?" In his personal life, Sheldon was committed to Christian Socialism and identified strongly with the Social Gospel movement. Walter Rauschenbusch, one of the leading early theologians of the Social Gospel in the United States, indicated that his theology had been inspired by Sheldon's novels. In 1892, Rauschenbusch and several other leading writers and advocates of the Social Gospel formed a group called the Brotherhood of the Kingdom. Members of this group produced many of the written works that defined the theology of the Social Gospel movement and gave it public prominence. These included Rauschenbusch's *Christianity and the Social Crisis* (1907) and *Christianizing the Social Order* (1912), as well as Batten's *The New Citizenship* (1898) and *The Social Task of Christianity* (1911).

with the novel socialist morality of the era. Socialism portrayed itself as a decided moral advance over traditional Christianity, which was relentlessly criticized and condemned for its allegedly selfish individualism and egoism. Christianity was bluntly condemned as the Religion of the Selfish.[168] Socialism, by contrast, was said to embody altruistic concern for others, for all human beings, not merely the individual or particular privileged groups. Certain Christian denominations accepted and assimilated the socialist critique of Christianity. Rather than defending their faith against such charges, they embraced the views of their critics, often becoming as socialist as the Socialists. Such assimilation is of course explicit in those denominations that embraced the Social Gospel, but prevailing trends influenced other Christian denominations as well. Christ himself was reinvented as a socialist and socialism held to be the true expression of Christian spirituality and ethics. The transcendent core of Christian faith was eviscerated or obscured, and spiritual aspirations redirected toward amelioration of material suffering in this world. The Kingdom of God was no longer conceived as "within" or beyond, as in orthodox Christian theology, but more or less identified with this world—the earthly or temporal realm of society, government, and material concerns.

Such conceptions resemble the similar exchange of "vertical" for "horizontal" transcendence embodied in the modern ideological movements. The Social Gospel movement was in the forefront of such efforts in the American context. The movement was a uniquely American expression of the existential drive that Eric Voegelin associates with modernity more generally, that is, the futile attempt to "immanentize the Eschaton." The Social Gospel, like the more virulent ideological movements, collapsed the tension between the transcendent and immanent dimensions of existence, attempting instead to materialize the Kingdom of God within history. The transcendent pole of human of experience was obscured and spiritual aspirations, traditionally oriented toward a transcendent God beyond time and history, redirected to exclusively worldly or mundane concerns.[169] Social

---

[168] ". . . Christianity gives to morality an essentially selfish character. . . ." J.S. Mill, *On Liberty and Other Writings*, ed, Stefan Collini (Cambridge: Cambridge University Press, 1995 [1859]), 51.

[169] See Linda C. Raeder, "Voegelin on Gnosticism, Modernity, and the Balance of Consciousness" (*Political Science Reviewer*, Vol. XXXVI, 2007).

Gospelers replaced the traditional transcendent orientation of the Christian faith not with the promised land of the Marxian vision—ideal communism—but rather various forms of immanent or this-worldly "social" ministry—food kitchens, medical uplift, education, and other forms of material welfare. Presbyterians, Congregationalists, Methodists, Northern Baptists and other denominations influenced by the Social Gospel developed various "social creeds" that emphasized the "social" significance of the Gospel. By 1912 eleven denominations pledged to carry out "social service" programs.

While such charitable assistance has long been regarded as a Christian obligation, the Social Gospelers moved far beyond traditional Christian concern for the less fortunate. An essential feature of the Social Gospel was its truncation of religious obligation to provision of mundane social welfare, typically of a material nature. Religious obligation was more or less reduced to intraworldly "service to Humanity"; traditional obligation to serve the transcendent God more or less faded from view. As Albrecht Ritschl explained, salvation, according to the new Social Gospel, "was not to be interpreted in terms of a future life, but in terms of service in a this-worldly kingdom of human goodness."[170] As Woodrow Wilson propounded the Humanistic social creed, "There is no higher religion than human service. To work for the common good is the greatest creed."[171] Wilson followed in the footsteps of earlier prophets of the Humanist evangel, such as J.S. Mill. Mill had decades earlier proclaimed the moral superiority of the Religion of Humanity to orthodox Christianity and "service to Humanity . . . the law of our lives." In all such constructs, the traditional Christian obligation to serve one's fellows in service to God, conceived as a triangular relation among God, the individual, and his fellow human beings, is replaced by a dualistic Service to Humanity, a relation forged solely between human beings. The third, most crucial, leg of the orthodox Christian conception—God, the Source of the Christian obligation to serve other human beings—more or less disappears from view. God, as Nietzsche had pointed out, is dead.

Social Gospelers shared with communist true believers not only an ultimate aim—the creation of the Kingdom of God on earth—but also

---

[170] Albrecht Ritschl, cited in Opitz, *LTF*, 16.
[171] Woodrow Wilson (December 28, 1856 - February 03, 1924).

mutual belief in the perfectibility of man by means of "social" change. From a strictly theological perspective, the Social Gospel and similar quasi-religious movements within modern and postmodern society, such as so-called Liberation Theology, represent a corruption and degeneration of Christianity. Their chief significance for modern political developments is the fact that all such movements were (and are) eager to employ the coercive force of government to achieve their ends, whether such are regarded as the will of History or God. Various Social Gospelers, for instance, advocated governmental redistribution of wealth in the name of social justice, said to be an application of the "teachings of Jesus" and the "law of love."[172] Others advocated outright socialism, including government ownership of significant resources such as land, water supply, mines, and so on.

Such proposals cannot be defended on traditional Christian grounds let alone said to follow from Christian teaching. Neither socialism proper nor political redistribution of wealth can be morally justified on the grounds of traditional Christian ethics. Such forms of economic organization and policy are strictly prohibited not only by the longstanding Judeo-Christian validation of the rule of law in general but the right to property in particular. As previously observed, the moral legitimacy of private property is established and presupposed by the absolute biblical injunction against theft. The prohibition against taking a person's property without his consent rules out the moral legitimacy of both socialism proper and political redistribution of wealth, neither of which can be achieved without taking someone's property without consent. The only way to avoid such a conclusion is the improbable if not impossible achievement of universal voluntary consent to any proposed policy involving political distribution or redistribution of wealth.

The radical relativism of the Social Gospelers, like that of their Progressive counterparts, however, did provide a way around such moral obstacles. The Progressives, as said, denied the validity of moral absolutes, Christian or otherwise. The Social Gospelers were Progressives. Accordingly, they denied the absolutely binding nature of the Judeo-Christian Decalogue. Historical criticism undertaken in the previous century, they argued, had made several important discoveries

---

[172] Opitz, *LTF*, 18.

that undermined the moral authority of the Ten Commandments. Not only had such research uncovered the "fact," previously noted, that Jesus was a social reformer or even an outright socialist but also that certain of the Commandments served a suspect, even nefarious purpose, namely, protecting the "haves" against the "have-nots." On the basis of such putative discovery, Social Gospelers and Progressives concluded that the Judeo-Christian prohibition of stealing must not be regarded as absolutely but only relatively or conditionally binding on the human conscience. Morality, as every other historical entity, must be regarded not as fixed and unalterable but rather evolving and progressing. In this instance, Progress requires the present age to advance beyond the self-serving interpretation placed upon the Ten Commandments in former centuries. The Decalogue must not be regarded as a set of absolute injunctions transcending time and space but rather relative moral rules whose significance and meaning vary (progress) over the course of history. Such a weakening of moral absolutes was widely embraced not only by Social Gospelers and Progressives but other Christian denominations influenced by their teaching as well.[173]

Proponents of the Social Gospel shared with their Marxist brethren not only the demand for political redistribution of wealth and even outright socialization of various resources but a deeper substratum of belief as well. At the core of both systems of thought lies a shared belief in *determinism*. Philosophical determinism has been formally defined as a "theory that all events, including moral choices, are completely determined by previously existing causes. . . [such] that humans cannot act otherwise than they do."[174] In other words, determinism is a broad and general category of philosophical thought encompassing various particular theories united by a defining attribute, namely, the belief that something other than free choice "determines" or "causes" individual experience. Modern determinism takes many forms, from the economic and historical determinism of Marx to the psychological determinism of Sigmund Freud to the genetic or biological determinism of contemporary science.

---

[173] *The Book of Resolutions of the United Methodist Church 2016* (Nashville: Cokesbury, 2016).
[174] Encyclopedia Britannica, 2016.

Karl Marx taught that prevailing economic relations in a society "determine" the consciousness and behavior of its members. Social Gospelers extended such determinism beyond the realm of economics per se to the social environment more generally. The environment of the individual, and not the individual himself, was said to determine his behavior. Determinism so conceived, conventionally if not surprisingly referred to as environmental or social determinism, is yet another distinguishing feature of the Social Gospel and one that further turns orthodox Christianity on its head. Traditional Christianity, as previously discussed, regards the battle between good and evil as occurring within the heart and soul of the individual, the locus of moral agency, freedom, and responsibility. The character of any given society, including both its characteristic social, political, and economic institutions and prevailing social conditions, manifests the character of the individuals who constitute it. The social "environment" is regarded not as "cause" of human experience but rather its "effect," the manifestation of the values, beliefs, and actions of the individuals who constitute society. Christianity, moreover, does not permit individuals to blame external or environmental conditions for their values, beliefs, actions, or experience. Eve's decision to eat the fruit could not be blamed on the serpent or apple tree. Her action was determined not by her environment—the existence of the serpent and tree—but rather individual choice, the exercise of free will. Both the priority of individual values to social conditions and the existence of free will lead to the conclusion that improvement of the "social environment" necessarily requires preliminary improvement of the individuals who shape it. No magic, political or otherwise, can create a good society out of bad people.

Modern Western determinism rose to prominence in the wake of the "death of God." One of the central elements of the biblical worldview is of course the conviction that human beings, made in the image of God, are endowed with free will, the capacity for voluntary choice. If God is dead, however, then so is the conception of individual free will. Indeed the existence of free will was a significant and much debated issue in nineteenth-century England, the period that witnessed both militant hostility toward Christianity and the accompanying rise of antitheistic social morality. So-called Christian Voluntarists of the era countered the arguments of anti-theological thinkers by pointing precisely to the existence of free will as definitive "proof" of the existence of God.[175] Such efforts would prove more or less in vain. The social success of the antitheistic forces led not only to evisceration of Christianity but its characteristic conception of free will as well. Determinism emerged to fill the void.

Accordingly, various modern determinists, from Rousseau to Marx to the Social Gospelers, reject the traditional view that conceives the social environment as reflecting prior individual values, belief, and practice, dependent as it is on the concept of free will. Evil is said to result not from individual moral choice, regarded as yet another illusion of the Judeo-Christian imagination, but rather the external social environment and/or faulty social institutions of one sort or another. Rousseau attributed the source of evil to the *ancien regime* and its institutions, Marx to the capitalist economic system. The Social Gospelers attributed it to the social environment. Moreover, just as the elimination of the evils perceived by Rousseau required transformation of existing French institutions and the evils perceived by Marx required transformation of the economic system, so the evils perceived by the Social Gospelers required transformation of the social environment. The elimination of evil and creation of a good society require not the transformation, conversion, or moral development of its individual members but rather reconstruction of the social environment believed to engender bad or vicious behavior. As Rev. Irving E. Howard summarized the Social Gospel view, "[i]nstead of the converted individual changing the environment, a changed environment was supposed to change the individual."[176]

The social or environmental determinism of the Social Gospelers took an ominous turn when conjoined with a belief acquired from their Progressive brethren, namely, that requisite change of the social environment could be achieved through judicious employment of the coercive power of government ("social engineering"). In 1885, Gladden attended a conference at which he was introduced to the idea of "using the force of the state to achieve . . . social righteousness . . ."[177] Arch-

---

[175] J.S. Mill, *An Examination of Sir William Hamilton's Philosophy*, vol. 9, *Collected Works of John Stuart Mill*, 33 vols, ed, John M. Robson, intro Alan Ryan (Toronto: University of Toronto Press, 1979). Hereinafter cited as *CW*.
[176] Opitz, *LTF*, 12.
[177] Ibid., 13.

Progressive Woodrow Wilson was in attendance at the conference, as was Richard T. Ely, the aforementioned Progressive economist who championed greater governmental intervention in economic and social life. Upon embracing the (anti-Augustinian) belief in the efficacy of coercive force with respect to moral reform, Social Gospelers joined hands with Progressives in a mutual effort to remove constitutional limits on the power of the federal government. The Progressives regarded such limits as obstacles to Progress; the Social Gospelers came to regard them as obstacles to establishing the Kingdom of God on earth. The achievement of the Kingdom thus required a reinterpretation not only of Christianity but also the U.S. Constitution. Progressives and Social Gospelers marched in step toward achievement of their mutual goals.

Proponents of the Social Gospel also united with Progressive and socialist fellow travelers in attacking capitalism. Marx's assault on the liberal economic order involved a frontal assault not only on capitalism but also its corollary religious traditions. Marx not only confessed his "hatred of the gods" but dismissed religion as the "opium of the people," an illusory and ultimately poisonous means of escaping the sufferings of this world.[178] The Social Gospelers, by contrast, did not advocate outright rejection of Christianity but rather its reinterpretation and identification with socialism. In 1889, the Society of Christian Socialists was formed in Boston to "show that the aim of socialism is embraced in the aim of Christianity." In the same year, Gladden spoke on the topic of "Christian socialism" at a council of Congregational churches. Although Gladden did not identify himself as a full-fledged socialist, he shared its denigration of individualism, which he, like his socialist brethren, linked to the market order. As Gladden put it, "It begins to be clear that Christianity is not individualism. The Christian has encountered no deadlier foe during the last century than that individualistic philosophy which underlies the competitive system." Other Social Gospel ministers agreed: "Business itself today is wrong . .

---

[178] The full quote from Karl Marx has been translated as follows: "Religion is the sigh of the oppressed creature, the heart of a heartless world, and the soul of soulless conditions. It is the opium of the people." The quotation originates from the introduction of Marx's proposed work "A Contribution to the Critique of Hegel's Philosophy of Right." The "Contribution" was never completed but Marx published the introduction (written in 1843) in his own journal, *Deutsch-Französische Jahrbücher*.

. based on competitive strife for profits. But this is the exact opposite of Christianity. We must change the system. . . ."[179] Rauschenbusch attacked both competition and business monopoly. In 1934 the Congregational-Christian churches established a Council for Social Action that summed up the anti-capitalist aspirations of the Social Gospel movement.

> [The Council resolved to work toward] . . . the abolition of the system responsible for these destructive elements in our common life [the competitive market system], by eliminating the system's incentives and habits, the legal forms which sustain it, and the moral ideals which justify it. The inauguration of a genuinely cooperative social economy democratically planned to adjust production to consumption requirements, to modify or eliminate private ownership of the means of production or distribution wherever such ownership interferes with the social good.[180]

The conclusion of Rev. Howard is to the point— "the Social Gospel as it developed in American Protestantism was not an application of the teachings of Jesus."[181] It represents, on the contrary, yet another manifestation of the tremendous "shift in faith" that took place in Western society during the modern period. Voegelin characterizes such a shift as the general eclipse of transcendence. Rev. Howard further specifies the characteristically modern dynamic as a shift "from God to man, from eternity to time, from the individual to the [collective] group, individual conversion to social coercion, . . . from the church to the state," and, not least, from individual spiritual freedom to social determinism.[182] Such are among the consequences of the "death of God" in its American expression.

Secular Messianism and the Social Religion

---

[179] Cited in Opitz, *LTF*, 14.
[180] Ibid., 20.
[181] Ibid.10
[182] Ibid., 11.

The Social Gospelers, like many self-described Christian socialists and Christian altruists to the present day, seemed unaware of the nature of the social creed they absorbed from Europe, including both its origin as an explicit rival to traditional Christianity and its fundamental incompatibility with biblical faith. Christianity and socialism cannot be reconciled. The Social Gospelers, as discussed, could only appear to do so by revising Christianity in certain fundamental ways, for instance, reinventing Jesus as a social reformer and relativizing the Ten Commandments so that they no longer represent absolute and universal moral prohibitions. As important, however, the Social Gospelers and their descendants among the so-called Christian Left seem oblivious to the profane and profoundly anti-Christian roots of the social morality they came to attribute to Christianity itself. The social religion and morality of the nineteenth century, later championed by the Social Gospel, was deliberately constructed as a rival to, and substitute for, orthodox Christianity and traditional biblical morality. The Social Gospel was an important carrier of the profoundly anti-Christian morality championed by socialists, Marxists, Positivists, and other representatives of the antitheistic impulse in the eighteenth and nineteenth centuries. The profane and anti-Christian roots of the novel social morality constructed in the era are clearly evidenced by the historical record.[183]

Ethical and social thought in the West is generally thought to have undergone a gradual process of secularization throughout the course of the eighteenth and nineteenth centuries. The term "secularization," however, is often employed carelessly, and, as Jacob Viner observed, "is liable to deceive." Viner himself defines secularization as a "lessening of the influence . . . of ecclesiastical authority and traditional church creeds, and a shifting of weight from dogma and revelation and other-worldliness to reason and sentiment and considerations of temporal welfare."[184] Viner's definition, however, is itself somewhat misleading. The notion that secularization represents a "lessening" of the influence of religious authority, creeds and the like fails to capture the essence of such change. As discussed in a previous chapter, the weakening of

---

[183] Raeder, *Religion of Humanity*.
[184] Jacob Viner, *The Role of Providence in the Social Order: An Essay in Intellectual History* (Princeton: Princeton University Press, 2015), 55.

Western religious belief did not result from a more or less autonomous process of social change but was rather impelled by militant activists determined to undermine, if not eradicate, the traditional theological orientation of the West and the social and political order it sustained. The aim of such activists, as James Crimmins observes, was to "extirpat[e] religious beliefs, even the idea of religion itself from the minds of men."

The "death of God" enacted throughout the nineteenth century was characterized by an aggressive and even militant anti-theological thrust. Marx was an important leader of the modern "revolt against God" but far from alone in that endeavor. Prodigious efforts were made throughout the nineteenth century not only to undermine the religious traditions of the West, in particular, Christianity, but also to establish one form or another of secular, social, or political religion to serve as its replacement. Marxism was not the only political religion developed during the period. Various fellow travelers also aimed to capture the spiritual energy traditionally channeled toward a transcendent God and personal salvation and reorient it toward the promise of collective salvation through secular and ultimately political pursuits. The propagation of such intramundane secular creeds, including Benthamite Utilitarianism and the previously mentioned Religion of Humanity, was infused with intense spiritual energy. Their founders and carriers invested such constructs with ultimate and salvific value, both regarding and experiencing their constructed "religions without a God" as full-fledged religion, a fact expressly acknowledged by their devotees.[185] In his *Autobiography*, for instance, J. S. Mill describes his conversion to Benthamite utilitarianism, which Bentham himself called "a new religion," as an experience that struck him with all the force of religious conversion.[186]

The roots of the quasi-Christian morality of the Social Gospel and American Progressivism can be traced to eighteenth-century France,

---

[185] Richard H. Crossman, *The God That Failed.* New York: Columbia University Press (2001).

[186] Mill, *Autobiography and Literary Essays,* vol 1, *CW*, ed, 1981, 68. Jeremy Bentham: "A new religion would be an odd sort of thing without a name—[I] propose . . . Utilitarianism." Cited in Mary Warnock, introduction, J.S. Mill, *Utilitarianism, On Liberty, Essay on Bentham* (Cleveland: World Publishing, 1962), 9.

especially the thought of Henri de Saint-Simon and his followers, the St. Simonians and Auguste Comte. St. Simon and Comte were two of the more influential of the various secular messiahs to emerge in the modern and postmodern world.[187] Neither social savior made a secret of their mutual aim: to usher in a new world defined in opposition to preceding stages of human intellectual and social history, the so-called "theological" and "metaphysical" stages of the human mind.[188] The terminology varied—St. Simon would have his "terrestrial . . . New Christianity," Comte his "Positive Religion" or "Religion of Humanity"—but the aspiration was identical in all cases. All the secular religions formulated by the French messiahs were variations on the same theme. As Frank Manuel put it, they all "represented . . . a deflection of love from the God of the Christians to mankind and a transfer of interest from the future of the immortal soul to man's destiny on earth."[189] They all preached the by-now-familiar gospel of social and political salvation to be achieved here and now, in this world.

The various new secular religions, as we have seen, were invariably accompanied by newly formulated moralities— "terrestrial," "positive," "social," "purely human"—intended to replace the "theological" morality bound up with mankind's earlier and now putatively obsolete stage of development. The secular messiahs thus pursued two related aims. First, spiritual aspirations were to be reoriented away from the traditional transcendent God and toward a worldly, mundane substitute of one kind or another. The proposed replacement for God assumed various forms—Comte's "Great Being" of Humanity, the Social Gospelers' "Kingdom of God" on earth; the communist paradise that was the End of History, and so on. All such constructs, however, share an essential and defining attribute, that is, they all relocate the ultimate object of religious devotion and obligation from God to Man. The second and related aim was the social establishment of a new religion

---

[187] Cf. de Lubac, *Drama*; Frank E. Manuel, *The New World of Henri Saint-Simon* (Cambridge: Harvard University Press, 1956); D.C. Charlton, *Secular Religions in France 1815-1870* (London: Oxford University Press, 1963); Eric Voegelin, *From Enlightenment to Revolution*, ed, John D. Hallowell (Durham: Duke University Press, 1975); Jacob Talmon, *Political* Messianism (NY: Frederick A. Praeger, 1960).

[188] Manuel, *The New World of Henri Saint-Simon*, 123.

[189] Ibid.

that embodied the new "terrestrial" spirituality and morality. Indeed, certain of the secular messiahs were driven by even more grandiose ambition—to secure the final eradication of theology and metaphysics and all such transcendent orientation implied for human existence.[190] The realization of the secular messiahs' mission, then, required both the establishment of a secular or intraworldly religion and simultaneous replacement of theologically grounded morality with a naturalistic substitute constructed not by God but rather man. It further required the reorientation of religious aspirations and sentiments away from otherworldly concerns toward those, as Mill said, "confined to the limits of the earth."[191]

The social morality preached by the Social Gospelers, American Progressives, and the Christian Left more generally ultimately derives from such efforts. The morality of altruism and Service to Humanity is not of Christian inspiration but rather the opposite—a construction deliberately devised to replace, and improve upon, traditional Judeo-Christian ethics. In order to facilitate its acceptance, moreover, the novel anti-theological or "purely human" morality was further and deliberately devised to resemble traditional ethics. The St. Simonians, for instance, well understood that most members of eighteenth- and nineteenth-century European society regarded themselves as Christian. Not only would they have resisted overt attacks on Christianity but, in the English context, Christianity was protected against public criticism by various laws prohibiting blasphemy. Efforts to undermine Christianity were thus often conducted in a surreptitious and manipulative manner. St. Simon for instance, cunningly developed the strategy of employing traditional Christian symbolism and sentiment and investing it with novel social and political meaning. Christian symbols were reinterpreted and manipulated in the hope that unsuspecting believers might thus be more easily persuaded to embrace the new naturalistic and humanistic (antitheistic) creed. J. S. Mill, a fellow traveler with the St. Simonians in

---

[190] According to James Crimmins, Jeremy Bentham's aim was nothing less than "to extirpat[e] religious beliefs, even the idea of religion itself from the minds of men." James Crimmins, "Religion, Utility, and Politics: Bentham vs. Paley," in *Religion, Secularization, and Political Thought: Thomas Hobbes to J.S. Mill* (London: Routledge, 1990), 140.

[191] J.S. Mill, "Utility of Religion," *Collected Works of John Stuart Mill*, (Toronto: University of Toronto Press, 1972), Vol. 10: 421. Hereinafter cited as C*W*.

this regard as in others, similarly employed traditional Christian symbolism, including the person of Christ, to advance the anti-Christian Religion of Humanity, the proximate source, as mentioned, of contemporary secular humanism.

The St. Simonians and other secular messiahs of the era were acutely aware that religion provides the essential bond and animating force of human society. The "critical philosophy" of the eighteenth century, they believed, had successfully undermined Christianity, a task they regarded as necessary and on the whole salutary. Such an achievement, however, only realized half of the historical mission. What remained was the articulation and propagation of a new creed, a new faith, a new and "higher" religion to replace Christianity, which perhaps had been suitable in former ages but was no longer in harmony with the presently advanced state of the human mind. As Mill expressed the common sentiment of the secular messiahs, "Christianity . . . is gone, never to return, only what was best in it to reappear in another, and still higher form. . . ."[192] Progress required the development or purification of Christianity. To that end, the St. Simonians proposed the "New Christianity" or "Religion of Love" developed by their leader. As St. Simon explains in *Nouveau Christianisme*:

> . . . God has related everything to a single principle, and deduced everything from a single principle. . . . Now, according to this principle given to men by God as a guide for their conduct, they should organize their community in the way which will be most advantageous to the greatest number; they should make it their aim in all their undertakings and actions, to promote as quickly and completely as possible the moral and physical welfare of the most numerous class. *I maintain that in that, and that alone, consists the divine part of the Christian religion.* . . . God has given to men a single principle. . . . He has ordered men to organize their community in such a way as to secure for the poorest class the quickest and most complete improvement of their moral and physical condition . . . . (emphasis added)

---

[192] Mill to Carlyle, October 5, 1833, *CW* 12: 180-182.

Christianity in the hands St. Simon is reduced to political and economic ideology, more or less the Utilitarian principle of the Greatest Happiness of the Greatest Number. It becomes nothing more than a tool of politics, exclusively concerned with social organization and material welfare. Salvation is reinterpreted as political or collective salvation to be attained through political and economic action; the spiritual and transcendent dimension of biblical religion disappears from view. St. Simon is the father not only of Christian Socialism and the Social Gospel but all modern religious movements that reduce religious obligation to the amelioration of human suffering in this world. Marxist Liberation Theology and its cousin, Black Liberation Theology, are characteristic, as are certain forms of Christian advocacy for social justice.

The essence of the "New Christianity" is its resolutely this-worldly character, its attempt to reinvent Christianity by eviscerating its transcendent orientation. Such an effort necessarily involved the reconstruction of biblical morality. Traditional Judeo-Christian morality is of course rooted in a transcendent Ground of Being, a divine Source beyond this world. Such is precisely the aspect of traditional morality—its transcendent or theological source—that must be eliminated if the goals of the secular messiahs were to be realized. St. Simon thus attacks traditional biblical morality as mere "celestial ethics" that must be replaced by "terrestrial ethics." Comte's version proposes the novel morality of "altruism" as the naturalistic moral standard to accompany the Positivist Religion of the Future. Bentham's version proposes the standard of nontheological utilitarianism. His acolyte, J.S. Mill, castigates "theological morality" as inferior to the "purely human" morality embodied in both his version of utilitarianism and the Religion of Humanity he intended to substitute for the "baseless fancies" of traditional religion.[193] Marx stridently proclaims man as the highest divinity, the author of right and wrong.

The Law of the Three Stages

A brief discussion of the underlying philosophy of history embraced by the French secular messiahs will further clarify their goals and methods, as well as their significance for subsequent American developments. One

---

[193] J.S. Mill, "Utility of Religion," in *CW* 10: 420.

of the characteristic developments of the nineteenth century was the production of various comprehensive philosophies of history. Authors such as Comte, Hegel, Marx, and others believed they had gained insight into the inexorable laws said to govern the overarching course of human history. History, it was claimed, possesses an immutable pattern, typically consisting of three stages leading toward a final goal or end. Voegelin attributes the source of such symbolism to the writings of the twelve-century monk, Joachim of Flora. The Marxist variant divided history into three phases, slavery, feudalism, and capitalism. Hegel also divided history into three stages, based on the degree of freedom achieved in various epochs (periods in which one was free, many were free, all were free).[194] The St. Simonian and Comtean versions had a different emphasis. As John Eckalbar explains,

> [The St. Simonians] drew a parallel between the growth of mankind in history and the growth of a human body. Both mankind and the body were said to develop from stage to stage by the 'law of progressive development'. Humanity . . . is a collective entity. This entity has grown from generation to generation as a man grows in the course of years, according to its own physical law, which has been one of progressive development. The human race 'grows progressively according to invariable laws'. . . . The 'law of the perfectibility of the human species' is key to understanding history. By the law of perfectibility, it is ordained that mankind pass from the miseries of savagery to the bliss of a secular paradise.[195]

In the progress toward secular perfection, according to the St. Simonians, political society passes through two alternating modes of historical existence—"organic epochs" and "critical epochs." Two "organic epochs" have previously appeared in history. The first was the

---

[194] For Hegel, the widest view of history reveals three most important stages of development: Oriental imperial (the stage of oneness, of suppression of freedom), Greek social democracy (the stage of expansion, in which some but not all were free, and Christian constitutional monarchy (which represents the reintegration of freedom in constitutional government (all are free).
[195] John C. Eckalbar, "The Saint-Simonian Philosophy of History: A Note." *History and Theory* © 1977.

period of Greek and Roman polytheism ending with Socrates in Greece and Augustus in Rome; the second began with the preaching of the Gospels and ended with Martin Luther. The first "organic" epoch was followed by the "critical" epoch of philosophy, during which polytheism was undermined by the classical philosophers. The close of the second "organic" epoch came with the Protestant Reformation. The second "critical" epoch would come to a close upon the rise of the new era of secular perfectibility proclaimed by Saint-Simon and preached by his disciples. The *Doctrine* was written to announce that "the times have been fulfilled and the hour about to strike when, according to the Saint-Simonian transformation of the Christian word, "all shall be called and all shall be chosen."[196] The Saint Simonians regarded themselves as heralds of the third and final "organic" epoch. As Saint-Simon said, "the transition which is now taking place . . . consists in the passage from the theological system to the terrestrial and positive system."[197] As we have seen, such passage is the defining attribute of St. Simon's "New Christianity"—the replacement of "celestial" with "terrestrial" Christianity, conceived as an intraworldly program of positivist social and political reform. Voegelin's "immanentization of the eschaton" is inevitably brought to mind.

Comte's version of a philosophy of history embodies the identical move. He also asserted the existence of an inexorable law of history, the so-called "law of three stages"—theological, metaphysical, and positivist. Comte's law of history, like Saint-Simon's, is identified with "laws of progressive development," more particularly, with laws governing the development of the human mind and especially its capacity for abstraction and generalization. According to Comte, the progressive development of man's mental capacity is reflected in humanity's evolving conceptions of God. Early growth in the capacity for abstraction and generalization enabled human beings to move beyond the most primitive stage, polytheism, in which the government of nature was attributed to many minds (gods), a stage Comte labels the "theological" stage of the mind. Further growth in the capacity for generalization led eventually to the recognition that nature is governed by one mind (god); monotheism is thus characteristic of what Comte

---

[196] Eckalbar, ibid.
[197] Saint-Simon, cited in Manuel, ibid. 227.

calls the "metaphysical stage" of the mind. At this stage, however, the growth of the human mind is not yet complete. Comte anticipates yet further mental development that will culminate in the final stage of the human mind and history, the so-called "positivist" stage. This third and final stage, unlike earlier stages, is based on true and final knowledge of the source of the government of nature. Final knowledge discloses that the actual source is not God but rather invariable law embodied in modern science. At this final stage, the human mind has developed to the point where it recognizes that the phenomena of nature are governed, not by divine agency, whether of many gods or one god, but rather by the invariable and impersonal laws of positive science. The final goal of history is thus identical for St. Simon and Comte—a post-theological, post-Christian society free from the theological and metaphysical superstitions that prevailed in earlier stages of human development. Progress, in both cases, involves movement beyond transcendent religion. The St. Simonian and Comtean "laws of progressive development" are clearly an important source of later American Progressivism.

For St. Simon, Comte, and the Progressives, Progress entails the movement from theology and metaphysics to post-theological or naturalistic positivism. In other words, Progress so conceived entails the ongoing demise of the traditional religious faith of the West, defined by its orientation toward a transcendent God. Such a conception of Progress also confirms the merely relative or provisional nature of all social institutions. All institutions, religious, moral, political, legal, and economic, are conceived as fluid constructs continually adapting to time and change. Every such change is further regarded as superior to that which it supplants, insuring that history "progresses" or advances toward the ever-greater perfection of human society. Paradoxically, such a conception, which identifies Progress with movement through time, simultaneously points to a final goal of one kind or another, an end to time and change, the End of History.

The most crucial element of the conception of Progress advanced by the St. Simonians, Comte, and their Progressive descendants, however, is the assertion that Progress necessarily entails the ongoing decline of the traditional religious framework of Western civilization. Such thinkers concede that earlier stages of human development, the polytheistic and monotheistic stages, were valuable and necessary within

140

their own historic contexts. Such was especially true of the monotheistic phase, particularly its medieval expression (Christendom). The beliefs and institutional manifestations of monotheism, however, cannot be regarded as eternal and absolute truth but only provisional stages on the road to the final stage of human development—post-theological positivism or "science." Elements of Christianity might be preserved in the final age, provided Christianity is "purified" or "improved" in line with the advanced state of knowledge that has been attained by human progress. The secular messiahs believed that they were poised on the threshold of a new era; the final stage of history was at hand. Indeed the nineteenth century was permeated with the expectation of imminent transformation, whether to the final stage of communism, as in Marx, or the final stage of post-theological positivism, as in St. Simon, Comte, and fellow travelers such as Mill. Such a sense partially accounts for the urgency with which they constructed the alternative religions intended to fill the spiritual void that ensued upon the "death of God."

Secular Humanism: The Religion of Humanity

The philosophies of history developed in the nineteenth century, whether of Comtean, Marxian, or Hegelian inspiration, generally share the assumption that Progess necessarily entails the elimination of faith in a transcendent Source beyond history. American Progressivism inherited such a belief and carried it forward in the American context, with effects that continue to the present day. Such influence is evident, for instance, in the rise in the United States of so-called Secular Humanism, the moral arm of modern-liberal Progressivism. Both trends, Progressivism and secular humanism, are of considerable importance for modern American developments, in particular, their mutual relation to the anti-theological considerations under discussion. We have discussed the relation of Progressivism to the speculation of thinkers such as St. Simon and Comte. Secular humanism emerges from the same spring. A closer examination of the Religion of Humanity, the proximate forebear of contemporary secular humanism, will serve to further illustrate the process whereby positivist and Progressivist assumptions were assimilated by Anglo-American consciousness, in particular, the manner in which Christianity was reconstructed and incorporated into the movement of Progress toward final immanent perfection.

We have discussed the confrontation between nineteenth-century Christianity and the new social ethics. The antitheistic social morality championed by Marx and other secular messiahs was portrayed as superior to traditional Judeo-Christian ethics and the free society it sustained. Traditional morality, the personal morality of the Bible, was condemned as individualistic, egoistic, and selfish, allegedly concerned only with the individual's personal salvation and not, like socialism, with the good of the whole. The novel social morality was championed not only by outright socialists and communists such as Marx, but also fellow travelers such as St. Simon, Comte, Mill, and others. The new Socialist Man would willingly serve the collective good of society; Comte's man of the future would similarly "Live for Others," as the slogan of the Positivist Religion of Humanity later put it. The virtue of altruism, associated with the Positivist faith, was juxtaposed to its opposite, the vice of egoism, associated with Christianity.

Straightforward Marxism was undoubtedly too rich a brew for American consumption, representing rejection of traditional religion ("the opium of the people"). The New Christianity and Religion of Humanity advanced by the French messiahs, however, would prove more palatable to American tastes. By the turn of the twentieth century, the period that also witnessed the rise of Progressivism and the Social Gospel, such quasi-religious constructs had achieved a measure of social success in both England and America. Temples to Humanity checkered the New England landscape, and positivist ethical injunctions such as "service to Humanity" were trumpeted from on high by persons no less influential than Woodrow Wilson. Over time, the aspirations embodied in the Religion of Humanity and similar intramundane spiritual constructs were widely assimilated by Anglo-American consciousness. Morality was transformed away from the personal and individual and toward the "social"—the "altruistic" and "terrestrial" morality first championed by the St. Simonians. The Social Gospel movement is characteristic. Indeed, as we have seen, the triumph of the nineteenth-century social ideal eventually led to conflation of the moral and social. Hayek has enumerated over a hundred different uses in modern ethical and political discourse of what he calls the "weasel word" ("social").[198] Everyone is familiar, for instance, with such concepts as social justice, social conscience, social responsibility, social morality, social democracy, social problems, social work, social service, and so on. Consequentialist "social" aims are widely regarded as self-evidently good. Indeed in many quarters social concerns have supplanted traditional morality, the biblically based personal morality that shaped the development of Western liberal society.

Millions of persons over the course of the past century were persuaded of the inferiority of traditional biblical ethics to socialist ethics, a conviction still passionately embraced by many members of contemporary society. The vast majority, certainly within Anglo-American society, did not absorb such a conviction directly from Marx but rather through other more culturally persuasive sources. Anglo-American thought was not particularly receptive to the more or less alien idiom of a Comte or a Marx, but the views they championed would nevertheless reach English and American shores through the efforts of fellow travelers and acolytes. The work of John Stuart Mill is representative.

The youthful Mill was enchanted by the St. Simonians and Comte and ultimately emerged as a militant advocate of their new religious worldview. In 1841 Mill converted to Comte's Religion of Humanity, which was remarkably similar in substance to the nontheological utilitarianism of Jeremy Bentham, Mill's first "religion."[199] Henceforth he never wavered in his passionate commitment to replace Christianity with a Religion of Humanity. Mill is conventionally regarded as a secular thinker who championed ethical naturalism in contrast to traditional supernatural (theistic) ethics. Although he did champion what he called "purely human" ethics over against what he called "theological" ethics, Mill was very far from a secular thinker, if secular is defined as areligious or indifferent to religion. Throughout his life Mill pursued what can only be regarded as a religious mission. In a letter to Comte, Mill

---

[198] F.A. Hayek, *The Fatal Conceit: The Errors of Socialism* (Chicago: University of Chicago Press, 1991*)*, 114-117. The usage of the adjective 'social' obscures rather than clarifies the meaning of the word it qualifies, casting a fog over the legitimate or traditional meaning attached to concepts central to Western and American moral and political discourse.

[199] J. S. Mill, *Autobiography* (Penguin, 1990).

recounts the spiritual transformation he experienced upon reading Comte's *Cours*, an experience indistinguishable from religious conversion.[200] Mill explains:

> Having had the rather rare fate in my country of never having believed in God, even as a child, I always saw in the creation of a true social philosophy the only possible base for the general regeneration of human morality, and in the idea of Humanity the only one capable of replacing that of God. But there is still a long way from this speculation and belief to the manifest feeling I experience today—that it is fully valid and that the inevitable substitution [of Humanity for God] is at hand.[201]

Such an experience committed Mill to a two-pronged and lifelong goal: the evisceration of Christianity and social establishment of the Religion of Humanity he adopted, with revisions, from Comte. Mill, like St. Simon and Comte, bent his prodigious talents and will to the progressive elimination of Christianity from society and its replacement with a secular, social, or this-worldly religion. One consequence of such efforts was the insinuation of the radical anti-Christianity of the French secular messiahs into Anglo-American consciousness. Mill, who characterized his views as those of "advanced liberalism," is a pivotal figure in the transformation of classical to modern liberalism. An examination of his religious thought and aims is thus helpful in

---

[200] Voegelin has described Comte's writing of the *Cours* as a "spiritual practice," an insight supported both by Mill's method of absorbing the material and his intense response to it. Mill meditated long and hard on the work. As he told Comte, it was "... by successive rereading's of your work at my leisure ... [that] I reached my final and decisive conception [of it] that was not only stronger but essentially new, since it is primarily of a moral nature." He discovered that Comte "had sown in the previous volumes such fertile seeds for all the main concepts of the last that even the most extraordinary ideas I read there seemed like friends I had always known" (*Corr*, 118). Mill's deep immersion in the *Cours* seems akin to the "spiritual practice" Comte himself undertook in writing the work.

[201] J.S. Mill, *The Correspondence of J.S. Mill and Auguste* Comte (New Brunswick: Transaction, 1995).

understanding the course of American social and political development over the past century, a development profoundly shaped by modern-liberal progressivism.

The first crucial issue concerns the meaning of a Religion of Humanity. The traditional God of the West is of course understood as both the ultimate Source of existence and value, and the ultimate End or goal of human existence (eternal salvation). The Religion of Humanity replaces God so conceived with the "Great Being" of Humanity. In other words, "Humanity" is henceforth to be regarded as the ultimate source of value and the ultimate end of human aspiration. The traditional religious obligation to serve God is replaced by the religious obligation to serve the intramundane abstraction Humanity, an obligation that becomes nothing less than the "law of our lives." Religious fulfillment is to be sought not in union with God but rather with Humanity, with one's fellow men, here and now, in this world. Indeed all religious yearning and impulse is to be reoriented away from the "baseless" conception of a transcendent God and toward the Great Being of Humanity. The Christian aspiration for immortality (vertical transcendence) is to be replaced by concern for the welfare of future generations on this earth (horizontal transcendence). Only the selfish, Mill says, will continue to yearn for personal immortality beyond this world; the morally cultivated will achieve fulfillment in knowing that their efforts live on in the well-being of future generations. Mill, following St. Simon and Comte, unequivocally proclaims the humanistic "religion without a God" vastly superior to any form of transcendent religion. All the secular messiahs universally and vigorously asserted the authentic and superior spirituality of secular to transcendent religion. The Religion of Humanity, Mill says, is not only a "real" religion but better and "more profoundly religious" than anything heretofore called by that name.[202]

A second important aspect of the Religion of Humanity or secular humanism concerns morality and law, and, in particular, its source. The traditional Judeo-Christian God is of course regarded not only as the source and end of existence but also the moral law. The significance of the Judeo-Christian conception of the "higher law" for the development of Western constitutionalism, limited government, and the rule of law

---

[202] Mill, *Utilitarianism*, 423.

has been well documented by scholarly research.[203] The replacement of biblical with humanistic, naturalistic, or "purely human" ethics extirpates all such significance at a stroke, as does legal positivism, the philosophy of law that corresponds to such replacement. As Humanity supplants God as the ultimate source and end of value, so Humanity supplants God as the ultimate source of law. Upon social establishment of the Religion of Humanity Man and not God henceforth determines the nature and substance of law, moral and civil. "Theological" morality, as Mill says, is replaced with "purely human" morality, in his case, his particular version of Utilitarianism.

Utilitarianism, in Mill's hands, comes to resemble the social or altruistic morality devised by the St. Simonians and Comte and which also implicitly informs its English counterpart, the nontheological utilitarianism of Bentham.[204] It is seldom recognized that Benthamite utilitarianism, famously revised and disseminated by the Mills, was itself consciously intended to serve as a quasi-religious and naturalistic substitute for traditional Judeo-Christian morality. Bentham expressly acknowledged such an intention; as he said, "I suppose a new religion requires a new name: I propose utilitarianism."[205] The Benthamite religion embodies aspirations identical to those of the French secular messiahs. It too replaces service to God with this-worldly or temporal Service to Humanity (achieving the "Greatest Happiness of the Greatest Number . . . confined to the limits of this earth").[206] It too constructs a naturalistic or terrestrial ethics to replace the theological ethics that heretofore had governed Western civilization. The St. Simonians, Comte, Bentham, and Mill united in their efforts to ensure that henceforth Man and not God would govern this world.

Much of this history has been obscured or lost as a result of the vast social success of the anti-theological movements over the course of modernity. Many of the goals envisioned by the secular messiahs have been more or less realized, and the assumptions they embody are widely held in contemporary society as more or less self-evident truths.

---

[203] Edward S. Corwin, *The Higher Law Background of American Constitutional Law* (Indianapolis: Liberty Fund, 2008).

[204] Ernest Albee, *A History of English Utilitarianism* (New York: Macmillan, 1957), 6.

[205] Cited in Raeder, *Religion of Humanity.*

[206] Ibid.

Traditional religion has largely been relegated to the sphere of private subjective belief, as Mill and others consciously intended. The tradition of the higher or natural law has been submerged in the rise of legal positivism and its variants. The moral has been supplanted by the social in many quarters; those who reject the moral obligation to Serve Humanity can only be regarded as selfish if not wicked. Altruism is widely championed even within nominally Christian circles. Significant numbers of persons in Western and American society have reoriented their religious aspirations away from a transcendent God and toward humanitarian service confined to the limits of the earth. We have discussed the quasi-religious nature of the modern ideological movements such as socialism, fascism, and communism. Millions of persons over the course of the past century channeled spiritual and religious aspirations into efforts to achieve a secular paradise on earth, whether conceived as the final communist or positivist state or the Kingdom of God of the Social Gospel. Through such efforts they hoped to find meaning and purpose in their existence, to achieve a kind of salvation through collective political action and reform. The hope, however implicit, was that such efforts would bring spiritual fulfillment. The hope, however implicit, was that union with Humanity would prove an existential substitute for union with God beyond this world, a God condemned as illusory by ideologues and fellow travelers.

Those who formulated or embraced one variant or another of the modern social or political religions clearly channeled what are self-evidently, and indeed self-avowedly, religious aspirations into the realization of ideals exclusively temporal. Such ideals—summarized by Mill as the "improvement of mankind"—were to be realized by moral, economic, and political reform and invested with religious—ultimate and salvific—significance and value. The religious valorization of worldly improvement, however, was not itself the ultimate goal of the various social messiahs and reformers but rather a by-product of their overarching end. The ultimate goal, in all cases, was the replacement of God with Humanity and theological with purely human, naturalistic, or secular morality of human construction. Voegelin and other scholars have characterized such aspirations, widespread in the nineteenth century, as attempts at the self-divinization of Man. We have seen Nietzsche's prophesy come to fruition: the replacement of God with Humanity did indeed lead to the redivinization of the state, the new

Idol. Henri de Lubac famously characterized the nineteenth century as enacting a "drama of atheist humanism," a drama unfolding to the present day.[207] Its players include not only the militant ideological movements but also their less virulent cousins such as the Social Gospel, American Progressivism, and the Religion of Secular Humanism.[208] All such actors embrace one variant or other of an intramundane Religion of Humanity that conceives human beings and not a transcendent God as the ultimate source and end of value.

The central tenets of modern secular humanism have been neatly summarized by J. Wesley Robb: "Man is his own rule and his own end."[209] Such a formulation succinctly expresses the twofold aims of the secular messiahs of the preceding centuries. Man is his own rule—morality is divorced from a transcendent source and henceforth regarded as of purely human construction. Such a conviction represents the triumph of the terrestrial or nontheological morality of the St. Simonians and Benthamites as well as the materialist morality of Marxism. The limits on human action entailed by the traditional notion of a law above the King—a God-given moral law superior to human preference—are abolished at a stroke. Man is entitled to construct whatever moral rules he chooses, in the spheres of both personal and political morality; he can become like God. Man is his own end: there is no goal or purpose to human existence beyond the subjective goals or values established by human beings. Humanity is an end-unto-itself. Man is free, as Nietzsche proclaimed, to "transvalue all values," to move Beyond Good and Evil, to exercise without restraint the "will to power."[210] No one can say the values of the Nazis or ISIS are inferior to the values of liberal democracy: man is his own rule and his own end.

The absurd and even demonic consequences of the modern drive to immanentization implicit in the modern political religions and related constructs are dramatically illustrated by the example of Auguste Comte, the founder of the Religion of Humanity. Comte went so far as to proclaim himself the new Christ, the "world-immanent last judge of

---

[207] De Lubac, *Drama*.

[208] J. Wesley Robb, *The Reverent Skeptic: A Critical Inquiry into the Religion of Secular Humanism* (New York: Philosophical Library, 1979), 6.

[209] Ibid.

[210] Walter Kaufman, *Nietzsche: Philosophers, Psychologist, Antichrist* (Princeton: Princeton University Press, 1974).

mankind, deciding on immortality or annihilation for every human being."[211] The memory of those persons who had made significant intramundane contributions, he pronounced, would forever be preserved in the annals of mankind; indeed, the especially illustrious would be honored with a place in the Positivist "calendar of saints."[212] Such recognition was intended to serve as a this-worldly replacement for the immortality promised by Christian faith. Those who failed to make an enduring contribution to immanentist human welfare, on the other hand, were to be consigned to social oblivion; their memories would simply be erased from the records of human existence.

Comte's ideas, as we have seen, were taken seriously by many eminent persons, including Mill, one of the chief architects of modern-liberalism. Few scholars have explored either Mill's lifelong goal to replace Christianity with a Religion of Humanity or the relation between the new Humanitarian faith and modern-liberal progressivism. Voegelin is one of the few thinkers to have done so. He draws attention to the relation between Comtean-Millian secular messianism and the ethos of secular liberal Progressivism, especially its ideal of ever-advancing immanentist Progress. Modern liberal Progressivism, he argues, manifests the existential imbalance characteristic of its virulent ideological brethren and is thus far less benign than generally believed. It impoverishes human existence by identifying progress with temporal material advance and obscuring the transcendent dimension of existence. Moreover, in relegating religious values to the private sphere of subjective preference, secular Progressivism creates a spiritual vacuum in the public square readily filled by messianic ideologues promising collective political salvation and ultimate fulfillment on earth. Voegelin warns, however, that the end of radically immanentist liberal progressivism is not the emergence of a realm of earthly perfection but rather the gulag and concentration camp. As he starkly if colorfully puts it, the "progressivist symbolism of contributions, commemorations, and oblivion draws the contours of those `holes of oblivion' into which the

---

[211] William C. Harvard, "Notes on Voegelin's Contributions to Political Theory," in Ellis Sandoz, ed., *Eric Voegelin's Thought: A Critical Appraisal* (Durham, NC: Duke University Press, 1982), 131.
[212] Ibid.

divine redeemers of the gnostic empires drop their victims with a bullet in the neck."[213]

Postmodernism, Multiculturalism, Tolerance

Over the past several decades American society has been engaged in what is popularly described as a "culture war," pitting secular "liberal" progressives against "conservative" traditionalists. The conflict is generally thought to involve various contested social issues, such as abortion, homosexuality and sexual expression more generally, education, the family, media, environment, and others. The focus on issue politics, however, tends to obscure the more fundamental and deeper divide in contemporary American society. Every culture is ultimately a product of the prevailing religious worldview held by members of that culture (*cultus*). The contemporary battle over the direction of culture in the United States is ultimately a battle not over discrete issues but rather conflicting religious worldviews. Modern liberal progressivism (the Left) generally embodies the novel secular or human-centered faith that, as has been discussed, arose in competition to traditional biblical faith, generally defended by contemporary conservatism (the Right). The division between the two camps could not be starker. Their respective views conflict at the most fundamental level, the level of religion, encompassing as they do conflicting views regarding the very nature of human being and purpose of human existence. Nor could the stakes involved in the culture war be more significant. What is ultimately at stake is not the substance of particular public policy but rather preservation or destruction of the characteristically American way of life, dependent as it is upon certain inherited religious values (culture) implicit in both its institutional structure and customary practices.

The contemporary culture war is a particularly American manifestation of the general topic under discussion, that is, the modern revolt against God and displacement of Christianity by one variant or other of a secular or innerworldly political religion. Contemporary cultural and political conflict in the United States did not begin with recent elections but is rather an outcome of trends and movements developed over several centuries. The nineteenth century, as we have

---

[213] Ibid.

seen, witnessed the construction of various forms of intramundane social or political religion intended to supplant traditional Christianity. The political Left is the chief carrier of the novel secular religiosity in the American context, beginning with such movements as the Social Gospel and Progressivism, the proximate forebear of modern liberalism.[214] Traditional religious values and institutions are typically defended by the Right, the conservatives whose general aim, as the term indicates, is the conservation of traditional American values and institutions in the face of modern challenges.

For well over a century the Left in both Europe and North America has led an assault on biblical religion and its civilizational manifestations. Such efforts have achieved substantial success; contemporary Western culture, including American culture, is saturated with the secular progressive worldview. The rising generation in the United States has been reared in a cultural environment profoundly shaped by nontheistic and even antitheistic assumptions, a society implicitly and explicitly informed by a post-Christian, post-theological, or postmodern worldview. Many members of American society are ignorant of the nature and history of Western civilization in general and American society in particular and increasingly unfamiliar with the religious worldview that impelled their development. The deracination of significant portions of the American populace, especially its younger members, may arguably be well-intended but is not accidental. It is rather the result of conscious efforts to transform American society, efforts typically spearheaded by secular or progressive elites. Advocates of such transformation, from Karl Marx through Antonio Gramsci to Saul Alinsky, have long understood that the success of their efforts depends upon transformation not only of particular political, economic, and legal institutions but culture more generally. As one prominent contemporary American public figure put it, such transformation requires a "change in our traditions, our history."[215] Culture is always and everywhere the product of the cult (*cultus*). Thus the transformative

---

[214] Cashdollar, *Transformation of Theology*; Gillis Harp, *Positivist Republic*; Raeder, *Religion of Humanity*.

[215] "Barack knows that we are going to have to make sacrifices; we are going to have to change our conversation; we're going to have to change our traditions, our history; we're going to have to move into a different place as a nation." Michelle Obama, Speech given in San Juan, Puerto Rico on May 14, 2008.

change sought by the modern American Left necessarily involves transformation of the religious and moral self-understanding of traditional American society, an understanding decisively informed by the biblical worldview.

The ongoing transformation of traditional American values and beliefs has been facilitated by the rise of several significant intellectual and educational trends, among the most important of which are postmodernism, multiculturalism, and relativism. Marxism and related modern ideologies are widely recognized to have sought explicit transformation of Western society. The relation between the fashionable doctrines of postmodernism, multiculturalism, and relativism and the goal of cultural transformation is less commonly perceived. The means employed by the latter are more subtle, indirect, and implicit than those advocated by classic Marxist ideology, but such doctrines serve to undermine traditional Western and American society as surely, if not as straightforwardly, as Marxist doctrine proper. The Fabians and fellow travelers were correct: the transformation of the free society in the direction of socialism or some other form of collectivism does not, as Marx suggested, depend on violent revolution. The same goal can be achieved by the gradual, evolutionary destruction of its foundational beliefs and values, as recognized by the British Fabians, their Progressive American counterparts, and later Communist strategists such as Gramsci. The realization of Communism, Gramsci maintained, requires destruction of the "cultural hegemony" putatively held by the capitalist ruling class—the false intellectual, philosophical, and religious ethos it has long perpetrated to maintain privilege and control. Such can be achieved by the patient and long-term reeducation of the populace within the framework of traditional social institutions, such as schools, universities, courts, and media. Communist student leader Rudi Dutschke famously reformulated Gramsci's evolutionary strategy as "the long march through the institutions."[216] We recall in this regard the

---

[216] In 1967, Rudi Dutschke, a German student leader, reformulated Antonio Gramsci's philosophy of cultural hegemony with the phrase, "The long march through the institutions." Instead of a long military march, such as the one undertaken by the Chinese Marxist Maoist Tse-tung, in the highly developed western countries the long march would be through the most culturally significant of our social institutions – that is, through schools, universities, courts, parliaments and through the media, through newspapers and television.

motto of the Fabians: "Make Haste Slowly." Postmodernism, multiculturalism, and relativism are three gradualist or evolutionary means advanced by the modern Left toward attainment, surely if slowly, of its transformational goals.

Postmodernism

Postmodernism is the general term used to describe the overarching cultural perspective that develops in the West after the decline of "modernity." Scholars disagree on the precise origin of the term, variously attributing its first use to one or another nineteenth or early twentieth century thinker.[217] The central attribute of postmodern thought, on the other hand, is more readily identified, namely, skepticism toward or outright denial of the existence of universal or absolute Truth—a "Big T" Truth that transcends both history and the subjective values and opinions of human beings. The Western tradition from classical Greece to modernity is of course saturated with the very outlook that postmodernism rejects—belief in objective and immutable Truth, including moral and religious Truth. Accordingly, the postmodern era, as previously noted, is often referred to as the "post-Christian" or "post-theological" era.

Postmodernism not only rejects the concept of absolute Truth but other conceptions central to the Western tradition as well. It rejects, for instance, the characteristic distinction between this-world and the world Beyond first apprehended by Plato, as well as the related distinction between nature (what is objectively given to humankind) and history (contingent human experience in time). On the postmodern view, Nature is more or less assimilated to History. Not only does the traditional concept of a given nature presuppose a metaphysical "Giver," which cannot be sustained on postmodern grounds, but the truth of nature can never be more than particular historical truth, the only form in which truth of any kind can or does exist. The postmodern restriction of truth to the various truths accepted by particular cultures and societies over time means of course that truth, like history itself, is continually in flux. Truth, as every other aspect of human existence in time, is and must

---

[217] The term originated as a critique of the putatively "modernist" scientific mentality of objectivity and progress associated with the French Enlightenment.

be provisional and contingent, relative and conditional. What is true for postmodern society may not have been true for ancient or medieval society or, for that matter, the eighteenth-century society of colonial America. What is true for one culture, say Western culture, is not necessarily true for other cultures. What is true for one ethnic group may not be true for a different ethnic group. Indeed what is true for one person may not be true for a second person. There is no eternal and universal Truth that transcends particular historical truths, no absolute, unconditional Truth that transcends the relative truths of particular historical cultures, groups, individuals, and so on.

Postmodernism so conceived therefore must, and does, reject the Truth-claims associated with the Platonic and Judeo-Christian worldviews, and indeed any religion or philosophy that claims to articulate a universal or absolute Truth that transcends the movement of history. For postmodern thinkers, such truths as exist are inevitably subjective, relative, and conditional, relative to and contingent upon the particular perspective of the perceiver, a viewpoint generally described as "perspectivism."

Nietzschean Perspectivism

Various postmodern thinkers regard themselves as descendants of Friedrich Nietzsche, the German philosopher, who famously announced the "death of God" at the close of the nineteenth century. Nietzsche's critique of Western civilization involved a thoroughgoing attack on the Platonic and Christian distinction between transcendence and immanence and the absolute Truth they claim to represent. According to Nietzsche, both conceptions are delusions or illusions. There is no Truth that transcends history, only the particular truths of particular perspectives. Nor is there a substantive reality transcending this world; remove the veil of illusion and one finds nothing but a void, a nothingness. The recognition of such hard truth, however, should not be met with despair but rather, Nietzsche proclaims, with courage and the will to create. The great majority of human beings, the weak and cowardly, will undoubtedly fall back on the comforting illusions of traditional philosophy and religion, but a few extraordinary individuals, the *Übermenschen* (Overmen or Supermen), possess the requisite courage and will squarely to face the truth of existence. The Übermensch responds to the metaphysical void not with despair but rather the realization that he himself must singlehandedly create the values, meaning, and purpose by which to orient his existence. Such are not given by God or a supernatural source, as Platonism and Christianity falsely maintain. Platonism and Christianity, again, represent mere illusions fit only to console and control the great mass of human beings, who, in fact, are little better than slaves. The Nietzschean *Übermensch* is superior to the mass. He alone does not flinch in the face of the void but rather accepts the challenge to endow his life with self-created value and purpose.[218] He alone has the strength to discard delusional crutches such as supernatural religion, suitable only for inferior human beings who lack the vitality and will truly to exist.

Nietzsche further maintains that the Truth-claims of Platonism and Christianity are not merely false and delusional but pernicious in yet another respect—they are hostile to life itself. Philosophy and religion posit a transcendent realm in eternity and a transcendent morality to which man is obliged to align his values and action. According to Nietzsche, such conceptions diminish the significance of this world and existence in time. The negative rules of Judeo-Christian morality are especially malignant, compressing, restraining, and enervating the life force. Obedience to such rules makes man mild, meek, passive—they make him slavish. Indeed, says Nietzsche, Christianity is the religion of slaves, its morality a "slave morality."[219] The *Übermensch* will not be constrained by such life-denying values. He rises up to "transvalue all values," to create his own morality and his own rules, "beyond Good and

---

[218] Elaborating the concept in *The Antichrist*, Nietzsche asserts that Christianity, not merely as a religion but also as the predominant moral system of the Western world, in fact inverts nature, and is hostile to life. "I call Christianity the one great curse, the one great intrinsic depravity, the one great instinct for revenge for which no expedient is sufficiently poisonous, secret, subterranean, and petty -- I call it the one immortal blemish of mankind. . . and one calculates time from the *dies nefastus* on which this fatality —arose— from the first day of Christianity! Why not rather from its last? From today? Revaluation of all values! Friedrich Nietzsche, Conclusion, *The Antichrist*, in Michael Tanner, ed, *The Twilight of the Idols and the Antichrist* (London: Penguin Classics, 1990).
[219] Ibid.

Evil."[220] He exerts what Nietzsche calls his "will to power"—his will to create his own existence.

According to Nietzsche, the metaphysical and religious tradition of Western civilization stemmed neither from disinterested search for Truth nor revelation by a supernatural God. It is rather a construction of human beings motivated by such a "will to power," the will to define or control reality through the creative act. Nietzsche generally employed the term in reference to the creativity of the artist. Certain of his descendants, most infamously the German Nazis, interpreted the will to power in a political sense, as the will to political power. Other postmodernists accept Nietzsche's critique of both metaphysics and absolute Truth—all truth is relative and conditional, dependent on the individual's perspective—but, unlike Nietzsche, tend to associate "perspective" with various neo-Marxist categories, especially the so-called "Marxian Trinity" of gender, race, and economic class. The truth perceived by a poor black woman, for postmodernists, is different from the truth perceived by a rich white man; truth is perspectival, relative, and conditional.

Postmodern theorists suggest, moreover, that the dominant traditions and values of Western civilization—Judeo-Christian morality, constitutionalism, the rule of law, capitalism—rose to dominance not because they are inherently true, in accord with nature, or conducive to human flourishing. Such "social constructions" were rather invented or devised by those persons or groups that historically wielded power in society and this for the purpose of controlling or "marginalizing" less powerful persons and groups. Indeed postmodernists believe that the power possessed by cultural and political elites in all eras includes the power to define language itself, which in turn has enabled such groups to define truth and reality itself. In the case of Western civilization, its dominant elites—more or less European white men—putatively exercised their power to define language to cast themselves as superior to those groups over whom they wielded power—ethnic minorities, women, homosexuals, and other groups historically portrayed as culturally or socially inferior. The similarity to Marxism, which attributes the power to form a culture's prevailing ideas and values to the

---

[220] Friedrich Nietzsche, *Beyond Good & Evil: Prelude to a Philosophy of the Future*, trans, Walter Kaufman (New York: Vintage, 1989).

capitalist ruling class, and for the exclusive benefit of that class, is striking and obvious.

Indeed, for staunch postmodernists, the entire Western Canon—the classics of literature, philosophy, religion, art, music, and other cultural expressions that traditionally formed the basis of higher education in the West—represents little more than the biased and self-serving perspective of the powerful. The power of white European men enabled them to define the very concepts of "superior" and "inferior" and do so in a manner that ensured the continuing power of their own class and kind. This explains why Shakespeare, for instance, has long been included in the Western Canon but Hildegard von Bingen, the female medieval writer and polymath, has not. Shakespeare was a white European man and his elevation simultaneously elevated all white European men; female writers, on the other hand, were marginalized, relegated to insignificance. This is why Plato has traditionally been more highly regarded than the Greek lesbian poet Sappho. White heterosexual men held the power to define what is of value and what is not, and Plato served their purposes far better than Sappho. In postmodernist reality, however, objective grounds for holding Shakespeare superior to Hildegard or Plato superior to Sappho simply do not exist. Such a conclusion follows from the postmodern rejection of objective trans-historical standards, the only means by which such judgments could be made. Who is to say that Plato is superior to Sappho? Who is to say that Beethoven is superior to Madonna? Who is to say that the Mona Lisa is superior to Mickey Mouse or Antigone to American Idol? Who is to say that Notre Dame Cathedral is more beautiful than a strip mall? No one can make such claims. There is no absolute truth or objective universal standard that permits judgments of absolute superiority and inferiority. There is only subjective perspective—only your opinion and my opinion. All opinions are equally based on personal perspective, and all opinions are equally valid. The traditional definitions of superiority and inferiority are mere self-serving inventions or social constructions of dominant elites or power-holders, typically, in the West, white men. Such definitions and judgments have nothing to do with truth but only the will to power.

Such postmodern logic extends beyond artistic judgments to morality, law, politics, economics, science, religion, and every other cultural phenomenon.[221] Who is to say that marriage should be defined as a union between a man and a woman? Who is to say that Christianity is superior to Wicca? Who is to say that women should be permitted to drive an automobile, travel, and receive an education? Who is to say that it is always morally wrong to steal or kill or lie? Who is to say that rationality is better than irrationality? Who is to say that scientific laws capture objective truth? No one, according to postmodernism, can make such absolute judgments. Even the valorization of rationality and science represents only another "privileged" perspective posing as Truth. Who is to define freedom, justice, rights, law, and other terms of Western political discourse? Who is to say that the rule of law is superior to the personal rule of men? Who is to say what the U.S. Constitution means? Who is to say that capitalism is superior to socialism? Again, no one can make such claims, for there is no objective trans-historical standard by which to evaluate competing perspectives. Even theory and history—reason and experience—are mere perspectival constructs without universal validity. For postmodernists, traditional definitions and standards, including the standards of rationality, logic, and evidence, do not capture the truth of experience but merely further the power of historically dominant elites. Arguments and evidence offered by scholars and scientists, no matter how scrupulously constructed, can hold no more claim to objective truth than the assertion that Beethoven is superior to Madonna. Scholarship and science, like all claims to truth, in fact and necessarily merely evidence the subjective perspective of the researchers and, indeed, may serve merely to oppress and suppress dissenting perspectives.

Postmodernism thus poses a radical challenge to the foundational principles of Western civilization in general and American society in particular. Western civilization developed precisely on the basis of beliefs, values, and convictions rejected out-of-hand by postmodern doctrine. From the Greeks to the Americans, Western thought and practice was oriented by an ideal of objective Truth, whether the Forms of Platonism or the Divine Truth revealed by the biblical God, a Truth conceived as absolute, immutable, and universal, transcending history and particular perspective. Man, the rational animal of the Greeks, the

---

[221] Postmodernism challenges the very concept of logic, regarded as yet another imposition of European man on other perspectives.

rational persona of the Romans, the being endowed with reason of the Judeo-Christian conception, was believed not only equipped but more or less obliged to employ his reason to uncover Truth, moral and natural. Such truth as is discoverable by human reason was supplemented in the Platonic conception by the truth apprehended by mystical insight and, in the Christian conception, by the Truth revealed in Scripture. Throughout the course of its development, Western society not only conceived the objective reality of Truth but regarded its pursuit as worthy, legitimate, and even obligatory. Indeed Aristotle regarded the contemplative life in pursuit of truth (*theoria*) as itself the Highest Good, the *summum bonum*, as the medieval world would later describe it, a belief he bequeathed to the Western world that followed in his footsteps.

Western civilization developed upon the ancient conviction of the objective and immutable Truth of the order of existence. Such includes the conviction of an objective and immutable order of law—the moral and physical laws of nature which man can potentially discover or recognize but which he himself does not construct or invent. It developed upon the belief that certain actions are right- or wrong-in-themselves, regardless of an individual's subjective opinion, preference, or perspective. It developed upon the further belief in an objective or given human nature that is not susceptible of human or social construction. It developed on the belief that there is a superior, higher form of existence suitable to human nature and an inferior, lower form of existence that violates that nature. Certain actions or ways of life are in accord with the unfolding of human nature and certain ways of life prevent the realization of that nature. Postmodernism denies the Truth-value of all such traditional Western convictions, dismissing them as mere privileged and self-interested perspectives of the dominant elites who invented them. In so doing, postmodernism takes aim at the very heart and soul of Western civilization.

Multiculturalism

One of the major carriers of postmodernist thought in contemporary American society is the fashionable doctrine of Multiculturalism embedded in the greater part of educational curricula throughout the United States. The term itself is inoffensive and even appealing by traditional standards. Western educational aspirations generally included the expansion of intellectual and imaginative horizons beyond the limited confines of a student's particular culture, the hope of learning from experience and wisdom embodied in other historical civilizations. The goals of contemporary Multiculturalism, however, are of an entirely different nature. Multicultural education furthers a purpose quite unlike that of traditional cultural studies—a social and political purpose that involves, indirectly if not directly, the evisceration if not destruction of Western civilization. The seemingly benign banner of multicultural education may prove to veil a Trojan Horse, offering putative gifts that prove pernicious if not disastrous in the long run.

The threat to Western society posed by the doctrine of Multiculturalism is most clearly perceived in light of the preconditions of cultural and social survival. Most persons, quite understandably, tend to assume that the society into which they are born will last forever: "There'll always be an England!" sang the British people in 1939.[222] Few persons ponder the origins of their own society or concern themselves with the means of its preservation and vitality. Even a cursory study of human history, however, clearly demonstrates that societies and civilizations are not permanent, self-sustaining entities guaranteed to endure over time but transitory phenomena that rise and fall, appear and disappear, come and go. Contemporary societies and civilizations, including American society, are not exempt from the possibility that they too will one day be relegated, as is said, to the "dustbin of history." They are no more immune to the threat of historical decline than now-vanished civilizations of the past. American society, like all societies, is a fragile growth whose existence and flourishing require cultivation and care. Failure to recognize or honor the conditions of its existence and vitality may unintentionally lead to its demise. Civilizational decline or destruction can occur, moreover, not only through carelessness or ignorance but also willful intention. Insofar as the latter holds true, a society may not only experience cultural decline but also be said to commit cultural suicide.

---

[222] "There'll Always Be an England" is an English patriotic song, written and distributed in the summer of 1939, which became highly popular upon the outbreak of World War II. It was composed and written by Ross Parker (born Albert Rostron Parker, 16 Aug 1914 in Manchester) and Hugh Charles (born Charles Hugh Owen Ferry, 24 Jul 1907 in Reddish, Stockport, Cheshire).

Contemporary Multiculturalism is a popularized offshoot of post-modernist thought. Both constructs embrace radical relativism, perspectivism, and a denial of universal Truth that transcends particular historical experience. Multicultural education, as said, purports to serve an important and unobjectionable purpose—to expose American students to cultural beliefs and values beyond their immediate range of experience. Such exposure is considered necessary, among other reasons, to overcome a putative American ethnocentrism—an exclusive focus or preoccupation with the American cultural perspective. The aim of multicultural education is often widened to include a critique of so-called "Eurocentrism"—the exclusive focus on the values and perspective of Europe, the home of Western civilization and mother of America. The actual content of multicultural curricula, however, does not typically involve the praiseworthy goal of exposing students to the achievements of other historical cultures. Multicultural education rarely includes exploration of, say, Confucian China, Shinto Japan, the Byzantine Empire, or the ancient civilizations of Egypt and India. Students generally learn very little about the actual historical experience of other world cultures. What they unfailingly "learn" is rather the postmodernist dogma that all cultural perspectives are relative. They learn that no objective standard exists by which to evaluate the contributions of various cultures to world civilization and thus no civilization may be regarded as intrinsically superior or inferior. They learn that there is only "your culture" and "my culture," your cultural perspective and my cultural perspective; one is as valid as the other. Any judgments to the contrary merely evidence a pernicious American or European ethnocentrism. They learn, moreover, that an exclusive commitment to the values of one's own culture—a conviction that its values are good, perhaps even superior to those of other cultures, and thus worthy of defense—is not merely ethnocentric but indeed the gravest of all multicultural sins: the sin of "intolerance."

The willful imposition of Multiculturalist dogma in contemporary educational institutions not only serves the intended transformation of American culture desired by its advocates but, insofar as it achieves its goals, can only be regarded as attempted cultural suicide. In the name of Multiculturalist value-constructions such as "diversity," "otherness," and "tolerance," students are steeped in a philosophy of radical cultural relativism. The road of relativism is anticipated to end in the glorious embrace and celebration of "diversity." The more probable end, however, is nihilism (nothingness). If all cultures—all values, beliefs, and practices—are equally and relatively true, then nothing is True. The multiculturalist claim inevitably undermines commitment to one's own particular culture, conceived as merely one alternative among many equally valid options. In light of multiculturalist assumptions, efforts to preserve one's particular society, one's particular way of life, seem misguided if not absurd. Radical cultural relativism undermines a society at its deepest level, the level of self-preservation.

Such a possibility calls call for reflection upon the general conditions essential to the preservation of any culture, society, or civilization. We have discussed the fact that every society ultimately manifests the implicit and explicit beliefs, values, and assumptions—the worldview—embraced by its members. Society is man writ large, and man is a being that seeks value fulfillment. The values jointly held and pursued by members of a particular society largely generate the facts of that society, a relation derived from the nature of things.[223] Although it may seem obvious and self-evident, it must nevertheless be emphasized that the first and most basic requisite of cultural survival is the desire of a people to maintain the values and beliefs that constitute their culture's foundation and spring of action. A people indifferent to the characteristic values of their culture, or a people weary of existence, will lack the will to sustain it. An apathetic people will not put forth the effort that may be required to preserve their way of life, especially in the face of opposition from competing cultural paradigms. Such is also true of a people who, for one reason or another, grow hostile to their own culture, who come to denigrate or despise its customary values, beliefs, and practices. They may become convinced that their way of life is bad or wrong, detrimental to the planet or flourishing of other cultures. Or they may simply be distracted, ignorant, or lazy, unwilling to expend the energy necessary to understand themselves or the larger culture of which they are part.[224] They may be unaware of their own personal values and beliefs or those characteristic of their own culture. In such a case, they

---

[223] "Values generate facts," in the words of F. A. Hayek.
[224] Neil Postman, *Amusing Ourselves to Death: Public Discourse in the Age of Show Business* (London: Penguin Books, 2005).

would be unable to recognize an attack on those values and thus disarmed from their defense.

The first condition for the survival of any society, then, is the conviction in the minds of the people that their particular society is worth preserving, that its characteristic values and beliefs are good and true, not merely relatively but absolutely. A people who despise themselves, hold themselves in contempt, or otherwise reject the enduring validity of their characteristic cultural values cannot and will not strive to preserve them. Such a conclusion seems self-evident. Thus one certain way to destroy a society is to convince the people that their society and culture, their way of life, is not good or special or grounded in Truth. Such is precisely the achievement of postmodern Multiculturalism.

Tolerance

Among the virtues preached by the gospel of Multiculturalism, perhaps none is accorded greater reverence than the virtue of "tolerance." On its face, the promotion of tolerance, like the promotion of multiculturalism, is unobjectionable and even praiseworthy. Both the virtue of tolerance and multicultural education have long been characteristic Western values. Multicultural tolerance, however, like contemporary Multicultural education in general, has little in common with the traditional Western virtue beyond a shared name. Tolerance is yet another characteristic Western value whose meaning has undergone significant transformation over recent decades. The traditional definition of tolerance, according to Merriam-Webster, is the "capacity to endure pain or hardship; sympathy or indulgence for beliefs or practices differing from or conflicting with one's own." In other words, throughout most of Western history, tolerance has implied "putting up" with something that causes one pain, enduring something that one personally dislikes or of which one personally disapproves. A person does not "tolerate" beliefs or behavior that he enjoys or finds praiseworthy but rather those he finds somehow offensive or repugnant. In the social and political sphere, tolerance thus means permitting other people to think and behave in ways that one personally finds objectionable, distasteful, or even morally wrong.

Tolerance so conceived has long been recognized as a Judeo-Christian virtue and enjoined on Christian conscience. Its classic Anglo-American defense was provided by John Locke in his celebrated work on religious freedom, *A Letter Concerning Toleration* (1689). Locke's work was inspired by the bloody conflict engendered throughout Western Europe in the aftermath of the Protestant Reformation, and, particularly, the English Civil War. Monarchs of the era claimed the right to control the religious beliefs of the populace. Religious division among the populace led various sects to fight long and hard to obtain political power, which was routinely employed to penalize members of dissenting sects. Locke identified the ultimate source of such religious conflict and violence— the claimed right of government to control the religious life of the people. The only way to end the violence, he said, was to remove the sphere of religion from political control. Religion and the Church, he said, should be recognized as voluntary associations and thus immune to the coercive reach of government. Religious sects must forego the use of coercion and agree to tolerate—put up with—one another's differences.

Toleration did not emerge in a spirit of graciousness or nobility but rather as a practical solution to the conflict of the era. The Western valorization of tolerance may have emerged as a pragmatic resolution of religious conflict but its significance extends far beyond religion and practical politics. Beyond securing peace, which of course is no mean accomplishment, the question is why persons should strive to be tolerant of thought, speech, and practice they dislike and perhaps even condemn, not only with respect to religion but social life more generally. The moral obligation of toleration in Western civilization, religious and otherwise, is not an autonomous or primary obligation but rather secondary and instrumental. The demand for toleration derives, in the end, from commitment to a higher and more fundamental Western value, namely, the primary value of human freedom. Members of Western society are obliged to tolerate much that they may personally dislike because such is a price of individual freedom. Every individual desires to be free to act on the basis of his personal values and purposes, values and purposes that others may find distasteful, offensive, or immoral. Every individual wants other persons to "put up with" his personal beliefs and idiosyncrasies. To recognize that one's personal desire for toleration is shared by all other human beings is to live by the Golden Rule. Justice—

equality under law—demands that toleration of one's own beliefs and behavior be extended to equal toleration of others' beliefs and behavior.

Moreover, in a free society on the American model each individual is held to possess a natural right to liberty, that is, to engage in voluntary actions that do not violate the equal rights of other individuals. The only behavior legitimately restrained by law is behavior that violates other persons' unalienable rights to life, liberty, and property, including related First-Amendment rights such as free speech and free exercise of religion. Such rights do not include the right to be free from merely offensive or objectionable behavior, behavior of which one personally disapproves but which violates no one's natural or constitutional rights. Individual freedom so conceived thus obliges every individual to tolerate, put up with, beliefs and behavior he or she may find objectionable, so long as such behavior does not infringe on the legitimate rights of another person.

Such, however, is emphatically not the understanding of tolerance propounded by contemporary Multiculturalism. As one contemporary dictionary succinctly defines the novel Multicultural meaning, toleration is said to be "a disposition to tolerate or *accept* people or situations (emphasis added).[225] The concept of toleration has been transformed from "bearing," "enduring," or "putting up with" objectionable behavior to "accepting" such behavior. Such is not a superficial but rather profound change that fundamentally redefines the meaning of toleration. Moreover, such is the meaning that saturates contemporary American culture. Members of contemporary society have been taught, explicitly and implicitly, to identify "toleration" and "acceptance," a lesson conveyed by both popular culture and formal education at every level, from kindergarten to post-doctoral training. To tolerate is to accept, without judgment. Such is without question the meaning attached to the concept of toleration by the overwhelming majority of contemporary students.

They have further been taught that "intolerance" so conceived, that is, the failure to accept—to express disapproval of the beliefs or behavior of other people—is among the most reprehensible of social crimes. Negative moral judgments are unpardonable, the very height of intolerance. A classic example is the issue of homosexuality. In the

---

[225] The Free Dictionary.

current cultural environment, persons dare not express moral disapproval of homosexual behavior, a disapproval, it should be noted, which has been more or less the norm within Western civilization since the ascendancy of Christianity. Multicultural toleration, however, means acceptance, without judgment, in this case to regard homosexuality as merely one lifestyle among various morally equivalent possibilities. Multicultural tolerance is thus related to other contemporary illiberal phenomena such as "political correctness," campus "speech codes," "hate speech," and the like. Even to think in traditional moral categories is condemned as wrong; indeed, such thought may be evidence of mental disease—"homophobia," "Islamophobia," and so on. Under such cultural pressure few persons are foolish or courageous enough to express conventional moral judgments or even employ common sense (consider, for instance, the contentious issue of "profiling" airline passengers).

Many college students and other young adults have been exposed to such a closed and repressive mental atmosphere since birth. One consequence is a disturbingly passive generation that seems incapable of making, certainly reluctant to make, moral judgments of any kind. Young people have been taught that to make such judgments is "intolerant" of other "perspectives." Self-censorship has become habitual among students shaped by Multicultural education, the mind unfamiliar with conceptual and moral discrimination.[226] To exercise the capacity for critical evaluation—to "judge"—is regarded as wrong, intolerant. (The irony of such strident moral condemnation of "intolerance" is striking: young people, largely forbidden to make moral judgments, have no difficulty condemning "intolerance" in no uncertain terms.) All behavior, all opinions, all cultures, must be regarded as more or less equal, relative to the individual's perspective. No one is able or entitled to say that certain beliefs and actions are absolutely right or wrong or that certain cultural norms are superior to others. Such judgments are dismissed as mere "opinion"; others may hold a different opinion. There

---

[226] The word "discrimination" has itself undergone transformation under the Multicultural dispensation. Contemporary usage tends to equate it with "prejudice" and injustice, implying that discrimination is always morally wrong. Merriam-Webster, however, retains the older definition, in which discrimination is defined as "the ability to recognize the difference between things that are of good quality and those that are not."

is no objective standard by which to judge between conflicting opinions and, in any case, to make moral or truth judgments would be intolerant.

Diversity

Students are implicitly taught that beyond tolerance (approval), the primary and absolute value, exists only the correlative value of "diversity"—the putative celebration of various and different perspectives and experiences, of "otherness." The multicultural conception of diversity, however, requires as careful analysis as its corresponding conception of tolerance. American society has traditionally represented one of the most authentically diverse societies in the course of human history. Between 1782-1956, the de facto motto of the United States, as every schoolchild once learned, was *"E pluribus Unum"*—"out of many, One."[227] During the Founding era, the motto generally referred to the welding of a single federal political order out of many individual political communities—originally colonies and then states united under the federal Constitution. Over time, however, it acquired further significance for American self-understanding. America, as the saying goes, is a "nation of immigrants," a "melting pot" enriched, one might say, by the diverse perspectives of people from a variety of cultural and ethnic backgrounds. American society is atypical for many reasons, among which is the lack of relation been American identity and kinship or ethnicity. American identity is not a function of birth or biology but rather commitment to certain general or abstract values and principles. American identity, unlike national or cultural identity in the majority of societies known to history, is not defined by race, ethnicity, or biological factors of any kind. Any person, from any ethnic or cultural background, can, in principle, be an American. The only requirement is the acceptance of certain value commitments, in particular, the moral and political principles that underlie the unique structure of American constitutional order. "One, from Many": the "Many" is inseparable from the "One"—the unity of moral and political principle that makes the diverse "Many" one people, the American people.

---

[227] *E Pluribus Unum* had been adopted by an Act of Congress in 1782 as the motto for the Seal of the United States and has been used on coins and paper money since 1795. Few of my undergraduate students have ever heard of the phrase.

The traditional economic order of American society further promotes a truly diverse society. Capitalism not only permits but encourages multiplicity—diversity of tastes, interests, and pursuits. The abstract legal framework comprised by the rule of law serves the same purpose. Law does not command individuals to pursue specific values or ends but merely structures the means they must employ in pursuing their diverse personal values and purposes. Indeed the hallmark of the free society is pluralism—the pursuit of diverse and individually self-determined values and goals and not a unitary purpose binding on every individual. A pluralistic society such as traditional America honors the fact that values and purposes vary greatly among persons and does not recognize a right of government to impose a uniform set of goals on the populace. The traditional American ideal—morally, legally, politically, economically—has long been diversity-within-unity, *e pluribus unum*.

American universalism—the conception that any person can in principle be an American—is yet another manifestation of the underlying Judeo-Christian vision that informs traditional American political order. Christian universalism teaches that all human beings share the same nature and possess equal spiritual worth, a worth that does not derive from their particular attributes but rather human nature itself: "There is neither Jew nor Greek; there is neither slave nor free; nor is there male and female, for you are all one in Christ Jesus" (Galatians 3: 28). A person is not defined by what might be classified as "secondary attributes" (concrete particulars such as ethnicity, gender, and so on) but rather his essential nature or substance, his abstract status as a human being.

Contemporary multiculturalism dramatically revises such traditional American ideals. More particularly, it eviscerates the elements of unity and universalism bound up with traditional American self-understanding. The multiculturalist perspective recognizes only "the Many"—"diversity," "difference," and "otherness"—and turns a blind eye toward a shared and unifying "One." Indeed it challenges and even rejects the view that American identity is defined by subscription to unifying moral and political principles. Such a view is dismissed, even reviled, as mere American ethnocentrism, regarded as yet another means by which dominant elites, including the Founders themselves, marginalize and suppress persons and groups who do not subscribe to traditional American principles and values. To assert allegiance to values such as constitutionalism, the rule of law, unalienable natural rights, and economic freedom is to assert a merely subjective opinion and, moreover, display "intolerance" of diversity and difference. We recall that both Postmodernism and Multiculturalism challenge or reject the concept of objective and universal Truth; such truth as exists is merely relative and perspectival. On such a view, American founding principles certainly do not represent an objective and abiding truth of existence. Such principles, as previously noted, are little more than historical relics or, worse yet, mere social constructions of the powerful that serve to silence the voices of less powerful groups. Indeed they are hardly more than mere "American propaganda."[228]

There is no more reason to honor such social constructions than the equally oppressive social constructions of Christianity, which similarly serve to suppress the perspectives of historically marginalized social groups. Postmodern Multiculturalism regards all traditional concepts and views—gender roles, sexual preference, family structure, morality, constitutionalism, the rule of law, economic theory, and beyond—in the same light. There is no objective reality or Truth that validates the superiority of the traditional family or heterosexuality. Such concepts, like constitutionalism and the rule of law, are merely cultural constructs invented throughout history by dominant and self-serving elites. Language controls reality and those who hold power control language. There is no objective reality given to man that language serves to describe, only the social construction of meaning. Language is regarded as eminently plastic and malleable, readily susceptible to human design. Moreover, insofar as reality is little more than a social construction defined by language, the proper manipulation of language can serve to change or transform reality itself. Thus the ongoing redefinition of the meaning of the central moral and political concepts of traditional Western and American society discussed throughout this book. And thus the endless charade of postmodern politics, its twisting and parsing of language, fantastic promises, and absurd observations that defy reality. Indeed postmodern political actors in the United States frequently appear to be outright liars. Such a judgment, however, is not quite accurate. In order to lie, one must first believe in Truth, which

---

[228] University professor of my acquaintance who would undoubtedly prefer to remain anonymous.

postmodern politicians do not. They are postmodernists, which means they regard reality as plastic and formed by language. They further believe, as we have seen, that he who has power—political power—controls language and thus reality. Thus the endless repetition of what appear as blatant untruths to members of society whose vision is informed by traditional ("pre-postmodern") presuppositions.

Postmodernism and Multiculturalism regard truth and reality as relatively meaningless concepts but attribute the greatest possible significance to language. Despite their intense preoccupation with language, however, such constructs fail to recognize one of the most important characteristics of language, which is not its role in the "social construction" of reality but rather transmission of the actual historical experience of a people. We have discussed the traditional American ideal of "diversity within unity." One requisite of achieving such unity among the culturally diverse members of American society is the acquisition of the historical language of that society—English. Contrary to postmodern assertions, the English language is not a constructed artifact but rather a spontaneously evolved carrier of cultural experience. To learn any language is simultaneously to learn a particular way of experiencing the world. In the case of the English language, it is to absorb the unique experiences that have shaped the development of Anglo-American society. An individual cannot fully understand or participate in American society (or any society) without understanding the language that carries its meaning. As any bilingual person will attest, to comprehend two languages is to perceive reality through two different lenses, to perceive two different worlds.

A common language is essential to a common culture, a fact long recognized in the United States. Historically, a primary goal of immigrants, if not for themselves then for their children, was to learn English, a goal also encouraged if not demanded by the larger culture—schools, churches, businesses, and so on. Postmodern Multiculturalism, however, dismisses the significance of language for cultural unity. Its proponents suggest, on the contrary, that to learn English is to be subjected to the ethnocentric social constructions of European culture, historically dominated by white Christian men and long serving to oppress women, homosexuals, people of color, non-Christians, and other minorities. Contemporary immigrants to the United States are rarely encouraged, indeed often implicitly discouraged, to learn its language, which is to say, absorb its traditions, values, and meaning. The absence of a shared language, however, eliminates an essential social bond. There can be no American people, no American society, without an element of unity, and a common language is central to such unity. The multicultural demand for diversity, extending even to language, can only shatter American society into disjointed fragments. Scholars warn of the "Balkanization" of America that looms large if present trends are not arrested.[229] The assault on the English language, however, is merely one skirmish within the greater battle fought by postmodern multiculturalists—the battle against traditional American society and the overarching civilization from which it emerged. Multiculturalism is an important phenomenon because it embodies at a popular level numerous currents implicated in the ongoing erosion of American and Western culture. The free society emerged in Western Europe in line with the particular values, assumptions, beliefs, and historical circumstances of the European peoples. Over time the Judeo-Christian worldview blended with elements of Greco-Roman and Germanic culture to form the unique civilization of Christendom. The spiritual foundation of that civilization comprises certain fundamental and related convictions, including the reality of a transcendent God who creates man in his image. Every human being is regarded as a being of inestimable spiritual worth, endowed with reason and free will, and charged with a profound personal mission—to earn eternal salvation. The biblical worldview further comprises a distinction between heaven and earth, this world and the world Beyond. It is also bound to the conviction of an omnipotent and omniscient God who is the source of order in existence, both natural and moral order, a God who rules the world providentially and administers ultimate divine justice in the world Beyond time. Western civilization is grounded on the belief in a creative Source who stands beyond history and who establishes the nature of things, the givenness of existence in this world.

The characteristic moral, legal, political, and economic practices and institutions of traditional American society presuppose all such convictions to varying degrees. Postmodernism dismisses all of them in one fell swoop. Indeed it dismisses the very concept of cultural, social,

---

[229] Merriam-Webster defines the primary meaning of Balkanization as follows: 1. To break up (as a region or group) into smaller and often hostile units.

or spiritual "foundations," which implies a rootedness transcending the flux of history. It challenges the concept of Nature as an index of objective reality beyond the reach of human subjectivity. The postmodernist view perceives no such reality, no givenness of existence impermeable to human will and action. Nature is dismissed as yet another social construction, leaving behind only History, only human experience in time, only particular cultures, particular religious beliefs, particular historical circumstances, and so on. Natural or Higher Law recedes from view along with the concept of universal and overarching Truth, convictions central to the Western tradition for millennia. For postmodernists as for Progressives, truth, including metaphysical and religious truth, consists solely in the relative and particular truths thrown up by particular historical experiences in particular cultures.

Although postmodernism rejects foundationalism, not every postmodern thinker always and necessarily rejects the particular cultural experiences that constitute the Western and American tradition. Thinkers such as Richard Rorty defend certain traditional values not on the ground of truth-in-itself but rather the ground of History.[230] The experiences and values that shaped Western civilization are recognized as definitive for American society, and insofar as the American people wish to preserve their way of life, says Rorty, they are obliged to honor them. Such values, however, cannot be regarded as representing the truth of reality but only relatively true—true for American or European society but not societies that developed on the basis of different cultural perspectives. Americans, then, are permitted to defend their particular society but only on the basis of History, not Nature or Truth. American traditions and values may be valid for Americans due to their particular historical experience but cannot be regarded as universally valid, true-in-themselves, or rooted in any foundation other than the vagaries of history. The majority of postmodern multiculturalists, however, are far less accepting of Western and American culture. They reject not only the concept of foundationalism, as does Rorty, but also the substantive values and traditions characteristic of Judeo-Christian civilization. Such values, as we have seen, are typically dismissed as self-serving social

---

[230] Richard Rorty, *Achieving Our Country: Leftist Thought in Twentieth-Century America* (Cambridge: Harvard University Press, 1998).

constructions of hegemonic elites who employ their power of controlling language to oppress or marginalize perspectives of the less powerful.

Many individuals who pursue the Multicultural agenda and educational curriculum undoubtedly do so on the basis of mere naivety or thoughtlessness, failing to consider either the sources or implications of such a paradigm. The doctrine, moreover, is not only popular and politically correct but a mandatory component of educational curricula in many public schools. Teacher training in the universities is saturated with Multicultural dogma, and public schoolteachers are often required to transmit its teachings regardless of their personal values or concerns. For various reasons, then, many advocates of Multiculturalism may be unaware that the doctrine is a spearhead of contemporary neo-Marxist movements in the United States and elsewhere. The leaders of such movements correctly perceive the utility of the Multicultural paradigm with respect to the fundamental transformation of Western society for which Marx once yearned and they themselves continue to yearn. We have mentioned the "long march through the institutions" anticipated by Gramsci and others.

Contemporary Multiculturalism, as previously observed, is not concerned with comparative study of various world cultures, as the term would imply. The actual content of Multicultural studies in the majority of American educational institutions is of Marxist inspiration, whether or not such is explicitly recognized or acknowledged. More particularly, the basic paradigm of postmodern Multicultural theory is saturated with the Marxian concept of class struggle. Postmodern thinkers, following Marx, tend to perceive class struggle or conflict—the conflict between oppressors and victims—as the essence of social relations. So-called cultural Marxists, however, move beyond Marx in broadening and extending that struggle beyond the economic antagonism between capitalist and worker to other dimensions of social experience as well, in particular, race and gender. The oppressors are generally portrayed as European elites of various kinds—"Dead White Men," such as the American Founders, who imposed their definition of reality on others. The victims comprise the myriad of putatively marginalized groups— women, people of color, Native Americans, non-Christians, homosexuals, non-western civilizations, and even the planet itself (endangered by Western science and greed). Indeed, on the Postmodern and Multiculturalist view, the very concept of civilization appears as a symbol of Western oppression, defined by powerful elites and imposed on those subject to their power. What is civilization or civilized behavior? Who is to say? The traditional meaning assigned in the West, like the meaning of its other traditional symbols, has no inherent validity but is merely one more language-construct foisted on the powerless by self-serving elites.

Postmodern Multiculturalism drives a stake into the heart of Western civilization. All traditional concepts and values are transformed or transvalued, if not denigrated and reviled. Western standards have no claim to objectivity or Truth or superiority to other cultural standards; indeed, they have been unmasked as the symbols of oppression they always were. Similar judgements extend to every value and institution associated with the West, including its central conception of a universal human nature shared by all human beings. Multiculturalism replaces Christian universalism with an atavistic tribalism that conceives personal identity as bound to one's specific racial, cultural, or other particularistic group (race, gender, class). It is thus related to the rise of so-called "identity politics" in the United States, the demand for recognition and status asserted by the myriad groups putatively marginalized and oppressed by Western civilization. American college campuses have seen the development of African-American Studies, Women's Studies, Queer Studies, Latino Studies; and so on. College courses in Western Civilization have largely been eliminated or replaced by courses such as Eurocentrism. Students and others are encouraged to identify with their particularity and not a universally shared humanity. There is no such universal human nature, on the Multiculturalist view, but only particular cultural forms shaped by history.

Multiculturalism thus challenges the Judeo-Christian or Western conception of what it means to be a human being, with potentially profound consequences for American moral, legal, and political order. Traditional American institutions are inseparable from the conviction of a universal human nature. Such a conviction lies at the root of the Founders' declaration that "all men are created equal," endowed with identical individual rights, and entitled to be judged by identical laws. The postmodern rejection of a universal human nature thus leads, among other consequences, to rejection of the traditional American ideal of the rule of law. Legal theorists influenced by postmodern Multiculturalism have argued that particular groups should be ruled by particular laws unique to their particular circumstances and experiences. Judges are encouraged to take into account the particular cultural experiences of plaintiffs and defendants in reaching judicial decisions. Judges may even claim superior wisdom based upon their personal membership in a traditionally "marginalized" group. The recent and controversial remark of Supreme Court Justice Sonya Sotomayor—"I would hope that a wise Latina woman . . . would more often than not reach a better conclusion than a white male who hasn't lived that life"—is saturated with such postmodern Multiculturalist assumptions.[231] Calls have been made for incorporation of traditional Islamic Sharia law into the American system of justice. On the Multicultural viewpoint, such inclusion is perfectly sensible—particular communities should be ruled by their own particular law. Such a view, however, is in utter conflict with central values of the American system of justice—the general ideals of the rule of law and equality under law, the universal application of identical rules to all manner of persons, without distinction. The same may be said for the Multicultural argument that judicial decisions should take into account the particular cultural circumstances of litigants. Traditional America has insisted, on the contrary, that "Justice is Blind," that the law, like God, is no respecter of persons.

Multicultural relativism and perspectivism lead not only to an explicit rejection of the traditional American conception of justice but also traditional views of religion, morality, marriage and the family, sex roles and practices, and capitalism, indeed every value and institution historically associated with American society. The premises of postmodern Multiculturalism preclude the defense of any traditional value on any grounds but the vagaries of history, a defense which itself runs the risk of condemnation as both ethnocentric and intolerant. The proper attitude is to be tolerant (accepting) and open to otherness and diversity. The disparagement or rejection of traditional values extends even to patriotism, said to be yet another manifestation of ethnocentric hubris. Americans must learn to overcome parochial attachments to their way of life and become "global citizens," celebrating the equal value of all cultural perspectives. They must overcome their traditional

---

[231] "I would hope that a wise Latina woman with the richness of her experiences would more often than not reach a better conclusion than a white male who hasn't lived that life." Sonia Sotomayor, 2001 speech at Judge Mario G. Olmos Law and Cultural Diversity Lecture, University of California, Berkley.

attachment to Christianity. Biblical religion must be recognized as merely one perspective or subjective preference among others of equal validity. They must overcome their traditional commitment to capitalism, which is similarly disarmed from claiming the status of objective truth, representing, on the contrary, the "false consciousness" or mere rationalization of capitalist oppressors. The Founders' idea of unalienable rights, as mentioned, should be dismissed as mere propaganda. History itself must be redefined, transformed, "changed." Conventional history represents not a true and accurate account of human experience but rather the selective and self-serving narrative of cultural and political elites. In the end, none of the values, beliefs, assumptions, traditions, institutions, or customs that constitute the traditional American way of life are left standing. The Fabian Socialists were right—violent revolution is far from necessary to transform and even destroy a society or indeed an entire civilization.

We thus return to the issue introduced at the outset—the issue of cultural survival. The fundamental requisite of such survival—the will to perpetuate one's particular culture—is difficult if not impossible to sustain in a society saturated with Multiculturalist assumptions. Contemporary Multiculturalism portrays all cultures as more or less equal and recognizes few if any intrinsic values beyond "tolerance-acceptance" and "diversity." Such doctrine inevitably undermines confidence in the worth of any particular way of life, including the American way of life. Americans are not entitled to regard their unique culture as anything more than one historical option among various others of equal validity. Such radical relativism and perspectivism inevitably weaken patriotic sentiment and the willingness or ability to defend traditional American values in the face of competing cultural constructs and worldviews. A people will only defend the characteristic values of their society if they believe they are good and worth preserving. Such conviction, however, is daily undermined by the explicit and implicit Multicultural message conveyed to members of American society, especially its youth, by both contemporary education and influential popular media. Indeed every dimension of contemporary American society—moral, religious, cultural, political, and historical—

is saturated with the belief-complex or worldview of postmodern perspectivism and relativism.

A particular manifestation of the relation of Multiculturalism to the decline of American patriotism is its explicit denigration of the traditional notion of so-called American Exceptionalism. From its inception, the American people generally regarded their new nation as unique among nations, charged with a special mission in accord with God's providential design. America, in the celebrated phrase of John Winthrop, was to be the "City upon the Hill," the shining example of a free people under God.[232] America was not like other nations, the overwhelming majority of which were founded on force and conquest. America was different, unique, exceptional. For the first time in history, human beings were given the opportunity to devise a constitutional order on the basis of rational reflection and not under pressure of force or compulsion. For the first time in history, human beings devised a political order that not only expressly acknowledged the equal worth of every individual but aimed to provide universal institutional protection of his unalienable rights, the moral treatment to which every individual is entitled by virtue of his human nature.[233]

On the view of postmodern Multiculturalism, American Exceptionalism so conceived can only appear preposterous, indeed precisely the kind of ethnocentric hubris Multiculturalism strives to overcome. Accordingly, Multicultural curricula often bombard students with a one-sided account of history that highlights the failures and flaws of the American experience. Students typically learn little about the actual historical circumstances and values that underlie the American founding or the significance of American achievements in world history. They learn instead that the Founders were slaveholders and oppressors, not only of African slaves but other marginalized groups such as women and Native American peoples. They learn little about the massive destruction of human life that resulted from the twentieth-century experiment with economic centralization (many have never heard of a gulag or a Mao Tse-tung), but are generally well acquainted with the so-called "Robber Barons" of the Gilded Age. They learn little about the laws of economics but are outraged by the "corporate greed" that permits

---

[232] Speech, John Winthrop, "A Model of Christian Charity," 1630.
[233] Preamble, U.S. Constitution

Nike to pay Chinese workers a fraction of their American counterparts and persuaded that the propaganda of Michael Moore's "Sicko" is worth the attention of serious persons. They learn little or nothing of the contribution of biblical religion to the development of Western civilization and Western values, values they generally take for granted, but unfailingly learn that religious conviction is mere subjective opinion and preference. American college students know little of the actual content of the United States Constitution; indeed about sixty percent of them believe the Marxist slogan "From each according to their ability, to each according to their need" is contained therein. They learn little about the structure, function, or purpose of the American federal government but are nonetheless convinced that health care is a universal or human right. They learn nothing of the purpose or function of law yet are quite sure that the Supreme Court should be culturally diverse.

Multiculturalism is far from the only contemporary trend that poses a threat to the preservation of American society. Its special significance arises from its role as a carrier, in a simplified and seemingly benign manner, of neo-Marxist aspirations. Multiculturalism as practiced in contemporary American society shares the purpose if not the methods of the ideological movements of the twentieth century, namely, the transformation of Western and American society. The experience of Europe is most instructive in this regard. American Multiculturalism was largely imported from European sources. The doctrine has to date advanced further in its birthplace than in America, allowing a glimpse of its longer-term consequences. Relativistic *Toleranz* (acceptance) has become a more or less absolute value in many Western European nations, one that dare not be challenged, while contempt for the religious tradition that formed the basis of Western civilization knows few bounds. Despite pleas and protests from religious leaders, for example, European political leaders refused to acknowledge, even cursorily, the Christian roots of European civilization in the founding documents of the European Union. The decline of Christianity and accompanying rise of Multicultural "tolerance-acceptance" has disarmed European peoples from defending their traditional values and way of life in the face of non-European immigrants who do not share Western values. In recent years—the massive influx of Moslem migrants from the war-torn Middle East—the situation has become progressively more unwieldy and even dangerous. Farsighted European statesmen and scholars warn that the resulting inability to assimilate the large influx of immigrants from non-Western cultures such as fundamentalist Islam, whose religious worldview is both alien and antagonistic to that of the West, may lead to the disappearance of Europe as a distinct civilization, perhaps within the lifetime of present inhabitants.[234]

---

[234] There are recent signs that Western leaders are awakening to the dangers posed by Multiculturalism and related paradigms, for instance, the criticism of multiculturalism by David Cameron in England, Angela Merkel in Germany, and Nicolas Sarkozy in France; publications such as Marcello Pera, *Why We Should Call Ourselves Christians: The Religious Roots of Free Societies* (NY: Encounter Books, 2011) and Bruce S. Thornton, *Decline and Fall: Europe's Slow Motion Suicide* (Encounter Books, 2007).

FOURTEEN

JURISPRUDENCE AND CONSTITUTIONAL RECONSTRUCTION

---

*Our peculiar security lies in the possession of a written Constitution. Let us
not make it a blank paper by construction.*   —*Thomas Jefferson*

The revolt against the Judeo-Christian worldview, along with the
ascendency of socialist ideals and related trends such as Progressivism,
Postmodernism, and Multiculturalism, have undermined crucial
presuppositions of traditional Western society, including its American
expression. One important manifestation of this ongoing process is the
marked transformation of the fundamental legal framework of American
political order, the United States Constitution. American Constitutional
reconstruction over the past century is not an autonomous development
but rather correlative to the movements and trends under discussion.
The widening influence of post-theological and neo-Marxist paradigms
led to the emergence of a novel form of constitutional jurisprudence, the
previously mentioned Progressive doctrine of the "Living Constitution."
Progressive jurisprudence has played, and continues to play, a central
role in the erosion of traditional American constitutional order.

Anglo-American constitutionalism, as we have seen, is inextricably
linked to the traditional ideal of the rule of law. Both constitutionalism
and the rule of law are further linked to the corresponding concept
conventionally known as *judicial review*. Judicial review is the doctrine
under which legislative and executive actions of government are subject
to review, and possible invalidation, by the judiciary. The validity of
judicial review in the United States is commonly held to have been
formally established in the celebrated case of *Marbury v. Madison*, argued
before the Supreme Court in 1801. In the United States, federal and

state courts at all levels, trial and appellate, are authorized to adjudge the constitutionality (agreement with the Constitution or lack thereof) of legislation that is relevant to any case properly within their jurisdiction. In the formal language of law, judicial review refers primarily to the adjudication of the constitutionality of statutes (written law enacted by a legislative body), especially by the Supreme Court of the United States. Less formally, the doctrine of judicial review means that all actions of the federal legislature and executive are valid only insofar as they cohere with the fundamental law of the U.S. Constitution. The overarching purpose of American constitutionalism, as we have seen, is the limit the actions of the federal government. One of the central means toward that end is the establishment of law that binds the government in advance and that government itself cannot change, that is, the higher law of the U.S. Constitution. Judicial review is essential to the realization of limited government.

Originalism and the Living Constitution

The principle of judicial review implies of course that judges and justices conducting such review possess intimate knowledge of the Constitution. Such knowledge, however, involves far more than familiarity with the explicit language of the Constitution. It further involves awareness of the *meaning* of Constitutional language, upon which the constitutionality of challenged legislation or action crucially depends.[235] The explicit language of the Constitution is beyond dispute and immediately accessible to any literate person. The second kind of knowledge—the meaning of the explicit language of the Constitution—is more problematic and, indeed, lies at the center of modern constitutional controversy. Over the past century, two schools of constitutional jurisprudence have emerged that embody different methods of constitutional interpretation or "construction" (in the language of the Founders). The first is the jurisprudence associated with the "Living Constitution," previously mentioned in the discussion of Progressivism; the second is the contrasting method of constitutional interpretation conventionally known as "Originalism."

---

[235] See Hayek, *Rules and Order*, 97-101, for a discussion of the significance of tacit knowledge with respect to jurisprudence.

The Originalist philosophy of constitutional interpretation holds that the proper method of establishing the meaning of the explicit language of the Constitution entails recurrence to one of two possible standards: either the meaning held at the time of its construction or the authors' intent in crafting a particular Constitutional provision. Originalism thus comprises two related theories, generally referred to as "original meaning" and "original intent." "Original meaning" refers to the view that interpretation of a written constitution or law should be consistent with the ordinary meaning attached to it by sensible persons alive at the time of its adoption or enactment. "Original intent," by contrast, refers to the view that interpretation of a written constitution should be consistent with the meaning (intent) attached to the document by the individuals who drafted and ratified it. Most Originalists embrace the former view, "original meaning." The major division between the two Originalist theories concerns the locus of authority, that is, whether the authoritative meaning should be attached to the original meaning of the text, as described, or the intentions of the authors or ratifiers. In either case, Originalism aims to prevent the imposition of novel constitutional interpretations, whether such are alien to the original meaning or authorial intention (or both). All Originalists deny that the judiciary is authorized to "make" law; its only legitimate role is to uphold the law as written and enacted by others.[236]

The chief antagonist of the school of Originalism is the school of constitutional interpretation commonly known as the Living Constitution. The term itself was first coined by Professor Howard McBain in a 1927 book of the same name.[237] As we recall from previous discussion, advocates of a Living Constitution maintain that the U.S. Constitution should be regarded as a fluid and evolving document whose meaning changes over time. The doctrine is associated with American Progressivism, which, as we have seen, embraces a philosophy of history that tends to equate forward movement in time with Progress. Progressivism embodies a radical and all-embracing relativism, rejecting, like Postmodernism and Multiculturalism, a belief in an overarching and

---

[236] Ibid.

[237] The term originally derives from the title of a 1927 book of that name by Prof. Howard McBain, while early efforts at developing the concept in modern form have been credited to figures including Oliver Wendell Holmes Jr., Louis D. Brandeis, and Woodrow Wilson.

transcendent Truth immune to historical change. On the Progressive view, the only constant in human experience is change itself. Beliefs and values change; morality changes; historical circumstances change; the groups that constitute society change; the meaning of language changes; everything changes through time—everything "progresses." Progressives argue that the overarching principle of change should apply to the U.S. Constitution as it does to all other aspects of human existence. In order to maintain the relevance of the Constitution to contemporary society, to have it "live" rather than die, it too must change with the times. Such evolutionary adaptation, moreover, may be accomplished not only by amendment, as anticipated by the Founders, but also by changed interpretation of the document's explicit text. Advocates for the Living Constitution thus reject the Originalist position that the authoritative meaning of the Constitution should be attached to its original intent or meaning. To do so, on their view, is to saddle American society with an antiquated and irrelevant Constitution, a relic of a bygone world with little significance for contemporary society. It is to stifle Progress itself.

The conflicting views embodied in the doctrines of Originalism and the Living Constitution are particularly instructive for students of American social and political development, mirroring as they do the conflicting worldviews that have shaped such development over the past century and beyond. The ongoing contest may loosely be represented as Traditionalism versus Progressivism (and related to the culture war previously discussed). The former camp consists of various defenders of traditional American society and its characteristic values and institutions, embodied as they are in the Founders' Constitution. Such values, as we have seen, include belief in the primacy of the individual endowed with unalienable rights; limited government and the rule of law; a market economy; traditional Judeo-Christian morality, including the notion of natural or higher law; procedural or rule-based justice; objectivity and universalism; moral and political absolutism; and embrace of American Exceptionalism. The latter camp consists of persons and groups eager to transform or change American society in the interest of Progress. Characteristic values and beliefs include a rejection of limited government and its replacement with rule by administrative elites; hostility toward individualism and elevation of group identity; rejection of natural or higher law and embrace of legal positivism, including such Progressive doctrines as "sociological jurisprudence" and "legal realism";

extensive governmental regulation or control of economic processes and outcomes; embrace of a naturalistic or secular humanism and denigration of traditional biblical faith; pursuit of social or distributive justice; postmodern rejection of objectivity, universalism, and Truth; multiculturalism; and radical relativism. The following table dichotomizes various conflicting views associated with the two schools:

Originalism	*Living Constitution*
Moral and political absolutism	Moral and political relativism
Fixed meaning	Fluid and evolving meaning
Truth and objectivity	Perspectivism
Strict Construction	Broad or Loose Construction
Enumerated Powers	Implied Powers
Higher or Natural Law	Legal Positivism
Judeo-Christian morality	Naturalism/Secular Humanism
Traditional justice/	Social Justice/
Procedural/deontological ethics	Consequentialist ethics
Negative rights	Positive rights
Objectivity/Universalism	Subjectivity/Particularism/
	Group Identity
American Exceptionalism	Multiculturalism – Globalization
Founders/Classical Liberalism/	Modern Liberalism/
Conservatism	Progressivism

The two schools of contemporary American jurisprudence embody divergent worldviews incapable of reconciliation. Advocates of Originalism and the Living Constitution differ not merely in their approach to Constitutional interpretation but on even more fundamental grounds, including conceptions of truth, morality, justice, rights, religion, and the nature of human existence. The two schools embody different conceptions of what it means not only to be an American but also a human being. The contest is thus far more profound than competition between judicial philosophies, penetrating as it does to the heart and soul of American identity. Its ultimate outcome cannot be predicted with certainty at this juncture in history. The only certainty is that the final victory of the Living Constitution would mean the unequivocal death of the Founders' Constitution and the traditional American way of life it secures.

We have discussed the nature of the U.S. Constitution as a kind of secularized higher law whose purpose is to structure and limit the actions of the federal government. It was intended as a fundamental law, "fixed," constant, and perpetual. The Founders recognized that future experience—trial and error—might suggest beneficial changes to the Constitution and thus incorporated procedures for its amendment. The Constitution can be changed if experience should prove it necessary but only with difficulty, through the amendment process specified in the Constitution. An amendment must be proposed to the states either by a two-thirds vote of both houses of Congress or a convention called by two-thirds of the states and ratified by three-fourths of either the states or state conventions, as the case may be. By such means, the Founders aimed to ensure that any changes to the fundamental law would be the result of deep reflection and deliberation and in accord with the settled opinion of the vast majority of the American people.

The Founders regarded the U.S. Constitution as a crucial guarantee of free government and the unalienable rights of the people. It was to serve as a law superior to the will of government and bind its actions in all cases whatsoever. Such a conception, as we have seen, is central to the traditional doctrine of the rule of law: a law that can be changed by those it governs is no law at all. Sam Adams succinctly expressed the general view of the founding generation: "In all free states," he said, "the Constitution is fixed."[238] The colonists, as we recall, believed themselves betrayed by the novel British constitution of the era, informed as it was by the innovative doctrine of Parliamentary Sovereignty. Ironically, the constitutional development that ultimately led to the American War of Independence bears close and curious resemblance to the Living Constitution of modern Progressivism. The British constitution, the colonists were informed, had evolved, changed over time; the Americans

---

[238] Samuel Adams, "In all free States the Constitution is fixed; and as the supreme Legislative derives its Power and Authority from the Constitution, it cannot overleap the Bounds of it without destroying its own foundation." Massachusetts House of Representatives to the Speakers of the Other Houses of Representatives (Feb. 11, 1768), in Cushing, ed, *Writings of Samuel Adams*, 185.

must now recognize Parliament as the locus of sovereignty. Colonial views were said to be antiquated, outdated; to insist on historical rights and liberties, as did the colonists, was to cling to relics of the past. The British constitution had adapted to the flow of history; the sovereignty of Parliament was now established doctrine and practice. The Americans, as we have seen, could not and did not accept such constitutional evolution. Indeed their bitter experience under the concept of a changing or evolving ("living") constitution fueled their determination to prevent a similar end to the American experiment in republican government, that is, violation of their rights by changes in the fundamental law of the land.

Toward that end, the Americans developed two novel safeguards. First, they invented the concept of a *written* constitution that enumerated or specified their rights and that was immune to change by government itself. The experience with England convinced them that the fox cannot be trusted to guard the henhouse. Constitutional law—the legal framework that provided security for their rights—was not to be constructed or established by government but rather *given* to, imposed upon, government. Second, they conceived the idea of calling special state conventions for ratification of the proposed Constitution. Both American inventions were novel means toward attainment of the overarching goal—to ensure the more or less perpetual validity of the fundamental or higher law of the Constitution. The Constitution, as the Founders reasoned, is meant to serve as a permanent and unalterable limit to governmental action and this means that government itself cannot be regarded as its author. The wisdom of their insight is clearly evidenced by the application of such reasoning not only to government but also the individual. Everyone recognizes the inefficacy of a rule of personal conduct assigned by an individual to himself. A person who regards himself as the author of the law governing his own behavior can readily justify changing that law if it should interfere with his present desires. It is obvious that law is only meaningful and effective if established by an entity superior to that which is to be governed; a self-imposed law, it might be said, is no law at all. Moreover, government in a political order of the American type possesses no autonomous right to create law, constitutional or otherwise. We have discussed the terms of the Anglo-American social contract, as defined by Locke and embraced by the colonists. In the American understanding "We the People" are the source and fountain of all governmental power, including the power of lawmaking and legislating. As Thomas Paine expressed the common view of the founding generation,

> A constitution is not the act of a government, but of a people constituting a government; and government without a constitution is power without a right. All power exercised over a nation, must have some beginning. It must be either delegated, or assumed. There are not [sic] other sources. All delegated power is trust, and all assumed power is usurpation.[239]

On the American view, as we have seen, government is merely the utilitarian trustee of the limited power delegated by the people to further the security of their natural and unalienable rights. Legitimate government, as Jefferson emphasized, is based on consent of the governed. The consent of the American people did not extend to the invention of law but rather was limited to the declaration, adjudication, and execution of the pre-existing moral law, the Law of Nature and of Nature's God, toward protection of their individual rights. For such reasons, the Founders concluded, government itself cannot be permitted to establish the constitutional law that is to govern its action. The law, and thus the lawmaker, must be superior to the entity it aims to rule, in this case, government.

The Founders thus faced a dilemma. On the one hand, the American people—the source of all political power—must establish the fundamental law of the land. Only thus would the Constitution be controlling on the government and immune to arbitrary change by those it is intended to govern. The only possible source of the law that binds governmental action is the people themselves. On the other hand, the Constitution is meant to bind not only government officeholders but the American people themselves. The people have no more authority to change the Constitution at will than government. To permit whimsical or willful constitutional change on the part of the people, or a majority of the people, is to subject the fundamental law not to the arbitrary power of government but the equally arbitrary vagaries of popular

---

[239] Thomas Paine, *Rights of Man* (Mineoloa, NY: Dover, 1999).

opinion. The Founders, as we have seen, regarded majoritarian democracy as a recipe for perpetual "violence and injustice," more particularly, violation of the rights of both individuals and minorities. The fundamental law of the Constitution can only serve as higher law if beyond the reach of human manipulation, whether exercised by government or the people.

The Founders' problem, then, was to devise a way to establish a fundamental constitutional law whose authority simultaneously derives from the people and remains superior to both the people (electoral majorities) and government. Only thus could the Constitution serve as an effective limit on the power of the federal government. Their solution was the establishment of a novel procedure for ratification of the U.S. Constitution, the aforementioned state conventions. Each of the thirteen new states was instructed to hold a special convention convened solely for the purpose of ratification. Delegates to each state convention were chosen by the people of their respective states and instructed to cast their votes for or against ratification. The Constitution would only take effect if nine of the thirteen states voted in favor of its adoption. "We the People" would thus be both the ultimate fount and ultimate architects of legitimate governmental authority. The fundamental law of the Constitution would be given to, imposed upon, government by authority of the people assembled within their respective states. Government was thereby constrained to act in accordance with their intentions, possessing no power but that delegated to it by the people and unable to alter the Constitution without their consent.

By such a procedure the people established limits not only on the new federal government but also and simultaneously on themselves. Upon conducting the vote for ratification, the special conventions were disbanded or dissolved. Once ratified, the people could no more change the law of the Constitution than could government, except by following the amendment procedure outlined in the Constitution, a procedure they themselves established. Everyone's hands were tied upon ratification of the Constitution, the hands of government and the people. While its ultimate constituent authority derived from the American people, once established, the U.S. Constitution bound rulers and ruled alike. The special ratifying convention was an ingenious and innovative method of securing a secular equivalent to the traditional religious conception of the higher law—a law given to man and unalterable by human authority—that implicitly served as its model. It reveals, moreover, the unqualified desire of the Founders and the American people to establish fixed and perpetual limits to both the power of the federal government and the people's power to achieve goals by means of federal governmental action.

Strict vs. Broad Construction

The Founders' Constitution, as we have seen, embodies various assumptions derived from their formative spiritual inheritance, the Judeo-Christian worldview. The Founders were decidedly not postmodern relativists, multiculturalists, or Progressives. First and foremost, they believed in Truth. They believed in the objectivity of morality, including justice, in the existence of right and wrong independent of subjective human preference. Indeed, they tended toward a kind of moral and political absolutism: the obligation to honor both the moral law and law of the Constitution is not contingent upon particular historical circumstances, social conditions, personal identity, or the flux of time but binding at all times under all circumstances. They believed that America is an exceptional nation, guided by Providence in both its founding and its promise. They believed in a constant and universal human nature that transcends history and culture. The U.S. Constitution was to be a Constitution not merely for the eighteenth century but rather for the Ages, embodying, as they believed, universal Truth that transcends the particularities of history.[240]

We have discussed, moreover, the Founders' skepticism of human nature armed with power, derived from their Augustinian view of human nature and shared alike by Federalists and Antifederalists of the day. The apprehension of the human lust for power, as we recall, was especially acute among the Antifederalists. Their keen awareness of the universal *libido dominandi* would eventually lead prominent Antifederalists to oppose ratification of the new Constitution, perceiving certain constitutional provisions as open invitations to abuse of abuse. Such a potential stemmed from the ambiguity of language characteristic

---

[240] The phrase *Novus ordo seclorum* (Latin for "New Order of the Ages") appears on the reverse of the Great Seal of the United States, first designed in 1782 and printed on the back of the United States one-dollar bill since 1935.

of the suspect provisions, which, the Antifederalists believed, would readily lend itself to manipulation by unscrupulous political actors bent on grasping power.

Antifederalist apprehensions of potential abuse of power under the proposed Constitution led to extensive discussion regarding the proper construction or interpretation of the fundamental law. Jefferson and other influential Antifederalists (or republicans, as they called themselves) championed a method of constitutional interpretation known as *strict construction*. Strict constructionists maintain that the meaning of a Constitutional word or phrase should be construed narrowly or closely, in a "strict" or even near-literal sense. A word or phrase, on such a view, means what it normally means in plain, everyday language; it is not to be imaginatively expanded or distorted into a meaning at odds with common usage. Strict construction so conceived is usually associated with a second traditional principle of American constitutional interpretation, the so-called doctrine of *enumerated powers*. Such a doctrine holds that the only powers delegated to the federal government are those specifically enumerated or listed in the U.S. Constitution itself, such as the authority to establish the postal service.[241] Any power not expressly granted is presumed beyond the reach of federal authority. The Tenth Amendment explicitly supports the doctrine of enumerated powers: *The powers not delegated to the United States by the Constitution, nor prohibited by it to the States, are reserved to the States respectively, or to the people.*[242] In other words, any powers not granted by the Constitution to the federal government, or prohibited by the Constitution to the states, are reserved to the states or the people. In contemporary American jurisprudence, the related doctrines of strict construction and enumerated powers are generally associated with Originalism and championed by traditionalists.

Not all of Jefferson's contemporaries accepted the doctrine of strict construction. Thinkers such as Alexander Hamilton, Jefferson's great antagonist among the Founders, championed an opposing doctrine

---

[241] Article I, Section 8, Clause 7 of the United States Constitution, known as the Postal Clause or the Postal Power, empowers Congress "To establish Post Offices and post Roads."

[242] The precise text of the Tenth Amendment is as follows: "The powers not delegated to the United States by the Constitution, nor prohibited by it to the States, are reserved to the States respectively, or to the people."

generally known as *broad or loose construction*. He and other advocates of broad construction argued for a flexible reading of the text of the Constitution, one that permits a wide range of meanings beyond the usual sense of a term. A classic example involves the so-called "Necessary and Proper Clause"("Elastic Clause") of the Constitution: *The Congress shall have Power – To make all Laws which shall be necessary and proper for carrying into Execution the foregoing Powers, and all other Powers vested by this Constitution in the Government of the United States, or in any Department or Officer thereof.*[243] In his landmark opinion in *McCullough v. Maryland* (1819), Chief Justice John Marshall adopted a broad or loose reading of the Necessary and Proper Clause. The word "necessary," he said, can mean "convenient" or, as Hamilton previously put it, "useful."[244] Thus the federal government possesses constitutional authority to make any law it finds "convenient" or "useful" for executing its delegated powers. Such an interpretation of course grants the federal government far greater power than would an interpretation based on the doctrines of strict construction and enumerated powers. "Convenient" and "useful" are broad and subjective concepts that may justify many acts of government that would be forbidden upon a strict or narrow reading of the text. Broad or loose construction is thus usually associated with the so-called doctrine of *implied powers*, the counterpart of the Jeffersonian doctrine of enumerated powers. Advocates of implied powers, such as Hamilton, Marshall, and other early Federalists claim that the Constitution grants extensive unstated powers to the federal government, powers implied by the express grants of power enumerated in the Constitution.[245] In contemporary society, the doctrines of broad

---

[243] Article One, Section 8, clause 18.

[244] And, moreover, is beyond the range of common meanings of the word "necessary." Necessary is typically defined as "absolutely essential," "required" to be done, and so on. A quick online search produced not one standard definition that includes the term "useful" but rather repeated definitions of 'necessary' as required to be done, achieved, or present; needed; essential; and so on.

[245] Randy Barnett, "The Original Meaning of the Commerce Clause" (68 *University of Chicago Law Review,* 101-147 (2001); "The Original Meaning of the Necessary and Proper Clause" (6 *University of Pennsylvania Journal of Constitutional Law,* 183-221 (2003).

construction and implied powers are usually associated with modern-liberal Progressivism and its notion of the Living Constitution.

Controversy over constitutional construction began shortly after ratification of the Constitution and has continued to the present day. Antifederalist apprehensions have proven to be well founded; constitutional developments over the course of American history, and especially the past century, have clearly confirmed their foresight. Not only the Necessary and Proper clause but other equivocal Constitutional provisions, such as the so-called General Welfare Clause and Commerce Clause, have been broadly interpreted by modern Courts, resulting in extensive grants of federal power that strict constructionists regard as unconstitutional.

A classic example of the extent to which modern courts have stretched constitutional language to justify far-reaching actions of the federal government is the landmark interpretation of the Commerce Clause provided by justices eager to validate the extensive economic legislation of Franklin Roosevelt's New Deal. The text of the Constitution states that the United States Congress shall have power *to regulate Commerce with foreign Nations, and among the several States, and with the Indian Tribes.* Strict constructionists interpret the Commerce Clause to mean that the federal government is vested with constitutional authority to "make regular" commerce, trade, or exchange among the several states, and between the United States and both foreign nations and the Indian tribes. For instance, Congress may legitimately prohibit individual states from erecting tariff or other barriers that would inhibit trade across state borders, and it has constitutional authority to impose tariffs on imported goods. As Thomas Jefferson explained. ". . . the power given to Congress by the Constitution does not extend to the internal regulation of the commerce of a State (that is to say, of the commerce between citizen and citizen), which remain exclusively with its own legislature; but to its external commerce only, that is to say, its commerce with another State, or with foreign nations, or with the Indian tribes."[246]

The New Deal Court, by contrast, interpreted the Commerce Clause in the broadest possible manner. It ruled, for instance, that the federal

---

[246] Thomas Jefferson, "Opinion on the Constitutionality of the Bill for Establishing a National Bank" (15 Feb. 1791), Founders Online, National Archives, last modified Dec. 6, 2016. Hereinafter cited as "National Bank."

government possesses constitutional authority to prevent a farmer from growing wheat on his own land exclusively for his own use. The Court determined that such action was legitimately considered "commerce" because a farmer's decision to consume his own wheat and not bring it to market affects the nationwide supply of wheat and thus its price, a consequence, said the Court, that may be construed as "commerce." It concluded, accordingly, that the farmer's personal decision to grow wheat for his own use legitimately falls under jurisdiction of the federal government, exercising its constitutional authority under the Commerce Clause. Such reasoning clearly involves a meaning of "commerce" very far from conventional or common usage and very far from the meaning articulated by Jefferson and other strict constructionists.

A similarly broad interpretation has been applied by the modern Court to the General Welfare Clause. The U.S. Constitution contains two references to the General Welfare, one in the Preamble and the other in the so-called Taxing and Spending Clause.[247] Strict constructionists from the outset insisted that neither clause was intended to grant to the federal government general powers of legislation. The legitimate reach of Congress extends only so far as the enumerated powers delegated to it by the Constitution. Justice Joseph Story affirmed such a view in his 1833 *Commentaries on the Constitution of the United States*. The Preamble to the U.S. Constitution, he wrote, "never can be resorted to, to enlarge the powers confided to the general government. . . . It cannot confer any power *per se*; it can never amount, by implication, to an enlargement of any power expressly given. It can never be the legitimate source of any implied power. . . ."[248] The same applies to the General

---

[247] "We the people of the United States, in order to form a more perfect union, establish justice, insure domestic tranquility, provide for the common defense, promote the general welfare, and secure the blessings of liberty to ourselves and our posterity, do ordain and establish this Constitution for the United States of America." Article 1, Section 8, Clause 1: "The Congress shall have Power To lay and collect Taxes, Duties, Imposts and Excises, to pay the Debts and provide for the common Defence and general Welfare of the United States; but all Duties, Imposts and Excises shall be uniform throughout the United States."

[248] Joseph Story, *Commentaries on the Constitution of the United States*, in *Founders' Constitution*, Vol. 2:18-19. The U. S. Supreme Court affirmed such an interpretation in *Jacobson v. Massachusetts* (1905): "Although that Preamble indicates the general purposes for which the people ordained and established

Welfare and Taxing and Spending Clause (*The Congress shall have Power To lay and collect Taxes, Duties, Imposts and Excises, to pay the Debts and provide for the common Defence and general Welfare of the United States*). As Jefferson explained,

> [T]he laying of taxes is the power, and the general welfare the purpose for which the power is to be exercised. They [Congress] are not to lay taxes *ad libitum* for any purpose they please; but only to pay the debts or provide for the welfare of the Union. In like manner, they are not to do anything they please to provide for the general welfare, but only to lay taxes for that purpose.[249]

Such was the traditional understanding of the Courts as well. The use of the phrase "general Welfare" in the Tax and Spending clause was not generally regarded as an independent grant of power but a qualification on the taxing power which included within it a power to spend tax revenues on matters of general interest to the federal government. As James Madison summarized the view of strict constructionists, "With respect to the words general welfare, I have always regarded them as qualified by the detail of powers connected with them. To take them in a literal and unlimited sense would be a metamorphosis of the Constitution into a character which there is a host of proofs was not contemplated by its creators."[250] Jefferson, as usual, succinctly expressed the heart and soul of strict constructionism: "Our peculiar security lies in the possession of a written Constitution. Let us not make it a blank paper by construction."[251]

---

the Constitution, it has never been regarded as the source of any substantive power conferred on the Government of the United States or on any of its Departments."

[249] Jefferson, "Opinion on the Constitutionality of the Bill for Establishing a National Bank" (1791) in *Founders' Constitution*, Vol. 3:245-247.

[250] Madison, James Madison to James Robertson, Jr. 20 April 1831. *The Founding Era Collection*, James Madison Papers Early Access (University of Virginia Press, 2009-2016).

[251] Jefferson, Thomas Jefferson to William C. Nicholas, Monticello, 7 Sept 1803. www.constitution.org

The course of American constitutional development, most emphatically throughout and beyond the twentieth century, has led, however, precisely to the result Jefferson feared. Under sway of the Progressive doctrine of the Living Constitution and related moral and intellectual trends, the fundamental law has become more and more a "blank paper" upon which justices write their personal subjective values, opinions, and partisan political agendas into law. The written Constitution has not substantially altered over the centuries since ratification; only seventeen amendments have been added beyond the Bill of Rights. The dramatic growth in the power and reach of the federal government has been achieved not by constitutional amendment but rather broad constitutional construction—loosely reinterpreting the language of the Constitution—precisely as Jefferson and Antifederalists feared. The text is left standing as written but given a meaning alien and often opposed to that intended by its authors.

Such a method of interpretation, as we have seen, is justified by advocates of the Living Constitution on the grounds that the fundamental law must be adapted to the ever-changing values and circumstances of history. To cling to the original meaning of the Founders or their contemporaries is to saddle the present generation with outworn and obsolete beliefs, to hold back Progress. Such a view, as we have seen, presupposes the radical moral and historical relativism at the heart of American liberal-Progressivism and postmodernism more generally. There is no universal or absolute Truth that transcends the flux of history. The alleged self-evident truths proclaimed in American founding documents are not in fact truth but, at best, representative sentiments of the era or, at worst, ideological constructs devised by dominant historical elites, who employed their power to define language and reality toward securing personal self-interest and interest of their class. Progressive thinkers, as we recall, at times concede that prevailing beliefs and values of eighteenth-century America may have been appropriate (relatively "true") within their historical context, that is, a relatively homogenous Christianized society without power or consequence on the world stage. They are not, however, considered valid or relevant with respect to contemporary American society. Contemporary America, it is argued, is quite different from America of the founding era, exhibiting, for instance, far greater religious and ethnic diversity. The change in American circumstances has been accompanied by changes in private morality and this must be reflected in changes in public morality, in constitutional law. The Constitution must further be adapted to America's changed status among the nations, that is, its contemporary role as "superpower" on the world stage. The twenty-first century is not the eighteenth century. If the Constitution is to remain a "living" law, it must be attuned to the beliefs, values, and circumstances of the contemporary era. Such is precisely the function of the modern judiciary. The role of judges and justices is not to uphold the antiquated and possibly oppressive worldview of an era long gone but rather ensure that constitutional law reflects the forward movement of history, the evolving "spirit of the nation," in the words of Progressive leader Woodrow Wilson.[252] One method of accomplishing such a task is to give new meaning to old language, to give the broadest possible construction to the text of the Constitution.

The Establishment of Religion

The so-called "religion clauses" of the First Amendment provide an excellent illustration of the manner in which the Progressive doctrine of the Living Constitution has impelled the transformation of the Founders' Constitution. The relevant text of the Amendment states that *Congress shall make no law respecting an establishment of religion, or prohibiting the free exercise thereof.* The significance that the Founders attached to religion is indicated by the primacy given to the religion clauses, the first two clauses of the First Amendment to the Constitution. Their purpose, as we shall see, was to prevent the federal government ("Congress") from interfering in the religious life of the people. The rights originally enumerated in the Bill of Rights, as we recall, are rights against the federal government. In the case of the religion clauses, the American people are guaranteed the right of religious freedom, that is, to hold religious belief and engage in religious practice free from coercive interference by the federal government.

The right of religious freedom was to be secured in two ways, first, by prohibiting an "establishment of religion" (Establishment Clause) and, second, by prohibiting interference with the "free exercise" of religion (Free Exercise Clause). The more controversial of the religion clauses in

---

[252] Woodrow Wilson, U.S. Declaration of Neutrality, 19 August 1914.

the modern era is the so-called Establishment Clause. The original purpose and meaning of the clause is amply indicated by the voluminous historical record of the period. The clause was intended to prohibit the newly established federal government from instituting what was conventionally referred to an "established Church," a term that held clear and unequivocal meaning at the time the Constitution was written. An established Church, as Evans explains, was understood to be an "official church that occupied a privileged position within the state, was vested with certain powers denied to others, and . . . supported from the public treasury" [taxes]."[253] Legally established churches of this nature were commonplace in the founding era. The Church of England was of course an established church so defined, as were various Churches established throughout the American colonies, including the Anglican Church in Virginia, the Congregational Church in Massachusetts, and the established churches in seven other colonies.[254] Inhabitants of the several states with officially established churches were required to pay taxes to support their respective Churches and clergy, whether members of that particular Church or not. Growing religious diversity within the colonies, and especially competition among various Protestant denominations, led over time to demands for disestablishment. The Baptists in Virginia, for instance, regarded the legal requirement to pay taxes in support of the established Anglican Church as unjust. Why should they be forced to support a Church to whose doctrine and practice they did not subscribe and, moreover, employ resources that could instead be spent on their own churches and ministry? The Baptists were in the forefront of efforts to disestablish the Anglican Church in Virginia and supported in such efforts by both Jefferson and Madison. The result was the celebrated "Virginia Statue for Religious Freedom," drafted by Jefferson in 1777 and enacted into law in 1786. Similar trends were developing within the other colonies and newly formed states. By the time the U.S. Constitution was proposed, many persons were concerned that the power of the new federal government might be employed to create in the United States a counterpart of the established Church of England. If such should occur, every American citizen would be compelled to pay taxes to support a national Church to which many

---

[253] Evans, *The Theme is Freedom*, 275.
[254] Ibid., 275-277.

of them did not belong, and members of the national Church would have special privileges denied to others. This was morally unacceptable to many of the Founders and their contemporaries. Jefferson regarded establishment, as he said in the Virginia Declaration of Religious Freedom, as an "infringement of natural right"; Madison considered church establishment a violation of the "rights of conscience."[255]

Jefferson and Madison were far from alone in this regard. As we have seen, the first natural right claimed by early American colonists was precisely the right of conscience. The religious clauses of the First Amendment were enacted to secure such a right, "the most sacred of all property,"[256] as Madison put it. Securing the right of conscience was thought to require two related prohibitions on the exercise of power by the federal government, both of which are established by the First Amendment. First, as discussed, the Amendment forbids Congress from instituting an Established Church.; as Madison pointedly observed, "[t]e Constitution forbids everything like an establishment of a national religion."[257] The explicit guarantee provided by the Establishment Clause was necessary to quell the fears of the newly independent states regarding the potential creation of a national church. Second, the federal government was forbidden to "prohibit the free exercise" of religion, that is, coerce religious belief and practice. Locke's *Letter Concerning Toleration* had stressed the impossibility of bending human conscience by means of coercion, a conviction widely shared within the American colonies.[258] A person's outward behavior may be influenced by the threat

---

[255] Madison, *Founders' Constitution*, Vol 5:24.

[256] Madison, "Property," March 29, 1792, *Founders' Constitution*, Vol. 1: 598.

[257] Detached memoranda, circa 1820. Madison's own original language for the proposed First Amendment included the phrase "nor shall any national religion be established": "The civil rights of none shall be abridged on account of religious belief or worship, nor shall any national religion be established, nor shall the full and equal rights of conscience be in any manner, or on any pretence, infringed." *Founders' Constitution*, Vol. 5: 24.

[258] Opening lines of the Virginia Act for Establishing Religious Freedom, "Whereas, Almighty God hath created the mind free; that all attempts to influence [the mind] by temporal punishments or burthens, or by civil incapacitations tend only to beget habits of hypocrisy and meanness, and therefore are a departure from the plan of the holy author of our religion, who being Lord, both of body and mind yet chose not to propagate it by coercions

of coercion, but such is powerless to touch the inner man. Governmental coercion of religious belief, of conscience, is not only morally wrong, a violation of natural right, but also futile. Religious belief and practice, Locke insisted, must be understood as strictly voluntary entities and a church as a voluntary society. The essential voluntariness of religious faith and practice can only be secured if government, the sword of organized coercion, is restrained from interfering in the private sphere of religion. As Madison put it,

> We hold it for a fundamental and undeniable truth that religion, or the duty which we owe our Creator, and the manner of discharging it, can be directed only by reason and conviction, not by force or violence. . . . The religion, then, of every man must be left to the conviction and conscience of every man: and . . . it is the right of every man to exercise it as these may dictate.[259]

Jefferson expressed similar sentiments: "Compulsion in religion is distinguished peculiarly from compulsion in every other thing. I may grow rich by art I am compelled to follow, I may recover health by medicines I am compelled to take against my own judgment, but I cannot be saved by a worship I disbelieve & abhor."[260] Such convictions were summarized in Madison's concise explanation of the meaning of the First Amendment: "Congress should not establish a religion and enforce the legal observation of it by law, nor compel men to worship God in any manner contrary to their conscience, or . . . one sect . . . obtain a pre-eminence, or two combined together, and establish a religion to which they would compel others to conform."[261]

The Americans embraced a Lockean distinction between coercive government and voluntary religion but also moved beyond Locke in a

---

on either, as was in his Almighty power to do. . . ." *Founders' Constitution*, Vol. 5:84.

[259] James Madison, "Memorial and Remonstrance against Religious Assessments," address to the Virginia General Assembly, June 20, 1785, *Founders' Constitution*, Vol. 5:82-84.

[260] "Notes on Religion" (October 1776), in *The Works of Thomas Jefferson in Twelve Volumes* (New York: G. P. Putnam's Sons, 1904), Vol. 2:266.

[261] Madison, *Founders' Constitution*, Vol. 5:93.

significant way: they were the first people in history to establish a constitutional framework that explicitly incorporates the longstanding Christian distinction between religion and government. They were the first to establish a constitutional framework that explicitly protects religion from governmental interference. The overarching purpose of the First Amendment's religion clauses was to shield religious belief and practice—the dictates of conscience and their outward expression—from the coercive force of the federal government. The general conviction was that religious belief, by its very nature, requires voluntary persuasion of the mind and thus preservation of true religion requires the absence of coercion, that is, freedom. Freedom is necessary to enable human beings to move beyond mere outward conformity toward attainment of a living faith that shapes heart and soul. As Madison observed, "[r]eligion flourishes in greater purity without than with the aid of government."[262]

It should again be emphasized that the Bill of Rights was intended as a limitation on the power of the *federal* government, not the several *state* governments. The First Amendment aimed to prevent the federal government from interfering with the religious traditions and customs of the individual states, not restrict state governments from regulating religion within their respective jurisdictions. We have seen that many of the original thirteen states maintained established Churches, some of which continued in existence well into the nineteenth century.[263] Such state-established churches were universally regarded as constitutionally legitimate (even if not universally regarded as desirable). Regulation of religion, including the establishment of an official state Church, was regarded as a power reserved to the states by both the Tenth Amendment and the general theories of divided sovereignty and enumerated powers underlying the American federal system. As Jefferson explained in his Second Inaugural Address (1805), "In matters of religion I have considered that its free exercise is placed by the Constitution independent of the powers of the General Government [i.e., the federal government]. I have therefore undertaken on no occasion to prescribe the religious exercises suited to it, but have left them, as the Constitution

---

[262] James Madison, letter to Edward Livingston, July 10, 1822, *Founders' Constitution*, Vol. 5:106.
[263] Evans, *The Theme is Freedom*, 278.

found them, under the direction and discipline of the church or state authorities acknowledged by the several religious societies."[264]

The Issue of Separation

It was widely if not universally agreed among the Founding generation that the First Amendment prohibited Congress from establishing a national Church (Establishment Clause) and also from interfering with individual religious belief and practice (Free Exercise Clause). Such agreement extended to the Tenth Amendment's prohibition of federal interference with state religious practice and custom. Such general consensus, however, did not extend to the *degree* of "separation" between religion and government demanded by such constitutional protections. John Witte has identified four prevailing views concerning religious liberty in the founding period—what he calls congregational Puritan, Free Church Evangelical, Enlightenment, and Civic Republican. Such classifications, he cautions, should not be regarded as mutually exclusive positions consistently advocated by distinct groups. The general tendency among thinkers of the era was rather to shift among the four perspectives or hold opinions representing some mix thereof. As Witte explains, "the "original understanding" of the founders respecting [the relation between] government and religion cannot be reduced to any one view. It must rather be sought in the tensions among the four prevailing perspectives and in the general principles that emerged from their interaction."[265]

Such general principles as did emerge, then, resulted from interplay among four distinct understandings of the proper relation between religion and government. The New England Puritans, descendants of the Calvinist theology of religious liberty, generally conceived church and state as two covenantal associations with distinct callings, both of which represented Godly authority. They established rules that aimed to

---

[264] March 4, 1805. The First Amendment's religion clauses, like various other restrictions on federal power listed in the Bill of Rights, were said by the Court to be "incorporated" by the post-Civil War 14th Amendment (1868) and thus applicable to the state governments as well as the federal government. See n296.

[265] John Witte, Jr., *Religion and the American Constitutional Experiment*, 2nd ed (Boulder: Westview Press, 2005), 23-24. Hereinafter cited as *American Constitutional Experiment*.

separate these associations to some degree, such as prohibiting Church officials from holding political office and political officials from either holding ministerial office or interfering with internal affairs of the churches. Separation of this nature was justified on the age-old Christian distinction between God and Caesar previously discussed; to mingle such offices, said the Puritans, "would confound those Jurisdictions, which Christ hath made distinct."[266] The Puritan tradition, however, also regarded church and state as complementary or coordinating ("close and compact") aspects of one unified society; they shared a similar nature and function and were both ordained by God. The Puritan view in this regard bears some resemblance to that of medieval Christendom, which also conceived spiritual and temporal rule as complementary and coordinating jurisdictions within a unified Christian society. The Puritans, then, were not strict separationists. They recognized a conceptual distinction between church and state but in practice permitted extensive intermingling of religious and political institutions. Government officials, for instance, assisted the churches by donating public property for use as church meetinghouses and other church functions and also employing government agents to collect tithes to support the congregational ministry. Church officials in turn assisted the government by permitting church meetinghouses to be used for town assemblies, to keep birth, marriage, and death records, and for other public functions. Moreover, despite their recognition of the distinct calling of religion and government, New England Calvinists also instituted Congregationalism as the Established Church of the community and did not recognize an obligation to tolerate other religions. Their position would change over time, partly in response to the influx of various religious nonconformists into the region. The eventual outcome was the enlargement of the Puritan understanding of liberty of conscience. By 1744, Elisha Williams could put the matter thus:

> Every man has an equal right to follow the dictates of his own conscience in the affairs of religion. Every one [sic] is under an indispensable obligation to search the Scriptures for himself . . . and to make the best use of it he can for his own

---

[266] Ibid.

information in the will of God, the nature and duties of Christianity. And as every Christian is so bound; so he has the unalienable right to judge of the sense and meaning of it, and to follow his judgment wherever it leads him; even an equal right with any rulers be they civil or ecclesiastical.[267]

The Massachusetts Constitution of 1780, drafted largely by John Adams, contains an even more generous guarantee of religious liberty:

> It is the right as well as the duty of all in society, publicly, and at stated seasons, to worship the Supreme Being, the great Creator and Preserver of the universe. And no subject shall be hurt, molested, or restrained, in his person, liberty, or estate, for worshipping God in the manner and season most agreeable to the dictates of his own conscience, or for his religious profession of sentiments; provided he doth not disturb the public peace or obstruct others in their religious worship.

The second set of beliefs regarding the relation between religion and government constitute what Witte calls the Evangelical view, rooted in sixteenth-century European Anabaptism. The Evangelicals, like the Puritans, held a theory of religious liberty. The Evangelical theory, however, led to a much stricter institutional separation of church and state than conceived or practiced by the Puritans. Indeed it led to the construction of a "wall of separation between the garden of the Church and the wilderness of the world," as Roger Williams put it in 1644.[268] The Evangelical view of religious liberty went beyond the Puritan in several significant ways. First, Evangelicals sought not only to protect the liberty of conscience of every individual but also the freedom of association of every religious denomination. The religious freedom of both individuals and particular denominations was to be realized not only by legal prohibition of established religion but any intermingling of religion and government whatsoever. Evangelicals denied that

---

[267] Ibid., 26.

[268] Roger Williams, "Mr. Cotton's Letter Examined and Answered" (1644), in *The Complete Writings of Roger Williams* (NY: Russell and Russell, Inc., 1963), 313, 392. See also Edward J. Eberle, "Roger Williams's Gift: Religious Freedom in America," *Roger Williams University Law Review* Vol 4:425, 1999).

government has any right either to interfere with the internal government of the church (assembly, worship, discipline, and so on) or be involved in the collection of religious tithes or taxes. They further condemned tax exemptions and other immunities for religion, property donations, and indeed any form of governmental support for religion. The Evangelicals seem to have recognized the wisdom of the old adage, "he who pays the piper calls the tune." As a Baptist Declaration of 1776 put it, If "civil Rulers go so far out of their Sphere as to take the Care and Management of religious affairs upon them, . . . Yea . . . Farwel [sic] to 'the free exercise of Religion'."[269]

The Evangelicals, then, demanded a strict and literal "separation" of church and state; "[t]he notion of a Christian commonwealth should be exploded forever," said Baptist preacher John Leland. Such views derived from the deep-seated voluntarism of the Christian Evangelical faith, the belief that "[n]othing can be true religion but a voluntary obedience unto [God's] revealed will." Evangelicals believed that every adult was called by God to accept the faith freely, that is, through voluntary choice. Governmental coercion would destroy such a possibility and in so doing violate both the individual and God. "Religious liberty is a divine right . . . immediately derived from the Supreme Being, without the intervention of any created authority. . . . [T]he all-wise Creator invested [no] order of men with the right of judgment for their fellow-creatures in the great concerns of religion."[270] One hears in such a conviction both the echo of Locke and the voice of Jefferson. One further perceives in the Evangelical demand for "separation" the enduring influence of Augustine and the experience of a persecuted sect that had suffered as a religious minority in colonial America for more than a century:

> God has expressly armed the magistrate with the sword to punish such as work ill to their neighbors, and our faithfulness in that work and our obedience to such authority, is enforced [by the Bible]. But it is evident that the sword is excluded from the kingdom of the Redeemer. . . . [I]t is impossible to blend church and state without violating our Lord's commands to both together. . . . [I]t has appeared for these thousand years

---

[269] Cited in Witte, *American Constitutional Experiment*, 29.
[270] Isaac Backus and Pastor Israel Evans (1747-1807), Ibid., 28.

that pure Gospel discipline in the church is very little if at all known in state establishments of religion and that instead of letting conformists thereto, and dissenters therefrom, grow together or enjoy equal worldly privileges, the sword has been employed to root up, and to prepare war against all such as put not into the mouths of the established teachers who are the means of upholding such rulers as pervert all equity.[271]

On the Evangelical understanding, established religion, enforced by the coercive arm of government, prevents "true religion," which must, above all, be voluntary. Christ himself had excluded the sword of coercion from religion, and the Christian faith by its nature must be accepted voluntarily, freely, or not at all; a coerced "faith" is not faith. Such convictions explain the urgency and passion of the Evangelical demand for limiting the power of government with respect to religion. Nothing less than salvation itself was at stake.

According to Witte, the third constellation of beliefs that influenced views on religious liberty in the founding era derives from the Enlightenment, usually associated with European thinkers such as Montesquieu, Condorcet, Voltaire, Locke, Adam Smith, and David Hume, and also Americans such as Jefferson, Paine, Franklin, and Madison. The Enlightenment theory of religious liberty complemented that of the Evangelicals. Locke is representative of the manner in which the two viewpoints occasionally blended. Locke, widely associated with Enlightenment thought of the eighteenth century, was reared within a dissenting religious environment (his father was a Puritan). The views expressed in his *Letter Concerning Toleration* are scarcely distinguishable from those of the Evangelicals: "Above all things, it is necessary to distinguish exactly the business of civil government from that of religion, and to settle the just bounds that lie between the one and the other." The church, Locke continues, must be "absolutely separate and distinct from the commonwealth." Such separation is mandatory because the church is "a voluntary society of men, joining themselves together of their own accord in order to the public worshipping of God in such

---

[271] Isaac Backus, *On Church State, and Calvinism, 1754-1789*, ed William G. McLoughlin (Cambridge, MA: Belknap Press of Harvard University Press, 1968), 351, 357-58, 373-75.

manner as they judge acceptable to Him, and effectual for the salvation of their souls." The Church is and must be recognized as a "voluntary association" whose members are free to enter or exit at will. The Church, unlike government, is forbidden to employ coercion: "[n]o force is to be made use of upon any occasion whatsoever. For force belongs wholly to the civil magistrate."[272] Religion differs from government as oil from water and voluntariness from coercion. Religion and government, moreover, deal with distinct dimensions of human consciousness, the inner man and his outward behavior. Governmental coercion may never legitimately be exerted over individual conscience; not only does coercion violate the individual's natural right of conscience but is also pointless. "The true and saving religion," Locke says, consists in the "inward persuasion of the mind" and, as such, is immune to coercive threats or the force of human law.

> For laws are of no force without penalties, and penalties in this case are absolutely impertinent, because they are not proper to convince the mind. . . It is only light and evidence that can work a change in men's [religious] opinions: which light can in no manner proceed from corporal sufferings, or any other outward penalties [inflicted by the government. . . . Every person] . . . has the supreme and absolute authority of judgment for himself [in matters of faith].[273]

Governmental coercion may be employed only within its legitimate sphere, the worldly sphere encompassing outward or external human behavior or action relating to mundane affairs.[274] The view of religion as a voluntary association beyond the reach of the coercive arm of government, classically articulated by Locke, was widely embraced in the American colonies. Over time it inspired efforts to eliminate various traditional governmental supports for religion, for instance, special tax appropriations or collections of tithes that provided aid, privileges, or protection to religious doctrines or groups; public donations of goods

---

[272] Locke, *Letter Concerning Toleration*, 223.

[273] Ibid., 219-20.

[274] Locke here echoes a longstanding conviction within Christian civilization; as Augustine and Aquinas put the matter, government deals only with "externals. See fn 341.

and realty to religious groups; special laws of religious incorporation; and civil laws against blasphemy, sacrilege and breaking of the Sabbath.[275]

James Madison, sometimes regarded, like Locke, as an Enlightenment figure, also sounded very much the Evangelical in 1822. The best arrangement, he said, is "a perfect separation between ecclesiastical and civil matters. . . . [R]eligion and government will both exist in greater purity, the less they are mixed together."[276] Despite such statements, however, neither Locke nor Madison demanded an absolute and utter "separation" of religion and government. Locke always assumed a community committed to a common Protestant Christianity. He refused toleration to those religions he believed did not themselves practice tolerance, among which he included Roman Catholicism; he regarded atheism as similarly beyond the pale. Madison's views also presupposed a common Christian culture. The Virginia Declaration of Rights (1776), partly written by Madison, states that ". . . religion, or the duty which we owe to our Creator and the manner of discharging it, can be directed only by reason and conviction, not by force or violence; and therefore, all men are equally entitled to the free exercise of religion, according to the dictates of conscience, and . . . it is the mutual duty of all to practice Christian forbearance, love, and charity, towards each other."[277] Madison, moreover, recognized the difficulty in precisely demarcating the respective spheres legitimately within the jurisdiction of government and religion, as medieval thought would frame it. Such was especially difficult with respect to the "unessential points" involved in the relation between church and state. In 1833 he wrote:

> It may not be easy, in every possible case, to trace the line of separation between the rights of Religion and the civil authority, with such distinctness, as to avoid collisions & doubts on unessential points. The tendency to a usurpation on one side, or the other, or to a corrupting coalition or alliance between them, will be best guarded against by an entire abstinence of the Government from interference in any

---

[275] Witte, *American Constitutional Experiment*, 31.
[276] Madison to Edward Livingston, 10 July 1822, *Founders' Constitution*, Vol. 5:106.
[277] Virginia Declaration of Rights, June 12, 1776, *Founders' Constitution*, Vol 5:3-4.

way whatever, beyond the necessity of preserving public order, & protecting each sect against trespasses on its legal rights by others.[278]

According to Witte, the aforementioned Virginia Statute for the Establishment of Religious Freedom, drafted by Jefferson, further exemplifies the Enlightenment formulation of religious liberty:

> Whereas Almighty God hath created the mind free; . . . all attempts to influence it by temporal punishment, or burthens, or by civil incapacitations, tend only to beget habits of hypocrisy and meanness, and are a departure from the plan of the Holy Author of our religion. . . . [Thus] no man shall be compelled to frequent or support any religious worship, place or ministry whatsoever, nor shall be enforced, restrained, molested, or burthened, in his body or goods, nor shall otherwise suffer on account of his religious opinions or belief; but all men shall be free to profess, and by argument to maintain, their opinions in matters of religion, and . . . the same shall in no wise diminish, enlarge or affect their civil capacities.[279]

Notwithstanding such convictions, Jefferson, like Locke and Madison, did not oppose in principle every conceivable intermingling of religion and government. He did not object, for instance, to various Virginia laws of clearly religious inspiration, such as those that punished disturbers of religious worship and persons who broke the Sabbath; that established days of public fasting and thanksgiving; that annulled marriages prohibited by Levitical law; and that established the mode of lawful

---

[278] Cited in Witte, American Constitutional Experiment, 31. Both Evangelical and Enlightenment views on religious liberty stressed the importance of liberty of conscience, freedom of exercise, and the equality of all faiths under the law.
[279] "Virginia, Act for Establishing Religious Freedom" (1785), Founders' Constitution, Vol. 5: 84-85. See also Thomas Jefferson, "A Bill for Establishing Religious Freedom," 1779, Founders' Constitution, Vol. 5:77. Jefferson drafted the Virginia Statute for Religious Freedom in 1777; it was enacted into law in 1786.

marriage (in church).[280] We have seen, however, that Jefferson regarded all such religious regulation as falling exclusively within the competence of *state* government. His antipathy toward governmental control of religion was largely directed at the newly formed federal government. Jefferson fully shared Antifederalist apprehensions of a federal grasp of power that would threaten the sovereignty of the several states, including their traditional authority over religion.

The final set of beliefs regarding religious liberty during the founding era constitutes what Witte calls the Civic Republican view. Representative thinkers include George Washington, John Adams, Benjamin Rush, and Oliver Ellsworth. Civic Republicanism derived from earlier Anglican and Puritan ideals of a Christian Commonwealth. Accordingly, such thinkers had much in common with their Puritan counterparts, as did Evangelicals with Enlightenment thinkers. Unlike the Evangelical and Enlightenment perspectives, and consistent with the Puritan view, Republican writers were greatly concerned to maintain a common religious ethos in the public square. Civic Republicans, however, unlike the Puritans, were not rigorous proponents of a particular religious denomination. They tended rather to emphasize the utility of religion, especially Christianity, for the general welfare and preservation of free government. "Religion and morality are the essential pillars of civil society," wrote George Washington.[281] "We have no government," said John Adams, "armed with power capable of contending with human passions unbridled by morality and religion."[282] Free government, they believed, depends upon general subscription to particular religious values and beliefs or at least to a "Publick religion" celebrating its civic ideals, symbolized by icons such as the Bible, the Constitution, liberty bells, and so on. [283]

---

[280] Witte, *American Constitutional Experiment*, 3.

[281] George Washington, "Letter To the Clergy of Different Denominations Residing In and Near the City of Philadelphia," March 3, 1797, in John C. Fitzpatrick, ed, *The Writings of Washington from the Original Manuscript Sources, 1745-1799*, Library Reprints, 1931 edition (2007), Vol. 35.

[282]John Adams, *The Works of John Adams, Second President of the United States*, ed, Charles Francis Adams (Boston: Little, Brown, 1854), Vol. IX:401, June 21, 1776.

[283] Witte, *American Constitutional Experiment*, 34.

Civic Republicans thus supported policies such as government appointment of legislative and military chaplains, government sponsorship of general religious education, and, occasionally, governmental enforcement of religiously based morality through positive law. The Continental Congress had supported many such measures. It authorized tax-supported chaplains for the military; tax appropriations for religious schools and missions; and recitations of prayer at its opening sessions and during the day of Thanksgiving. Its Northwest Ordinance of 1787 acknowledged that "religion and morality and knowledge, being necessary to good government and the happiness of mankind, schools and the means of education shall forever be encouraged."[284] Civic Republicans, then, were largely in favor of governmental support for religious institutions, regarding them not only as useful but essential to good government. They endorsed tax exemptions for church properties and tax support for religious schools, charities, and missionaries; donations of public lands to religious organizations; and civil laws against blasphemy, sacrilege, and interruption of religious services.[285] The strength of the Civic Republican tradition is indicated by the continuing existence of various provisions advocated by its supporters, for instance, tax-supported chaplains for the military and recitations of prayer at opening sessions of Congress. The U.S. tax code offers tax-exempt status to religious institutions and churches to the present day.[286]

Each of the four designated views informed the American conception of religious liberty that prompted the demand for the First Amendment. The viewpoints differed to some degree in inspiration and prescription

---

[284] Article III.

[285] Witte, ibid.

[286] The Massachusetts Constitution of 1780 is a good example of the Civic Republican effort to balance freedom of religion with what John Adams called a "mild and equitable establishment of one public religion." There is to be freedom of religion but also a public "religion at the fore and floor of society and government. . . Statesmen may plan and speculate for liberty, but it is religion and morality alone which can establish the principles upon which freedom can securely stand. . . Religion and virtue are the only foundations, not only of republicanism and of all free government, but of social felicity under all governments and in all combinations of human society." John Adams, *Works*, 8:232; 9:635; Letter to Abigail Adams (1775), cited in Edwin S. Gaustad, *The Religious History of America* (San Francisco: Harper, 1966), 127.

but nevertheless shared a commitment to certain uncontested general principles. They all advocated liberty of conscience and equality under law for a variety of religions, and they all opposed both theocracy and religious establishment. More particularly, they all embraced what the founding generation considered the "essential rights and liberties of religion":

1. *Liberty of conscience:* the right to be free from governmental coercion of religious belief.

2. *Free exercise of religion:* the right to act publicly on the choices of conscience, so long as such action does not violate the public peace or the rights of others.

3. *Religious pluralism:* Government is not to decide which religions ought to flourish or wither. Evangelicals regarded such matters as God's prerogative. Enlightenment thinkers looked to reason and persuasion. Puritans and Republicans looked to a plurality of private associations; families, schools, charities, learned and civic societies were the schools of religion and deserved the protection accorded to religious liberty.

4. *Equality of religion before the law:* The founders supported equality of all religions before the law. They mainly had the various Protestant denominations in mind but also Catholicism and Judaism. They were not generally concerned with equality between religion and non-religion, between believers and nonbelievers, as is often the case in contemporary society.

5. *"Separation" of church and state*: Although the phrase itself does not appear in any founding document, all four viewpoints advocated an institutional division between religion and government, as guaranteed by the First Amendment's prohibition of an establishment of religion. Their differences, as we have seen, regarded the degree of separation between political and religious concerns, not the distinction itself.

All four viewpoints defended the institutional division of religion and government on grounds of religious liberty, although such justifications typically involved different emphases and particulars.

First, the division between religion and government was invoked, like the medieval demand for "freedom of the church," as a means to protect the Church from governmental interference in its concerns. Second, it was sometimes invoked to protect government from an overreaching Church; seven states banned ministers from political office. Third, it was invoked to protect the natural and unalienable right of conscience; and, fourth, to protect individual states from interference by the federal government in local religious affairs. Jefferson, as we have seen, denied federal jurisdiction over religion, which belonged exclusively to the several states. States could patronize and protect religion, establish or abridge religion, but the federal government could not.[287] Finally, various half-hearted efforts to protect society from religion—to remove traditional forms of religion from law, politics, and culture at large— arose toward the end of the eighteenth century. Such efforts, however, were novel and controversial at the time, far from the general consensus regarding the meaning of the First Amendment.

6.   *Disestablishment of religion.* Jefferson understood disestablishment to mean the prohibition of "intermeddling" on the part of the government "with religious institutions, their doctrines, discipline, or exercises."[288] The general meaning of "establishment" at the time of the founding was "to settle, fix, define, ordain, enact, [or] set up" the religion of the community, its doctrines and liturgies, religious texts and traditions, clergy and property.[289] The model for religious establishment so conceived was of course the Church of England, which required by law use of the King James Bible and prescribed liturgies, rites, and prayer, including *The Book of Common Prayer.* It also demanded subscription to the Thirty Nine Articles of Faith

---

[287] As governor, Jefferson himself supported religion in various ways, including making religious pronouncements. He never did so as president.

[288] Jefferson, Letter to Rev. Samuel Miller, Jan. 23, 1808, *Founders' Constitution,* Vol. 5:98.

[289] Madison: Government meddling in religion "implies either that the Civil Magistrate is a competent judge of religious truth; or that he may employ religion as an engine of civil policy. The first is an arrogant pretension falsified by the contradictory opinions of rulers in all ages, and throughout the world; the second an unhallowed perversion of the means of salvation." "Memorial and Remonstrance against Religious Assessments," *Founders' Constitution,* Vol. 5:83.

and loyalty oaths to the Church, Crown, and Commonwealth of England.[290]

Religious establishment on the British model had led at times to governmental control of the church and repression and coercion of religious dissenters. The First Amendment aimed to prevent a repetition of such experience in the United States. The Americans had come to believe that an established national religion violates every principle of religious liberty—liberty of conscience, religious equality under law, religious pluralism, and the institutional division of church and state. The federal government was thus forbidden to impose any mandatory form of religious belief, doctrine, or practice. As Thomas Paine put the common view,

> All religions are in their nature mild and benign, and united with principles of morality. They could not have made proselytes at first, by professing anything that was vicious, cruel, persecuting or immoral. . . . Persecution is not an original feature in any religion; but it is always the strongly marked feature of all law-religions or religions established by law. Take away the law-establishment, and every religion reassumes its original benignity.[291]

The lingering question that remained unanswered at the time of the American founding is a question of major concern to contemporary American society. That is, does disestablishment of religion absolutely prohibit any form of governmental support for religion or simply require that any such support be distributed among all religions in a non-preferential manner?[292] The founders were divided on this issue. Evangelical and Enlightenment thinkers tended toward the absolutist view that government should be prohibited from extending any and all

---

[290] Witte, *American Constitutional Experiment*, 58.

[291] Thomas Paine, *Rights of Man*, Pt. 1 (1791), *Founders' Constitution*, Vol. 5:95-96.

[292] It should be noted that at the time of the framing, the character of American society was predominantly Christian, indeed Protestant, and the Founders gave little thought to accommodating, for instance, Native-American or African religions.

financial support to religion. Puritan and Republican thinkers took a less absolutist position; they would prohibit only direct financial support for the religious worship or practice of one particular group. As we have seen, they tended to regard general governmental support for religion— tax exemptions, land grants, taxes appropriated for missionaries and military chaplains, and so on—as necessary for the preservation of civil society and free government.[293] Such support, moreover, was generally held to be the responsibility of the state governments, not the federal government (although the Continental Congress, as mentioned, did provide governmental support for religion in various ways).

It is clear that the absolutist position associated with Evangelical and Enlightenment thought on religious liberty did not prevail at the time of the founding or throughout the major portion of subsequent American political development. Eighteenth-century America was marked by governmental support for the Christian religion in a variety of ways. We have seen that state governments at times donated land for churches, religious schools, and religious charities; collected religious taxes and tithes for ministers; supported Christian education in schools and colleges; enacted religious laws such as those outlawing blasphemy and sacrilege, as well as Sabbath laws, religious test oaths, and so on. Both established and other churches received such support in the eighteenth century. Moreover, government support for religion, both federal and state, continued well into the nineteenth and twentieth century, and, indeed, continues in a limited form at the present time. Contemporary federal taxpayers, for instance, support a Congressional chaplain who opens Congressional sessions with prayer, military chaplains in the armed services, and the federal mint that issues currency declaring "In God we Trust."

"Separation" and the Modern Court

Having examined the original meaning and intent of the religion clauses of the First Amendment, we next explore the modern Court's interpretation of those clauses. The discussion will illustrate and highlight the ongoing tension between the two contemporary schools of constitutional jurisprudence previously discussed, Originalism and the

---

[293] Witte, *American Constitutional Experiment*, 61.

Living Constitution. The contemporary controversy surrounding the religion clauses, especially the Establishment Clause, stems from the great divide between the interpretation offered by modern-liberal Progressive justices and the meaning historically attached to the clauses from the founding until the second half of the twentieth century.

The interpretation that prevails in contemporary society was famously formulated by Justice Hugo Black in the landmark case *Everson v. Board of Education* (1947). Black therein states:

> The 'establishment of religion' clause of the First Amendment means at least this: Neither a state nor the Federal Government can set up a church. Neither can pass laws which aid one religion, aid all religions or prefer one religion over another. Neither can force nor influence a person to go to or to remain away from church against his will or force him to profess a belief or disbelief in any religion. No person can be punished for entertaining or professing religious beliefs or disbeliefs, for church attendance or non-attendance. No tax in any amount, large or small, can be levied to support any religious activities or institutions, whatever they may be called, or whatever form they may adopt to teach or practice religion. Neither a state nor the Federal Government can, openly or secretly, participate in the affairs of any religious organizations or groups and vice versa. In the words of Jefferson, the clause against establishment of religion by law was intended to erect 'a wall of separation between Church and State'.[294]

Much of Black's opinion is in accord with the original meaning of the First Amendment but much else is not. A close reading of the ruling, sentence by sentence, will clarify the substantive departures from previous interpretation.

1.   *Neither a state nor the Federal Government can set up a church.* Such a statement departs from the original meaning attached to the First Amendment, which prohibited only the *federal* government from establishing or "setting up" a church. We have seen that the general

---

[294] 330 U.S. 1, 15-16. *Everson v. Board of Education*

view of the founding era acknowledged the constitutional authority of the several state governments to regulate religion, including the institution of an established church, within their respective states. Although the movement within the states was toward disestablishment, several states continued to support their established churches even after ratification of the U.S. Constitution in 1788.[295] Black's opinion in *Everson* is based on the modern interpretation of the Fourteenth Amendment ratified in 1868. On the constitutional doctrine of so-called "selective incorporation," the Fourteenth Amendment is said to have nationalized certain provisions of the Bill of Rights such that henceforth they are binding not only on the federal government but the state governments as well.[296] The novel judicial doctrine of "selective incorporation" substantively altered the U.S Constitution and vastly increased the power of the federal judiciary. Prior to the 1890s, the Bill

---

[295] South Carolina disestablished its state church in 1790. The Congregational Church of Connecticut was disestablished in 1818, and the established church of Massachusetts was not abolished until 1833.

[296] A constitutional doctrine whereby selected provisions of the Bill of Rights are made applicable to the states through the Due Process Clause of the Fourteenth Amendment. The doctrine of selective incorporation makes the first ten amendments to the Constitution—the Bill of Rights—binding on the states. Through incorporation, state governments are largely held to the same standards as the federal government with regard to many constitutional rights, including the First Amendment freedoms of speech, religion, and assembly, and separation of church and state; the Fourth Amendment freedoms from unwarranted arrest and unreasonable searches and seizures; the Fifth Amendment privilege against self-incrimination and the Sixth Amendment right to a speedy, fair, and public trial. Some provisions of the Bill of Rights—including the requirement of indictment by a Grand Jury (Sixth Amendment) and the right to a jury trial in civil cases (Seventh Amendment)—have not been applied to the states through the incorporation doctrine.

Until the early twentieth century, the Bill of Rights was interpreted as applying only to the federal government. In the 1833 case Barron ex rel. *Tiernon v. Mayor of Baltimore*, 32 U.S. (7 Pet.) 243, 8 L. Ed. 672, the Supreme Court expressly limited application of the Bill of Rights to the federal government. By the mid-nineteenth century, this view was being challenged. For example, Republicans who were opposed to southern state laws that made it a crime to speak and publish against slavery alleged that such laws violated First Amendment rights regarding freedom of speech and freedom of the press.

of Rights was held to apply only to the federal government, as the Founders intended. Under the "selective incorporation" doctrine, however, and equally novel interpretations of the Fourteenth Amendment's "Due Process" and "Equal Protection" clauses, various provisions of the Bill of Rights are held by the modern Court to apply to levels of government beyond the federal.

2. *Neither can pass laws which aid one religion, aid all religions or prefer one religion over another.* The founders, as we have seen, were divided on this issue. Evangelical and Enlightenment thinkers would tend to agree with Black's interpretation, but Puritans and Civic Republicans would not. The latter groups were not opposed to general governmental support for all Christian religions but only that which discriminated in favor of, or against, particular denominations.

3. *Neither can force nor influence a person to go to or to remain away from church against his will or force him to profess a belief or disbelief in any religion.* Such a statement fully accords with the original meaning of the First Amendment and the universal interpretation of its framers. Black, however, again applies it not only to the federal government, as originally intended, but also to the states, based on the Fourteenth Amendment as discussed above.

4. *No person can be punished for entertaining or professing religious beliefs or disbeliefs, for church attendance or non-attendance.* The Framers would agree, so long as the public peace is not disturbed.

5. *No tax in any amount, large or small, can be levied to support any religious activities or institutions, whatever they may be called, or whatever form they may adopt to teach or practice religion.* Evangelical and Enlightenment thinkers of the founding era would be more sympathetic to such an absolutist position than Puritans or Civic Republicans, who supported general governmental support for religion for the reasons discussed.

Black's interpretation may be in sympathy with Evangelical and Enlightenment positions as characterized by Witte, but it contradicts the historical experience of the American people. From the earliest colonial settlements until Black's ruling in *Everson*, government at all levels provided various kinds of taxpayer-funded support for religion. Christian religious symbols, funded by taxpayers, abounded in the public square. Taxpayers, for instance, funded Christmas displays at local city halls and the U.S. Capitol; the teaching of Christian precepts and the Bible in public schools at all levels; exhibitions of the Ten Commandments in courtrooms and other forms of public property; the use of Christian symbols such as the cross in various municipal logos; and so forth.[297] The use of taxpayer funds to support Congressional and military chaplains, as well as Congressional prayer and federally minted coins and currency bearing the motto of the United States, "In God We Trust," has previously been mentioned.[298] During the War of 1812, Congress authorized the printing of Bibles at taxpayer expense; the Northwest Ordinance of 1787 set aside funds for the teaching of religion in the newly settled territories.[299] The U.S. Supreme Court to the present day presides beneath a frieze (paid for by taxpayers) representing Moses receiving the Ten Commandments on Mount Sinai. The list could be extended almost indefinitely because American society from the outset supported general measures, funded by taxes, expressing its traditional religious heritage and commitments in the public square. Such was the dominant and uncontroversial practice of both the American people and American courts throughout most of their history. General taxpayer-funded support of American religious traditions was ubiquitous until the *Everson* ruling in 1947. No previous Court interpreted the First Amendment in the manner of Justice Black.

---

[297] Undeniable: *The Survey of Hostility to Religion in America* (Plano, TX: Liberty Institute, 2014). Hereinafter cited as Undeniable. In 2012, for instance, the city of Steubenville, OH, agreed to retire its new seal, which includes, among other symbols, a Latin cross atop a chapel (representative of the local Franciscan University). The decision followed a complaint by the Freedom from Religion Foundation, which claimed that the cross violated the Establishment Clause of the First Amendment.

[298] "In God We Trust" was adopted as the official motto of the United States in 1956. It is also the motto of the U.S. state of Florida. The phrase has appeared on U.S. coins since 1864 and on paper currency since 1957.

[299] Not only was religion to be taught but taught in publicly supported schools. See footnote 9 of Justice Douglas' concurring opinion in Engel v. Vitale, the case which removed prayer from public schools in the United States. Douglas there acknowledges that "[r]eligion was once deemed to be a function of the public-school system. The Northwest Ordinance, which antedated the First Amendment, provided in Article III that 'Religion, morality, and knowledge being necessary to good government and the happiness of mankind, schools and the means of education shall forever be encouraged'."

6. *Neither a state nor the Federal Government can, openly or secretly participate in the affairs of any religious organizations or groups and vice versa. In the words of Jefferson, the clause against establishment of religion by law was intended to erect 'a wall of separation between Church and State'.*[300] Black here asserts an absolutist doctrine of separation at odds with the original views of various founders, as well as the historical experience of the American people. The manner in which Black justifies his ruling is also noteworthy: an appeal to the authority of Jefferson, who, Black says, "intended" the Establishment Clause to erect a "wall of separation between Church and State." Such a justification has had far-reaching consequences for American society, consequences still unfolding at the present time, and the question of its validity must therefore be explored with some care.

We begin by observing that Black's ruling in *Everson* has firmly embedded the phrase "wall of separation" within popular consciousness. Most students, and perhaps most Americans, believe that the First Amendment does in fact erect a "wall of separation" between religion and government and, moreover, attribute that express language to the Constitution itself. Neither view is accurate. The express language of the First Amendment, as we have seen, forbids an "establishment of religion" and interference with the "free exercise" of religion. The phrase "wall of separation" to which Black refers does not appear in the text of the Constitution but rather derives from a personal letter Jefferson wrote to the Danbury Baptist Association in 1802, many years after ratification of the Constitution. In that letter, Jefferson says,

> Believing with you that religion is a matter which lies solely between Man and his God, that he owes account to none other for his faith or his worship, that the legitimate powers of government reach actions only, and not opinions, I contemplate with sovereign reverence that act of the whole American people which declared that their legislature should 'make no law respecting an establishment of religion, or prohibiting the free exercise thereof', thus building a wall of separation between Church and State. Adhering to this expression of the supreme will of the nation in behalf of the rights of conscience, I shall see

---

[300] 330 U.S. 1, 15-16. *Everson v. Board of Education.*

with sincere satisfaction the progress of those sentiments which tend to restore to man all his natural rights, convinced he has no natural right in opposition to his social duties.[301]

Jefferson's employment of the term "wall of separation" accurately captured neither the general interpretation of the First Amendment nor his personal views but makes perfect sense in light of his Baptist correspondents. The phrase, as we recall, was first employed in 1643 by theologian Roger Williams, who founded the oldest Baptist church congregation in America. It thus had special resonance within the Baptist community, which had long demanded an absolute separation between religion and government, suffering as it had for a century under religious establishment. We have seen, however, that such an absolutist position was not universally held among those who enacted the First Amendment (drafted by Madison). Moreover, during his tenure as governor of Virginia, Jefferson himself supported various religiously based measures authorized by the state government. His settled belief, as we recall, was that the First Amendment established limits solely on the power of the *federal* government. Jefferson's remarks in his Second Inaugural Address (1805), written three years after the Danbury letter, bear repeating:

> In matters of religion I have considered that its free exercise is placed by the Constitution independent of the powers of the General Government. I have therefore undertaken on no occasion to prescribe the religious exercises suited to it, but have left them, as the Constitution found them, under the direction and discipline of the church or state authorities acknowledged by the several religious societies.

Although Jefferson employed the absolutist metaphor of a "wall of separation" in his private correspondence, a decade or more after ratification of the U.S. Constitution, such sentiment represented neither his public position nor public interpretation of the First Amendment.

---

[301] Thomas Jefferson, "Letter to Danbury Baptist Association," Jan. 1, 1802, *Founders' Constitution*, Vol. 5:96. Jefferson's wording ("Wall of Separation") was several times upheld by the Supreme Court as an accurate description of the Establishment Clause: *Reynolds* (98 US at 164, 1879); *Everson* (330 US at 59, 1947); *McCollum* (333 US at 232, 1948).

His choice of language seems rather to reflect his finely honed political and artistic sensibility. Jefferson's public pronouncements on the issue of church-state relations were always in accord with the prevailing view that general support of religion by the state governments was constitutionally permissible (if perhaps not desirable).

Despite such facts, Black in *Everson* elevates Jefferson's private remark to the level of constitutional absolutism, contrary to both Jefferson's own stated views and the general historical interpretation of the First Amendment prior to *Everson*. Two elements of Black's opinion are of particular importance. First, *Everson* is the first Supreme Court ruling to apply the religion clauses of the First Amendment to the *state* governments. Prior to that ruling, the Courts uniformly upheld the traditional view that the First Amendment binds only actions of the federal government, not state governments. *Everson*, then, is the first Supreme Court case to "incorporate" the Establishment Clause of the First Amendment as binding upon the states through the Due Process Clause of the Fourteenth Amendment. It thus marks a turning point in Constitutional interpretation.

Second, and as important, Black unequivocally asserts in *Everson* that *[n]o tax in any amount, large or small, can be levied to support any religious activities or institutions, whatever they may be called, or whatever form they may adopt to teach or practice religion.* This provision alone has led to sweeping changes in American society: on its basis, all public (taxpayer-funded) expression of the American religious heritage has been condemned as unconstitutional. Among the more controversial consequences of Black's ruling is the prohibition of prayer in American public schools, prayer that was considered constitutionally permissible from the founding until 1947. In 1962 the Supreme Court ruled on a second landmark case, *Engel v. Vitale*. By a vote of 6-1, it held that school-wide, non-denominational prayer at the start of the public school day violates the Establishment Clause of the First Amendment.[302] In an opinion again written by Justice Black, the Court ruled that agents of government are constitutionally forbidden to compose an official school prayer and require its recitation in public schools. The prayer in question is as follows: "Almighty God, we acknowledge our dependence upon Thee, and we beg Thy blessings upon us, our parents, our teachers and

---

[302] 370 US 421.

our country. Amen."[303] According to the modern Court, such prayer, however nondenominational and innocuous, violates the Establishment Clause of the First Amendment. Public schools are of course funded by taxpayers.

The Court's rulings in *Everson* and *Engel* have entailed consequences far beyond the particular issues that led to the rulings, consequences that involve the progressive elimination of America's Judeo-Christian heritage from the public square. Such rulings have led, for instance, to the replacement of municipal Christmas trees with "holiday trees"; "merry Christmas" with "happy Holidays"; and, in the classroom, "Silent Night" with "Frosty the Snowman." Certain public schools have replaced the Easter Bunny with a novel "spring Bunny." Postal workers may not legally post the Ten Commandments in their office cubicles. Cities and municipalities are compelled to remove any Christian symbols from official logos. Public high schools are ordered to remove any reference to God from their honor codes. Students attending high school football games are forbidden to pray or give "religious speeches" over a public-address system prior to the games. A kindergarten assistant in the Pennsylvania public schools is fired for wearing a cross necklace to school. The Supreme Court of Alabama is forced to remove a granite monument displaying the Ten Commandments from the rotunda of the state courthouse. All such activities are of course supported, directly or indirectly, by taxpayer funding. Thus, according to the modern Court, they are absolutely prohibited by the First Amendment's Establishment Clause.[304] All such activities, however, were regarded as constitutional prior to Black's rulings.

Over the past several years, the First Amendment's religion clauses have been interpreted in an ever-more militantly anti-religious manner. The First Amendment has been invoked, for instance, in cases involving the rights of traditional Christians to practice their faith within the public square of commerce ("free-exercise of religion"). The question is

---

[303] Cited in Evans, *The Theme is Freedom*, 270.

[304] Bible readings at public schools were ruled illegal in a 1963 case, and school-approved prayer by a rabbi at a graduation ceremony was barred in *Lee v. Weisman* (1992). The court, however, has seemingly contradicted this expanded understanding of the Establishment Clause at times, for instance, the 1983 decision *Marsh v. Chambers*, which approved of prayer before sessions of Congress and state legislatures.

whether religious liberty includes the right to refuse service to potential customers on religious grounds, more particularly, whether traditional Christians have the constitutional right to refuse wedding services to homosexual couples. The Courts have ruled against religious liberty so conceived, and various Christian business owners have faced a variety of penalties, including massive fines and imprisonment, for refusing to submit conscience to governmental control.[305]

Persons who oppose the modern Court's reinterpretation of the Establishment Clause sometimes defend its original meaning by arguing that America is a "Christian nation," a view vehemently denied by those who support it. Both assertions contain an element of truth. The latter view correctly perceives that America is not a "Christian nation" in the sense that Iran, for instance, is a "Muslim nation." Iran, and other countries that practice Islamic fundamentalism, are theocratic societies that make no practical institutional distinction between religion and government. Religious authorities simultaneously exercise political authority and vice versa; the Koran is enforced by both religious and human ("secular") law. As we have seen, however, the United States, and the larger Western tradition from which it emerged, unequivocally reject such a theocratic conception of society. America is emphatically not a Christian nation in the sense that Iran is a Muslim nation. It constitutionally forbids secular authority to intervene in matters of religion let alone enforce religious belief and practice.

The opposing viewpoint, however, which perceives America as a "Christian nation," also expresses a partial truth. America is a Christian nation in an important if qualified sense. As the present work has aimed to show, its characteristic values, institutions, and customs—moral, legal, political, economic, and social—presuppose the Judeo-Christian worldview broadly conceived. America is an offshoot of a civilization whose very identity was definitively informed by biblical religion. American conceptions such as limited government, natural and unalienable rights, the Constitution as higher law, reverence and concern for the individual person, and the Lockean social contract make little sense in the absence of the implicit spiritual vision that informed them.

---

[305] *Undeniable*, 2013.

We have seen, moreover, that the conceptual and institutional distinction between religion and government, a distinctive attribute of Western civilization, is of Christian inspiration. One of the great contributions of the American founders was to have established this longstanding Western principle as constitutional or fundamental law, to have established a constitutional foundation for religious liberty. The federal government, unlike the Iranian government, is not authorized to enforce the Bible or indeed interfere with religious belief or practice in any manner whatsoever. The Americans, as we have seen, did not invent the distinction between God and Caesar, religion and government. But the historical development of such a conception, rooted in more than a millennium of Christian experience, reached its apogee in the American founding. In this qualified sense, America must indeed be regarded as a Christian nation.

In the Western or Judeo-Christian understanding, government is restricted to worldly, temporal, or earthly concerns; the entire dimension of the spirit, inward conscience as well as its outward expression, is regarded as beyond the legitimate reach of governmental coercion. Such was the general meaning of religious liberty within the founding era, and the First Amendment aimed to secure it. The religion clauses were certainly not intended as a grant of authority to the federal government to systematically remove any vestige of Christian belief and practice from the public square. We have seen, on the contrary, that American government at all levels, federal, state, and local, traditionally enacted various measures in support of religion, from military chaplains to the printing of Bibles to prayer in the public schools, all of which were regarded as constitutionally permissible until 1947. It is absurd to suggest that every generation of Americans up to 1947, including the founding generation, were so ignorant as not to recognize the unconstitutionality of such measures. They of course were not regarded as unconstitutional because until 1947 the First Amendment was generally interpreted as Originalists demand and as the Framers intended: to prevent both the establishment of an official national Church and the federal government from interfering with the free exercise of religious belief and practice. The novel interpretation offered by Black and fellow Progressive justices is among the more dramatic transformations of constitutional law effected by the jurisprudence of the Living Constitution.

The most important effect of the modern Court's rulings in *Everson, Engel* and similar cases has been the successful and ongoing removal of Christianity from the American public square. Such an effect cannot be regarded as coincidental or unintended but rather the very purpose of such rulings. It is perfectly congruent with the overarching thrust of modern and postmodern developments as previously described: eclipse of the transcendent dimension of existence and redirection of spiritual aspiration toward one form or other of intramundane or political salvation. We have discussed the religious dimension of the secular messianism embodied in the modern ideological movements. The assault on Western liberal economic and political institutions was invariably accompanied by assault on the spiritual and religious values that constitute their ground—Judeo-Christian values. The realization the ideological goal—replacement of the free society with some form of politically organized collectivism—necessarily involved the evisceration or elimination of religious convictions that stood in its way.

The ideological movements of course reached their most virulent expression in regimes such as Stalinist Russia, Hitlerite Germany, and Maoist China. Western liberal-democracies, however, including the United States, have been far from immune to the impulses that fueled radical ideological demands in the related spheres of politics, economics, and religion. Enemies of Western liberal society clearly understood, and understand, its profound historical and existential relation to the biblical worldview. They well understood, and understand, that their yearning for a fundamental transformation of Western and American society can only be realized by a correspondingly fundamental transformation of its religious or spiritual values. We have discussed various major carriers of such aspirations over the past century and beyond, including communism, socialism, positivism, Progressivism, Social Gospel, postmodernism, and Multiculturalism. To such a list must be added the constitutional jurisprudence advocated by modern-liberal Progressivism, its concept of a Living Constitution.

At first glance, modern Progressive jurisprudence may seem far removed from the overarching theme of the present work: freedom as historically conceived and practiced within American society. Such a legal development, on the contrary, is intimately bound up with the fate of the free society. We have seen that the overarching contest within modern and postmodern society involves rival and incompatible conceptions of human existence. Divergent and irreconcilable worldviews underlie the struggle between limited and unlimited government, capitalism and socialism, natural law and legal positivism, justice and social justice, traditional biblical faith and humanistic or secular religion. The modern Court's re-interpretation of the First Amendment must be viewed in light of that contest. So framed, the successful revision of American constitutional law appears as a major victory for antitheistic and illiberal forces in their battle with traditional religion and its political and cultural manifestations—individual freedom, limited government, and corollary institutions and values. The Judeo-Christian heritage has been dismissed as irrelevant to contemporary political order and traditional faith relegated to the private sphere of subjective preference.

Contrary to the modern Court, however, the debt of Western civilization to the biblical worldview, which gave rise not only to its characteristic values and institutions but its very identity, is both incalculable and beyond dispute, as is the indebtedness of the United States to biblical religion. The U.S. Constitution and other founding documents, as we have seen, presuppose the Judeo-Christian vision of human existence, as do traditional American conceptions of morality, law, economic order, and other values, including and especially individual freedom. To strike at biblical religion is to strike at the very root of the customary American way of life. The modern Court's revision of the meaning of the First Amendment is an effective tool toward realization of such a purpose.

The Court's dismissal of biblical religion from the public square, however, does not override the fact repeatedly emphasized throughout this study: the cult, in one form or another, is the root of all culture. Some cult, some conception of the ultimate truth of existence, must always lie at the basis of any society. The question that faces contemporary American society is which cult shall prevail. The evisceration of traditional biblical religion has not, and will not, lead to the rise of an areligious or apolitical secularism capable of sustaining freedom in the long run. Freedom, in the end, is a spiritual value derived from biblical sources. The demand for freedom presupposes a conception of the human person as a being entitled to special treatment, symbolized of course in the American tradition by the assertion of unalienable right. Such a conception, as we have seen, emerged from the

Christian revaluation of the human person and ultimately remains dependent upon some such spiritual vision. Not only is humanistic secularism incapable of justifying traditional institutions of freedom but the spiritual void created by the "death of God" has been, and continues to be, filled by rival nontheistic, antitheistic, or neo-pagan "religions" of one form or other that do not, and cannot, endow human being with comparable significance and value.[306] Denominational choices include communism, Marxism, socialism, fascism, secular humanism, Liberation Theology, radical environmentalism (worship of Gaia), modern-liberal Progressivism, and other naturalistic expressions of modern antitheistic and collectivist impulses.

The modern and postmodern effort to replace the transcendent God of the Western tradition with Humanity or some other intramundane abstraction is inseparable from the rise of twentieth-century totalitarianism and concomitant decline of limited government and individual freedom. Not only did biblical teaching implicitly limit the value of mundane politics but also imposed limits on human aspiration and striving: Thou shalt not. On the biblical view, God, the Source and End of existence, is the author of law, moral and physical, which, accordingly, is immune to human preference or will. Man must align himself to an objective or *given* order of being. All such limits, constraints, and duties are removed at a stroke by the "death of God." Man henceforth may regard himself as free to create the world in his own image, to exert his own will, to impose his own ideas of goodness and justice on the social order, come what may. There is no given reality, no higher authority or power to which Man must defer, no need to temper human aspirations or impulses, including and especially the lust for power. The "Triumph of the Will" proclaimed by the Nazis completes the "death of God."[307] In the end, as Voegelin and others have observed, the "crisis of modernity" is inseparable from the crisis of faith.[308]

---

[306] Evans, "The Rise of Neo-Paganism," in *The Theme is Freedom*, 113-30.

[307] Leni Riefenstahl, "Triumph of the Will" (*Triumph des Willens*), Nazi propaganda film directed, produced, edited and co-written by Leni Riefenstahl (Germany, 1935).

[308] Augusto del Noce, *The Crisis of Modernity* (McGill-Queen's University Press, 2015). There is a vast scholarly literature on the so-called 'crisis of modernity'; representative authors include Alasdair MacIntyre, Allen Bloom, Charles Taylor, David Walsh, and others.

As the present work has attempted to show, the erosion of the traditional spiritual foundation of the West, comprised by the biblical worldview, must inevitably lead to the erosion of the characteristic civilization that emerged in response to it—the Free World. Growing ignorance among the American people of the substance of the Judeo-Christian heritage, along with a growing and militant hostility toward biblical faith, thus present discouraging prospects for a people who would be free. The great concern with respect to American society is that the unimpeded advance of contemporary trends will only sustain its tragic and already well-progressed movement, in the prescient phrase of Hayek, down the "road to serfdom." There is no way around the fact that the free society—traditional American society—is the product of a unique spiritual vision of existence and crucially dependent upon it. As that vision grows dim, so must its finest earthly fruit, the political and social order of a free people.

Bibliography

Acton, H.B. 2003. *The Illusion of the Epoch: Marxism-Leninism as a Philosophical Creed.* Indianapolis: Liberty Fund.

_____. 1993. *The Morals of Markets and Related Essays.* 2nd. Indianapolis: Liberty Fund.

Altizer, Thomas J. 1982. *Eric Voegelin's Thought: A Critical Appraisal.* Edited by Ellis Sandoz. Durham: Duke University Press.

Aquinas, Thomas. 1988. *On Law, Morality, and Politics.* Edited by William P. Baumgarth and Richard J. Regan S.J. Indianapolis: Hackett Publishing Company.

Augustine. 1962. *The Political Writings of St. Augustine.* Edited by Henry Paolucci. Washington: Regnery Gateway.

Berlin, Isaiah. 1969. "Two Concepts of Liberty." In *Four Essays on Liberty*, by Isaiah Berlin. Oxford: Oxford University Press.

Berman, Harold J. 1983. *Law and Revolution: The Formation of the Western Legal Tradition* . Harvard.

Billington, James. 1980. *Fire in the Minds of Men: Origins of the Revolutionary Faith.* New York: Basic Books.

Bingham, Tom. 2011. *The Rule of Law.* London: Penguin UK.

Bracton, Henry of. 1903. *A History of English Law.* Edited by W. S. Holdsworth. London: Methuen & Co., Ltd.

Brent, Allen. 2009. *A Political History of Early Christianity.* New York: T&T Clark International.

Capaldi Nicholas, Theodore Roosevelt Malloch. 2012. *America's Spiritual Capital.* South Bend, IN: St. Augustine's Press.

Carey, George W. 1995. *In Defense of the Constitution.* revised and expanded. Indianapolis: Liberty Fund.

Cashdollar, Charles D. 1989. *The Transformation of Theology, 1830-1890.* Princeton: Princeton University Press.

Charlton, D.G. 1963. *Secular Religions in France, 1815-1870.* London: Oxford University Press.

Cicero. 1998. *The Republic and The Laws.* Translated by Niall Rudd. New York: Oxford University Press.

Cohn, Norman. 1970. *The Pursuit of the Millenium.* New York: Oxford University Press.

Corwin, Edward S. 2008. *The Higher Law Background of American Constitutional Law.* Indianapolis: Liberty Fund.

Coulanges, Fustel De. 1956. *The Ancient City: A Classic Study of the Religious and Civil Institutions in Ancient Greece and Rome.* New York: Doubleday and Company, Inc.

Crimmins, James E., ed. 1990. *Religion, Secularization, and Political Thought: Thomas Hobbes to J.S. Mill.* London: Routledge.

Crossman, Richard H., ed. 2001. *The God That Failed.* New York: Columbia University Press.

Dalberg-Acton, John Emerich Edward. 1907. *Historical Essays and Studies.* Edited by J.N. Figgis and R.V. Laurence. London: Macmillan.

Dawson, Christopher. 1954. *Medieval Essays: a Study of Christian Culture.* Garden City, NY: Image Books.

_____. 1991. *Religion and the Rise of Western Culture.* New York: Image Books.

_____. 1967. *The Formation of Christendom.* 1st. Sheed and Ward.

_____. 2002. *The Making of Europe.* Washington, D.C.: The Catholic University of America Press.

Diaz, Howard. 2012. *A Charter of Negative Liberties: Defining the Bill of Rights and Other Commentary.* Bloomington, IN: Westbow Press.

Dicey, A. V. 1915. *Introduction to the Study of the Law of the Constitution.* London: Macmillan and Co.

Dostoyevsky, Fyodor. 1993. *The Grand Inquisitor: with Related Chapters from the Brothers Karamazov.* Indianapolis: Hackett Publishing Comany, Inc.

Ellul, Jacques. 1979. "Politization and Political Solutions." In *The Politicization of Society,* edited by Kenneth S. Templeton. Indianapolis: Liberty Press.

Evans, M. Stanton. 1994. *The Theme is Freedom: Religion, Politics, and the American Tradition.* Washington, D.C.: Regnery Publishing, Inc.

Franz, Michael. 1992. *Eric Voegelin and the Politics of Spiritual Revolt: The Roots of Modern Ideology* . Baton Rouge: Louisiana State University Press.

Frohnen, Bruce, ed. 2008. *The American Nation: Primary Sources.* Indianapolis: Liberty Fund.

_____. ed. 2002. *The American Republic: Primary Sources.* Indianapolis: Liberty Fund.

Gamble, Richard M. 2014. *The War for Righteousness: Progressive Christianity, the Great War, and the Rise of the Messianic* Nation. Wilmington, DE: Intersollegiate Studies Institute.

Glendon, Mary Ann. 1991. *The Impoverishment of Political Discourse* . New York: The Free Press.

Hall, Daniel L. Dreisbach and Mark David, ed. 2009. *The Sacred Rights of Conscience.* Indianapolis: Liberty Fund.

Hamburger, Joseph. 1999. *John Stuart Mill on Liberty and Control.* Princeton: Princeton University Press.

Hamburger, Philip. 2002. *Separation of Church and State.* Cambridge, MA: Harvard University Press.

Harp, Gillis. 2005. *Positivist Republic: Auguste Comte and the Reconstruction of American Liberalism, 1865-1920.* University Park, PA: Penn State University Press.

Hayek, F. A. 2007. *The Road to Serfdom.* Edited by Bruce Caldwell. Chicago: University of Chicago Press.

Hegel, G. W. F. 1929. *Hegel: Selections.* Edited by Jacob Loewenberg. New York: Scribner's Sons.

Hoffer, Eric. 1951. *The True Believer: Thoughts on the Nature of Mass Movements.* San Bernardino: Borgo Press.

Jefferson, Thomas. 1904. *The Writings of Thomas Jefferson.* Edited by Thomas Lipscomb and Albert Bergh. Vol. 10. 20 vols. Monticello: The Thomas Jefferson Memorial Association of the United States.

Kirk, Russell. 2003. *The Roots of American Order.* Wilmington, DE: Intercollege Studies Institute.

Koenker, Ernest B. 1965. *Secular Salvations: The Rites and Symbols of Political Religions.* Philadelphia: Fortress Press.

Lerner, Philip B. Kurland and Ralph, ed. 1987. *The Founders' Constitution.* 5 vols. Indianapolis: Liberty Fund.

Locke, John. 1980. *Second Treatise of Government.* Edited by C. B. Macpherson. Indianapolis: Hackett Publishing Inc.

———. 2003. *Two Treatises of Government and a Letter Concerning Tolera*tion. New Haven: Yale University Press.

Lubac, Henri de. 1995. *The Drama of Atheist Humanism.* San Francisco: Ignatius Press.

Lutz, Donald S., ed. 1998. *Colonial Origins of the American Constitution: a Documentary History.* Indianapolis: Liberty Fund, Inc.

_____. 1988. *The Origins of American Constitutionalism*. Baton Rouge: Louisiana State University Press.

Löwith, Karl. 1949. *Meaning in History*. Chicago: University of Chicago Press.

Manent, Pierre. 1998. *The City of Man*. Translated by Marc A. LePain. Princeton: Princeton University Press.

Manuel, Frank E. 1983. *The Changing of the Gods*. Hanover, NH: Brown University Press.

_____. 1956. *The New World of Henri Saint-Simon*. Cambridge: Harvard University Press.

Marx, Karl. 1978. *The Marx-Engels Reader*. 2nd. Edited by Robert C. Tucker. New York: W. W. Norton & Company.

Mazlish, Bruce. 1976. *The Revolutionary Ascetic: Evolution of a Political Type*. New York: McGraw-Hill.

McIlwain, Charles Howard. 2010. *Constitutionalism: Ancient and Modern*. Indianapolis: Liberty Fund.

Molnar, Thomas. 1988. *Twin Powers: Politics and the Sacre*d. Grand Rapids: William B. Eerdmans Publishing.

Moots, Glenn A. 2010. *Politics Reformed: the Anglo-American Legacy of Covenent Theology*. Columbia: MO: University of Missouri Press.

Neusner, Jacob, ed. 2006. *Religious Foundations of Western Civiilization: Judaism, Christianity, and Islam*. Nashville: Abingdon Press.

Niemeyer, Gerhart. 1971. *Between Nothingness and Paradise* . Baton Rouge: Louisiana State University Press.

Nisbet, Robert. 2010 [1953]. *The Quest for Community: A Study in the Ethics of Order and Freedom*. Wilmington DE: Intercollegiate Studies Institute.

Opitz, Edmund A. 1996. *Religion: Foundation of the Free Society*. Irvington-on-Hudson, NY: Foundation for Economic Education, Inc.

_____. 1999. *The Libertarian Theology of Freedom*. Tampa: Hallberg Publishing Corporation.

Orwell, George. 2010. *Politics and the English Language and Other Essays*. Oxford: Benediction Classics.

Paine, Thomas. 2000. *Common Sense: and Related Writings*. Edited by Thomas P. Slaughter. New York: Bedford/St. Martin's Press.

Pera, Marcello. 2011. *Why We Should Call Ourselves Christian*. New York: Encounter Books.

Pestritto, Ronald J. 2005. *Woodrow Wilson and the Roots of Modern Liberalism*. Lanham, MD: Rowman & Littlefield Publishers, Inc.

232

_____. and William J. Atto, eds. 2008. *American Progressisvism: A Reader.* Lanham, MD: Lexington Books.

Raeder, Linda C. 2002. *John Stuart Mill and the Religion of Humanity.* Columbia, MO: University of Missouri Press.

Raico, Ralph. 2012. *Classical Liberalism and the Austrian School.* Auburn, AL: Ludwig von Mises Institute.

_____. 1985. *Liberalism in the Classical Tradition.* 3rd. Cobden Press.

Robinson, J.H. 1905. *Readings in European History.* Edited by J.H. Robinson. Boston: Ginn.

Rutherford, Samuel. 1998. *Lex, Rex, or The Prince and the Law.* Berryville, VA: Hess Publications.

Rutland, R.A., ed. 1976. *The Papers of James Madison.* Vol. 14. Chicago: University of Chicago Press.

Ryn, Claes G. 1990. *Democracy and the Ethical Life.* 2nd. Washington, D.C.: The Catholic University of America Press.

_____. 1992. "Political Philosophy and the Unwritten Constitution." *Modern Age* 303-309.

Sandoz, Ellis, ed. 1991. *Political Sermons of the Founding Era.* Indianapolis: Liberty Fund.

_____. ed, *Eric Voegelin's Thought: A Critical Appraisal* (Durham: Duke University Press, 1982),

Schumpeter, Joseph. 1954. *History of Economic Analysis.* New York: Oxford University Press.

Sebba, Gregor. 1981. "History, Modernity, and Gnosticism." In *The Philosophy of Order: Essays on History, Consciousness and Politics,* edited by Peter J. Opitz and Gregor Sebba. Stuttgart: Ernst Klett.

Shah, Timothy Samuel and Hertzke, Allen D., ed. 2016. *Christianity and Freedom. Vol. 1: Historical Perspectives.* II vols. Cambridge: Cambridge University Press.

Shaw, G. Bernard. 1889. *Fabian Essays in Socialism.* London: Fabian Society.

Siedentop, Larry. 2014. *Inventing the Individual: The Origins of Western Liberalism.* Cambridge, MA: The Belknap Press of Harvard University Press.

Smith, Ronald Gregor. 1966. *Secular Christianity.* New York: Harper and Row.

Sokolowski, Robert. 2006. *Christian Faith & Human Understanding: Studies on the Eucharist, Trinity, and the Human Person.* Washington DC: The Catholic University of America Press.

Sowell, Thomas. 1987. *A Conflict of Visions: Ideological Origins of Political Struggles.* New York: William Morrow & Co.

Talmon, Jacob L. 1960. *Political Messianism.* New York: Frederick A. Praeger.

Thornton, Bruce S. 2007. *Decline and Fall: Europe's Slow Motion Suicide.* San Francisco: Encounter Books.

Thucydides. 1993. *On Law, Power, and Justice.* Indianapolis: Hackett Publishing Company, Inc.

Tierney, Brian. 2008. *Christianity and Law.* Edited by John Witte and Frank S. Alexander. Cambridge: Cambridge University Press. 1988.

_____. 1988. *The Crisis of Church and State 1050-1300.* Toronto: University of Toronto Press.

Turner, James. 1985. *Without God, Without Creed: the Origins of Unbelief in America.* Baltimore: Johns Hopkins University Press.

Viner, Jacob. 2015. *The Role of Providence in the Social Order: An Essay in Intellectual History.* Princeton: Princeton University Press.

Voegelin, Eric. 1987. *Order and History.* Vol. V: *In Search of Order.* Baton Rouge: Louisiana State University Press.

_____. 1986. *Political Religions.* Translated by T. J. DiNapoli and E.S. Easterly III. Edwin Mellen Press.

_____. 1968. *Science, Politics, and Gnosticism.* Chicago: Henry Regnery Company.

_____. 1990. Voegelin, *Published Essays, 1966-1985.* Edited by Ellis Sandoz. Vol. 12 *The Collected Works of Eric Voegelin.* Baton Rouge: Louisiana State University Press.

Walker, Graham. 2014. *The Moral Foundations of Constitutional Thought: Current Problems, Augustinian Prospects.* reprint. Princeton: Princeton University Press.

Watkins, William J., Jr. 2016. *Crossroads for Liberty: Recovering the Anti-Federalist Values of America's First Constitution.* Oakland, CA: Independent institute.

Wills, Garry, ed. 1982. *The Federalist Papers by Alexander Hamilton, James Madison and John Jay.* New York: Bantam Books.

Witte, John Jr. 2005. *Religion and the American Constitutional Experiment.* 2nd. Boulder: Westview Press.

Wright, T.R. 1986. *The Religion of Humanity: The Impact of Comtean Positivism on Victorian Britain.* Cambridge: Cambridge University Press.

Made in United States
Orlando, FL
03 December 2021

11087156R00150